MECHANICS·
MERCANTILE
LIBRARY.

Arthur F. Mathews '06

"Socialism Is Great!"

Atlas & Co.
New York

"Socialism Is Great!"

A Worker's Memoir of the New China

Lijia Zhang

Atlas & Co. *Publishers*
15 West 26th Street, 2nd floor
New York, NY 10010
www.atlasandco.com

Distributed to the trade by W. W. Norton & Company

Printed in the United States

Atlas & Co. wishes to acknowledge Creative Work
for their support in publishing this work.

Interior design by Yoshiki Waterhouse
Typesetting by Sara E. Stemen

Grateful acknowledgment is made to the following for permission to
reprint previously published material: Yale University Press: "Assembly
Line" by Shu Ting, translated by Michele Yeh, from *The Anthology of
Modern Chinese Poetry*.

Atlas & Co. publications may be purchased for educational,
business, or sales promotional use. For information, please write:
Atlas & Company, 15 West 26th Street, 2nd floor,
New York, NY 10010.

Library of Congress Cataloging-in-Publication Data
is available upon request.

ISBN-13: 978-0-9777433-7- 7
13 12 11 10 09 08 1 2 3 4 5 6

To Zhou Fang, who did most of the pushing
to get this frog out of the factory well.

A frog in a shallow well says to a turtle from the Eastern Sea: "How happy I am! Sometimes I jump into the well; at other times I rest on a broken brick inside. When I swim, the water in the well comes up under my arms and supports my chin; when I leap, the mud covers my feet. I look around and see that none of those insects, crabs, or tadpoles are better off than me. Besides, I alone have the whole well, the whole pleasure of the well. This is the highest plane in life! Why don't you often come here to visit and broaden your horizon?"

The turtle accepts the invitation. He lowers his right leg into the well. But before he can put his left leg in, he realizes the well is too small and has to give up. Then the turtle tells the frog in the well about the sea. "The long distance of ten thousand *li* is not enough to describe the greatness of the sea; eight thousand inches is not enough to describe its depth. During the Dayu period, there were floods for nine out of ten years, yet the sea didn't rise. During the reign of Emperor Tang in the Shang Dynasty, there were droughts for seven out of eight years, yet the sea didn't fall. The sea will not change over time and will not rise or fall because of floods or drought. It is the joy of living in the Eastern Sea!"

Upon hearing this, the frog is truly surprised. It then feels disappointed and lost for a long time.

—Zhuang Zi, Chinese philosopher, fourth century BCE

Chapter 1

Inheritance

"Would you like to be a worker, if you have a chance?"

"Of course not, Ma. Why?" I answered my mother flatly, without even looking up from my homework. To be a worker? What an odd question! I was only sixteen, in my first term at senior middle school, and I was doing well.

Across the table, Ma tugged threads into a tassel for an Islamic prayer mat, made for export. For years we had been taking in embroidery work for sorely needed extra cash. Nai, my grandma, also clutched a prayer mat to embroider, but had dozed off. She dozed off more often now. If we asked her to go to bed she would straighten up and resume her work, only to fall asleep again within minutes.

"Not even working at a first-class enterprise like Liming, a real 'iron rice bowl'?" Ma had spent her entire working life at Liming Machinery Factory, the largest state-owned enterprise in our city, Nanjing. Under the authority of the Ministry of Aerospace Industry, our factory had nearly ten thousand employees. Its prestige derived from not only its scale but also its status as a military factory. With free services from nurseries to cremation, and countless bowls of rice in between, the life of a state employee meant cradle-to-grave security. Plus free showers and subsidized haircuts.

"Not even Liming." Finally I raised my head to look at Ma, who was frowning in my direction. I liked to look at Ma. She was pretty—when she didn't frown. She had lovely high cheeks, and bright, slanted eyes. Her arched eyebrows were like two new moons. Her name was fitting too: Yufang, fragrance of cloud.

Now she seemed at a loss for words. After a while, she added: "I would think twice if I were you, Little Li." That was my pet name at home, though I hardly merited its meaning, "little beauty."

It was the beginning of December 1980. Winter had come early. My hands, swelling red with chilblains, were carefully copying English words into an exercise book. How fascinating! This language system, reintroduced to schools recently, was completely different from Chinese. Our characters developed from pictographs, real pictures of actual things. *Jia*, for example, means home, where a roof shelters a pig and reveals our farming roots. Hunched over a naked bulb of low wattage, just about bright enough for our tasks, three generations of Chinese women, bundled up in padded cotton jackets and trousers, sat around three sides of a table pushed against a window. The lack of heating was geographic fate: the Communist central planners permitted no central heating south of the Yangtze, the river that splits China in two. The "southern capital" Nanjing lies on the lower reaches of its southern bank, where, though temperatures never fall as low as in cities to the north, the damp cold goes straight to one's bones. To fight the chill, we stuffed our feet in a straw basket warmed by a copper hot-water bottle. I could always tell which pair were Nai's—the tiny, bound ones. A warm, womanly intimacy hung in the air.

There were others in my family, but they weren't around. My father had spent his whole working life in another city. My elder sister Weijia was studying at her college in a far corner of the city. My naughty brother Xiaoshi was out playing in our village, Wuding New Village, the largest residential area for Liming employees.

Located just outside Wuding Gate, one of the thirteen city gates that once defined and guarded Nanjing, the village was still classed as rural, although the sprawling urban landscape was slowly swallowing up the green patchwork of fields that surrounded it. With few trees and little green space, there was none of the rustic beauty or tradition that the word "village" suggests. There were several thousand villagers, packed into three dozen or so concrete blocks, identical but for being either three or four stories high, depending on the year of construction.

Our flat, on the second floor of a four-story block, felt matchbox-sized, with low ceilings, one main room, and one side room. The walls of peeling yellow paint were bare but for a factory calendar and the two school certificates of merit that my sister and I earned each year without fail. Two beds took up much of the main room where we sat, but the bedding was neatly folded, for the beds also served as seats and worktables. An old wardrobe, a wedding gift from my mother's in-laws, gave off distorted reflections in its full-length mirror. The once intricate carvings were cracked, like an old worn face. A white tablecloth, crocheted by Weijia with sewing threads, covered a coarsely made cupboard. On top sat a colorful biscuit tin, long empty, but kept for decoration. Beside it stood a "hero" clock. "The masses are the real heroes" read one of Chairman Mao's quotations, printed on the clock face. A worker grasping a hammer, a peasant her sickle, and a soldier his gun were painted waving aloft his Little Red Book.

Looking at the painted worker, I smiled to myself. A worker? How funny I would look if I wore his canvas uniform and peaked cap.

Three weeks later, I was summoned after supper for a "little talk" in Ma's bedroom. I knew it was serious when she shut the door. Our last closed-door session had been nearly four years earlier, when I was in my last year at primary school. My teacher had recommended I study at Nanjing Foreign Languages School, an exclusive place whose graduates all went on to university, and were later trained as diplomats or interpreters for high-ranking leaders. "Would you like to go there to study?" she had asked. I had jumped up with joy. But my happiness was premature: I failed the political censorship—my father had "political problems." I was therefore rejected.

Ma's room was always so dim—high wattage would use too much electricity. When I started middle school, she arranged for me to sleep with her, thinking I was too big to share a bed with my brother and Nai. While Ma, next door, made endless tassels into the night, I was scared on my own—the eight-watt fluorescent lamp flickered in the darkness like a jack-o'-lantern. To forget my fear, I began to read books. Within months the characters on the school blackboard became as blurred as crawling ants. A pair of black-framed glasses came to reside on my small nose. When Ma discovered why, she banished me back to Nai's bed—it would have been wasteful to install a bright light just for my reading. I slept better, holding Nai's thin legs.

Now I looked expectantly at Ma as she sat down on the bed. What could it be this time? Even in the semidarkness, I could see her "two new moons" knitting together in a frown.

"Remember I asked if you would like to be a worker?" she began, her voice husky and low. She cleared her throat. "You are going to take over my job."

The sentence fell like thunder from a bright blue sky.

"What?! NO!" I jumped up again, this time in protest. "Why? I'm still young!" I pleaded.

"I became a worker myself at your age, only half a year

older," she said matter-of-factly. I remembered Ma once boasting that she had been a promising student, too, but was forced to give up school because her family was too poor.

"But surely, Ma, you can support me to finish school, then…"

"Poverty is only part of the reason." Then, calmly, she began to explain the rest. When the Cultural Revolution ended in 1976, China was a mess, its economy on the brink of collapse. To tackle the soaring numbers of jobless, a temporary policy appeared called *dingzhi*, literally, "replacing job." If parents could secure retirement, their children could take over their jobs. Several rounds of dingzhi had followed until it was strongly rumored that December 1980 was the last such opportunity. Despite excellent health at forty-three—some seventeen years away from the normal retirement age for women—Ma had decided to take advantage of the opportunity. When she first raised the issue with me, she had already applied to retire early on the grounds of poor health: she had been working for many years on the hazardous acid-pickling line. My poor reaction had not deterred her in the least, and now her application had been approved.

"I don't want to be a worker!" I insisted, stamping a foot in disgust.

In my mind's eye, I saw the blue canvas uniform and Ma's coarse hands. A worker? I knew it was the likely fate for children from our village, but I had grand plans for myself.

"I want to be a journalist!"

"I told you before, don't even dream about it," she replied. "A journalist? Writing is a dangerous thing to do in this country. Your dad is a good example." She frowned: the sheer mention of my father seemed to vex her. "Anyway, becoming a journalist is just one of your flights of fancy.

You also wanted to be a pilot, a barefoot doctor, and an interpreter, just to name a few!"

Ma had a glib tongue, but I was far from convinced.

"I'm good at writing, my literature teacher said so." At school, teachers often read out my compositions, and fellow students copied my prose. "Whatever happens in the future, I want to go to university first," I added assertively.

"Getting into university is harder than climbing to heaven!" she retorted. "I know you're a good student, but your school is very bad. Look, this year they 'drew an egg' again—not a single student passed the university entrance exam."

That much was beyond dispute. My middle school, like my primary school, had been established by Liming for its employees' children. Only later was the school's administration transferred to the city's education authority and children from nearby areas allowed to attend. No self-respecting teacher would choose to work at either of these remote and poorly equipped schools. After the humiliating failure of last year, the school introduced a new strategy—streaming students into classes based on their abilities, so that the most resources and attention would be spent on pupils with the greatest hope of reaching university.

But I was in the fast class, wasn't I? As if reading my mind, Ma continued in a crisp and clear voice, with a fluency that spoke of many rehearsals in her mind. "Even if you do pass the entrance exam, your bad eyesight will probably fail you. Look at Weijia, she scored quite well but only got into a teacher-training school."

A fair point. My sister Weijia was training as a primary school teacher at Xingzhi Secondary Normal College, not a "proper" university and hardly a place for an ambitious youth. However, poor sight (as in my sister's case) or any other physical defect was held against you. The university entrance system, only reintroduced in 1977 after the chaotic years, demanded almost perfect physical health—a useful way to reduce the pool of candidates. China's proper universities could accommodate fewer than 4 percent of those who took the entrance exam. In other words, only one out of six hundred Chinese children was lucky enough to experience higher education.

"But at least I can try, and if I score really high, some university will surely accept me. Can you wait for three years, Ma?" I knew someone from Weijia's class had gotten into Beijing University, China's Oxford, despite his bad eyesight. I didn't need to remind Ma that university was one of few guaranteed routes to success for an ordinary family like ours.

"Wait? I can, but not dingzhi. You know government policy is like a child's face—three changes in a day."

I wasn't good at arguing with Ma. To be a good child meant *tinghua*, "to listen to words," a phrase that conveyed obedience, the most desirable quality for Chinese children. So I listened, obediently, to the words of my teachers at school and my mother at home.

Barely comprehending, I listened as she went on. If I failed the university exam I would end up one of those jobless youths, or get a job in a collectively owned factory, if I was really lucky. A good job with Liming? No chance!

The prestige of state-owned firms remained high. "The working class leads everything!" newspapers reminded us. "Workers are our elder brothers" and "the masters of the nation."

"Look at this house. We are so poor," grumbled Ma, kicking her bedside table. One of the legs slipped from its brick support. That table and a bed were the only furniture in the cramped room. "We can't rely on your dad. He is useless, and Nai is getting old. She nearly died from the stroke. It hurts me to look at her hunched over the embroidery, like an old shrimp. After you become a worker, I can find another job, and our lives will be better."

Irritated by my wooden expression, Ma raised her voice. "But above all, Little Li, let me tell you I'm doing you a big favor! I simply don't understand why I have to beg you to take over my treasure." She blew her nose. "Your mouth still smells of breast milk; you don't know what's good for you! You'll go to work at the factory next week. That's it!"

She got up and walked out, her back straight and erect. For me, her back always spoke volumes about her proud, stubborn nature. Once she had set her mind on something, a four-horse cart couldn't hold her back.

I followed her lamely to the main room and met Nai's concerned look. Wide-awake in her usual place, she was still clutching her embroidery.

Ma banged and clattered around the flat for a while, voicing her displeasure, and then went into her room.

"You didn't agree?" Nai whispered.

I didn't answer. If I'd been wearing a hat, the force of my rage would have shot it into the air. Agree? What was the difference if I agreed or not? Everything had been decided. Although it was common practice for parents to decide what was best for their children, I still felt shocked, even wronged. But how could I bring myself to say anything unkind to Nai, the dearest person in my life? After raising Ma, her only surviving child, Nai had cared for her grandchildren like a faithful servant. We called her Nai, slang for paternal grandmother: Chinese people held paternal grandmas dearer than maternal grandmas.

"Dingzhi is the best for you," said Nai, her soft eyes focusing on me as I sat down heavily. "If you can't go to university, no point in finishing senior middle school, right?"

My semiliterate grandma would not make such a connection herself. Ma must have fed her the lines.

Despite myself, I thought she must be the most beautiful grandma in the world. Since no manufacturer still produced garments as elegant as her traditional-style jacket, which buttoned to the right, she had to seek out a village dressmaker. But she clung to her dressing habit like a child to its comfort blanket, regardless of how tricky it was to tie the butterfly button. My sister and I loved admiring a particular black-and-white picture of her in her youth—one of the few pictures to survive ransacking by the Red Guards—and wondering why Nai's striking good looks hadn't been passed down to us. In that yellowing image, Nai's beauty had a nostalgic quality. Her perfect oval-shaped face, sweet dimples, and naturally wavy hair recalled the stylish film stars of 1930s Shanghai. Now well into her sixties, she still had smooth skin and pitch-black hair. Even the mild stroke she'd suffered the year before had failed to leave any marks on her.

I knew there was no point in asking Nai to plead my case since she absolutely respected Ma's authority in the household. Ma was the queen, the sole decision-maker. Even when Father was around, his opinions rarely counted.

"I'll have to think about it," I said.

Chapter 2

The Weight of Adulthood

At sixteen, I still shared a bed with my brother and grandma, but when Weijia was away at college, I was upgraded to her single bed. For once, however, I couldn't enjoy the treat of sleeping alone. The bed's creaking legs groaned in complaint as I tossed and turned. There had to be some way out of this.

Would Weijia like to take over Ma's job? I brushed the idea aside. After two years' study, she would be assigned a teaching job. My thirteen-year-old brother was too young. So, just about old enough, I was the only candidate.

How I envied my older sister's certain future! She even had a boyfriend in the village, which was why she tried to sneak home whenever possible. I thought about that Foreign Languages School. If only I had passed the censorship, I would have been studying there, on the way to university. My future would look rosy and certain, too. If only, if only.

Instead, my life was about to take an unwelcome turn.

So far, it had been highly uneventful, despite the drama convulsing China. I was only two years old when the Great Proletarian Cultural Revolution broke out in 1966. My earliest recollections were of lighthearted, even comic moments: muddling along behind Nai as she tried to mimic the "loyalty dance" steps to express her devotion to our great leader Chairman Mao, neighbors up and down the street gathering in the morning to bow three times before his portrait; catching cicadas in the treetops with my brother.

An inch long, with big, globular eyes and transparent wings, the cicada chirps loudest when the world swoons under the midday sun. My brother and I used to roast the ones we caught over a small bonfire. The slightly burnt smell was so inviting that we often devoured them before they were properly cooked.

But the tidal wave of politics and terror soon began to sweep China's citizens. In Nai's arms, I was too young to remember, but later I learned enough to imagine the scene at the public struggle session: the accused would line up on a raised platform, their hands tied behind their backs, their heads bent low by placards around their necks that read "capitalist roader"—that is, one who has chosen the capitalist road—or "counterrevolutionary." Activists from neighborhood committees, the lowest and most interfering arm of state control, would invite everyone, including the family and friends of the accused, to denounce them, spit on them, or kick them. Already troubled by Parkinson's disease, my granddad was nervous, like a bird that could be startled by the mere twang of a bowstring. He feared that his business background would land him in one of these struggle sessions. One morning, Nai woke to find the old man's stiffened body hanging from a wooden beam in the communal hall of the traditional courtyard they shared with several families.

A year later, Ma secured a flat in Wuding New Village. I was too young to understand the pain caused by Granddad's suicide. Indeed, the adults had tried hard to shield us from troubles. Sometimes there was no hiding place.

In 1971, a group of young workers with red armbands burst into our flat and ransacked it. They took pictures from a photo album, Nai's antique porcelain bowls, even a spoon carved with the letters "USA." Harmless in normal times, these items were suspect in a nation wild with xenophobic and anti-feudal rage. Then, they took my mother. We children hid behind Nai, terrified into silence, fearing the sky was going to collapse.

It was a ghostly version of Ma that finally came back to us, half of her hair missing, her face death-white, and her body bruised and purple. The ghost acted strangely too, hugging us tight—as a typical Chinese parent, Ma had rarely showed emotion to her children. "I would have committed suicide if not for you," she said between sobs. For several months, she was locked in a dark room inside the factory. Interrogations stretched for days to deprive her of sleep and weaken her resistance.

Ma had been accused of being a member of the so-called "May Sixteenth Faction," a counterrevolutionary group that might never have existed, except in the minds of Mao's ever-more-hysterical disciples. She stubbornly denied involvement. She was lucky to get out alive—millions lost their lives during the Cultural Revolution. Makeshift courts were set up everywhere, and executions often took place without any legal proceedings. All in the name of making revolution.

Yet this was the only dark shadow on my childhood memories.

There was usually enough to eat, though the cicadas we roasted revealed a craving for meat not sated by the one gram of pork rationed monthly for each of us. Everyone was poor, and we were only a little poorer than our neighbors. We didn't have any toys, but we didn't know to miss them. Father was away; our indulgent grandma let us do whatever we wanted; and Ma, if not in trouble, might not have let us run wild in the rice paddies and vegetable fields of Red Flower Commune, the real village just a slingshot away from the concrete of Wuding New Village. On hot summer afternoons, I would sneak ut with Xiaoshi and other boys to swim and play in the Pig Pool, a small tributary of the Yangtze. Soaking on the other bank, water buffalo watched our tanned naked bodies slip in and out of the water like eels. There were shrimp too, delicious to stir-fry, if you dared to stick your hand in their holes below the bank. Xiaoshi had once pulled out a water snake. In 1972, I went to the village primary school, and later its middle school. By then, the revolutionary fever that could turn children against their parents or students against teachers was cooling.

On the first day at school, my teacher asked me to shout: "Stand up!" when she entered the room. Only later did I realize this was my appointment as class head. I guessed this was partly because Weijia was doing so well, and in any case I didn't let my teacher down. Good memory was the key to success in a system that demanded learning by rote, not creativity.

My reward was political. At the age of twelve, I was chosen to lead the school's Young Pioneers, the Chinese communist version of Girl Scouts or Boy Scouts. My family's less than pure background did not count against me here: so many parents had black marks on their records that their children usually were not affected at school. Only prestigious places like Nanjing Foreign Languages School enforced strict political censorship.

For me, this honor meant wearing the Young Pioneers' red scarf to school each day, giving speeches, and holding flags at open-air ceremonies. There were plenty of them that year. Our "great leader Comrade Mao Zedong" passed away in September 1976. Then the radical Gang of Four was arrested, convenient scapegoats for Mao's worst excesses. It would come to mark the end of the Cultural Revolution.

I could remember grieving over Mao's death—he had been the only leader my generation had ever known.

But I grieved more for the time wasted embroidering at home when other kids played outside. With little financial support from Father, our family was obliged to try all sorts of ways to make ends meet, from peeling garlic and making matchboxes to shelling peanuts and babysitting. Eventually, we settled on embroidery: the work was demanding but stable, and the pay better. To reward my siblings and me for our efforts, Nai would make us sunflower seeds or sweet potatoes. When she was empty-handed, she told scary stories full of ghosts and fox fairies. "Suddenly, there was a gust of wind. The young scholar put his book down and saw a beautiful girl in front of him, smiling sweetly…"

"Is she that fox fairy?" I would ask keenly. There were two types of fox fairy, good and evil, but both were beautiful women skilled at seducing men. The good ones would fall in love with young scholars and even bear them children; the evil ones would suck out scholars' souls so that they could live longer themselves. Sometimes, I was so lost in Nai's stories that I would stab my finger with a needle. Nai, like most women of her generation, never went to school. Her only education spilled forth in countless folktales passed down for generations through word of mouth. I found such tales, officially regarded as "feudal poison," deliciously entertaining.

As the four years following Mao's death slipped by, China sought to "bring order out of political chaos," the state-run newspapers explained. Many of those wronged in previous political movements, like my parents, were rehabilitated. Once Deng Xiaoping, China's most pragmatic leader, was back in power, he launched dramatic economic reforms, opened closed doors to the outside world and demanded the "Four Modernizations" in agriculture, industry, science and technology, and defense. I sensed that a better education would bring more opportunities in this new environment. The rest of my class would charge ahead with the rest of the country. But Ma wanted to drag me out of the race.

In Weijia's single bed, self-pity gripped me, and I began to weep, silently at first. Not satisfying enough. I left the room and went out to the toilet down the corridor, the only place that guaranteed some privacy. Squatting over the smelly hole, I had a good cry, letting my tears flow freely. My eyes grew swollen and red. Resolved to savor my right to play the tragic drama queen, I wanted to rest my head against the wall, completing the melancholic image. But the wall was coated with dried phlegm and worse.

I went to the kitchen to wash my hands and face. We shared both the small toilet and spacious kitchen with two other families, although we had individual sinks so we could pay for water separately. Before I could use the tap, I had to shift a large basin brimming with water—Ma had been stealing it for years. She would place the basin under a tap dripping too faintly for the meter gauge to notice. I had tried to dissuade her: water cost next to nothing, and a whole month's hassle probably saved just a few *fen* (cents), enough for just one oily breakfast doughstick. But every morning she saw herself getting that huge basin of water for free.

So typical of Ma, I murmured to myself resentfully. She thought she was smart, yet she failed to see the bigger picture. Why couldn't she see that I was a brilliant student? If she let me stay at school and get a good education, I might become successful, even rich, and then I would give her more money and pools of free water! My eyes began to water again.

Roused by my noise, Nai padded quietly into the kitchen. She poured some hot water into another basin, and handed me a hot towel. "Tinghua!" Patting my thin arms, Nai added, "Arms will never be as strong as legs."

I returned to bed chewing over her idiom. Why can't the weak contend with the strong? What if I disobeyed? Ran away? But where to? Our relatives in another province? Even if I could make my way there, why would they keep me? Why run away anyway? I just wanted to continue my studies, live the life I was living.

If I absolutely refused, Ma would probably throw me out, as she had Xiaoshi, several times. Spoiled by Nai, he tried his first cigarette, stolen from Father, when he was just eight. He engaged in countless fights and caused endless headaches for the family. Just a few months earlier, after he smashed up our home in an argument, our heartbroken mother tried to disown him and leave him in a juvenile delinquent center. But he was too young. If she disowned me, I wouldn't be able to support myself.

When I calmed down, I reached the sad conclusion that I had no choice but dingzhi. I never had many choices anyway. Ma decided on my hairstyle and chose clothes for me. She owned me.

Eventually I drifted into sleep, with a Russian hero as my comfort blanket. Pavel Korchaguin was the inspirational character in *How Steel Is Made*, a Soviet revolutionary classic set in the Great Patriotic War. Pavel's motto became mine, too: "One's life should be spent like this: when a man recalls his life, he will not regret wasting his youth or achieving nothing. He will be proud that he has devoted all his life to the magnificent cause of Communism."

I had written out this motto in large characters and posted it on the wall beside my bed—or rather our bed. I loved Soviet literature, not that I had much choice, for China's isolation was such that foreign literature basically meant Soviet literature. Pavel's creator, author Nikolai Ostrovski, never went to university either. Perhaps my firsthand experience with the sweat of the proletariat would enrich my life and writing too?

No farewell party for me. I was too embarrassed to tell my classmates from Number Forty-two School that I was about to become a worker.

The last day of 1980, sunny but cold. In the morning, I went to the factory to register and the world went on as normal.

Three dozen new workers gathered at Liming headquarters. Some looked young, fresh from school, but most were considerably older. With darker skin and coarse hands, they had clearly been "repairing the earth"—their scornful term for tilling the land. Now they looked happy, and with good reason. In 1968, after using the young Red Guards to spark the fire of Cultural Revolution, Chairman Mao decided to send all students, upon graduation, to the countryside to be reeducated by the peasants. Maybe the Great Helmsman felt his disciples had caused enough trouble; maybe it was just an easy way to keep them productively occupied. At the end of the 1970s, millions of sent-down youths somehow made their way home and found themselves competing for what few jobs were available with recent graduates. The dingzhi policy was initially aimed at resolving their unemployment.

I was too young to be sent to the countryside. Without tasting the hardship of rural exile, or the bitterness of unemployment, I couldn't appreciate the joy of holding this "rice bowl" in the city. Sitting among my fellow workers inside a meeting hall, I observed the proceedings as if watching a play.

With a speech of welcome and an air of importance, a factory official lectured us on the rules. One aim was to instill us with a sense of secrecy. Under no circumstances could we reveal to outsiders that the Liming factory produced rockets, nor could we say its code name, "105" (like all military factories in China, ours had a code). "For any violation, severe punishment will follow, as it may jeopardize national security," the official warned. I paid greater attention to his unusual hooked nose. He reminded me of a parrot and behaved like one, constantly repeating government slogans.

He told us not to come to our posts late and not to leave early. Each new worker had to serve three years' apprenticeship, during which time courting was strictly forbidden. Any violation, once discovered, would delay the apprenticeship. All factory property belonged to the state. Anyone picking a flower or taking a nail home would be heavily fined.

"*Aiya*, are you from another planet?" hissed my fellow villager Chen Songling, furiously scribbling down notes. I was pleased to have bumped into him that day. "To leave a good impression on the leaders, get yourself a notebook and scribble something!"

New employees all had to go through such a training session. Mine had only just begun.

My mind soon wandered with my gaze out of the meeting hall, and up the high walls that encircled the compound. Since this was a military factory, security was tight, with armed soldiers guarding the gate leading to the production area. It all looked so forbidding and grown up.

Later that evening, my mother held a symbolic handover ceremony at home. With two hands, she passed her toolbox to me, as if it were a treasure chest. "Take it," she ordered solemnly. "Working at a factory, you can always make use of these tools. I no longer need them." I thought I saw tears lingering in her eyes, and I wondered why.

In my dreams, I always saw myself grasping a pen, writing beautiful, compelling things. Now I was holding a rectangular metal box, its green paint peeling around the edges. A metallic smell rose as I opened the lid: no shining jewels or treasure lay within, but pincers, pliers, wrenches, and screwdrivers, plus half a dozen bicycle wheel spokes—Ma never wasted anything. I picked up a wrench and shivered at its cold touch. The tools coated my hands in a thin layer of grease. Had Ma been happy as a young turner, standing in front of a turning machine; then as a foreman's assistant; and finally as a middle-aged acid-pickling worker?

When I lifted the box to put it away, I felt its heft again. As a young girl, I was ever so impatient. "When can I grow up, Ma? When, when?" Now. At this moment. Unwilling and ill prepared, I was thrust into the adult world.

Chapter 3

Masters of the Nation

Out of the tall workshop buildings black chimneys rose higher, interrupting the skyline like legs of a spider dead on its back. Smoke seeped out, lingering awhile in the cold air, then dissolving slowly into nothing.

At school, we wrote about factory chimneys whenever teachers assigned compositions on our country's great achievements. With stock phrases such as "magnificent chimneys soaring into the sky," children across China reinforced these symbols of socialist progress. But viewing the real thing, I found them abrupt and ugly.

On the last day of our monthlong training session, we were taken for a walking tour around the Liming production area. Although my mother worked there all her life, I had never gone inside: no one was permitted entry without an official photographic pass. The tangle of pipelines at ground level struck a discordant note. Some were bandaged with white plastic, others hissed violently as the gas fought to escape like a trapped animal. At turns in the pipeline, white mist oozed out.

The tour started in the farthest corner of the southern compound and continued to the main compound in the north, crossing a railway line that divided the factory in two. I didn't expect the immense scale of the factory, nor its utter bleakness in winter. Vast, impersonal, and downright ugly in parts, Liming mixed the monumental and the plain messy—coal dumps, slag heaps, and massive buildings black with dirty windows. In one corner, I was surprised to find an isolated stretch of railway line where steam trains puffed to and fro, transporting heavy goods.

On the tarmac roads, there were few people but plenty of slogans. "Warmly congratulate the successful launch of the carrier rocket" read a massive sign papered over one side entrance, the bold red characters fading into pink. Other slogans hung from wires across the road and decorated the walls. "Work hard, build a beautiful socialist country," "Thoroughly clear away the poison of the Gang of Four," and "Unite our thoughts, follow the Party."

"The building to the right-hand side is Unit Twelve, the foundry," droned the Parrot. "Opposite is number thirteen, the forge." After walking around for the whole afternoon, we eventually stopped in front of an elegant facade. "Comrades, this is the oldest building in the factory. Look carefully—you can still see the date on the plaque. It was a typical construction of the late nineteenth century, wooden structure inside, brick and stone outside." He paused to find a satisfactory conclusion. "I'm proud to say that few other plants boast such a long history!"

If there was pride in Liming's history as a pioneer in China's military industry, it was tempered with shame. After a humiliating defeat at Britain's hands in the Opium War, the Qing government decided China must learn Western technology, and launched the Self-Strengthening Movement, China's first modernization program, to spur industrial development. In 1886, the "Jinling Machinery Manufacture Bureau" was established in Nanjing—using the city's alternative name, Jinling, or "Gold Mountain." With imported machinery, the factory made cannons, guns, artillery pieces, and cannonballs packed with dynamite.

The Korean and Cold Wars accelerated the development of China's defense industry and transformed Jinling from a small, workshop-style operation to a major military player, the Liming that I knew. Fearful of U.S. threats in the 1950s, China turned to its Soviet elder brother for help. Though the Parrot played down the role of the army of Soviet experts who had descended on China, everyone knew that China's first missiles were Soviet-designed, or modified versions of Soviet models.

Standing in the looming shadows, I was tired and cold. The factory's past glory and continued prominence, both exaggerated by our tiresome guide, failed to inspire. I wished I were at home, doing my homework, or even my embroidery.

My glasses steamed up as soon as I entered the workshop. Before I could see again, the smell of grease, unlike any smell I had known before, filled my nostrils.

I was being led to my new post. After one month's training at headquarters, we were assigned jobs in different factory units. High marks in the exam for new workers won me a desirable job—checking pressure gauges at Work Unit Number Twenty-three, which dealt with meters and measurements in the factory. My new world was hidden upstairs at the very end of Unit Twenty-one, by the back gate of the main compound.

"This is our new apprentice, Little Zhang," began Wang Dengshi, the short and energetic man who delivered me to my new life. In a Chinese factory, all young people are addressed as Little, plus one's family name, while older people are known as Old something, to their peers at least. The "little ones" can't address their elders directly, but only with the respectful "Master."

I cleared my glasses to see three men in the pressure-gauge workshop. "This is Master Lin Decai, Master Cheng Jingming, and Master Lan Houling," introduced Boss Wang. I shook their outstretched hands awkwardly. Another new ritual to learn.

"Welcome, welcome!"

"Sit, sit down!"

The masters all stared at me, smiling politely.

"*Hao, hao, hao,*" said Master Lin—"Good, good, good"—"Eh, looks like someone who's got *wenhua*!"

"Actually, I only graduated from junior middle school," I confessed, pushing back the big glasses that slipped down my small nose. I was embarrassed to claim the culture and education that "wenhua" implied.

"That's not bad," said Master Lan. Pointing at Lin, he went on in a high-pitched voice, "Before, he knew only the two characters for man and woman, so that he wouldn't go to the wrong toilet!" Lan revealed that Lin was a farm boy from neighboring Anhui province, recruited because the factory suddenly needed more staff during the Great Leap Forward. Lin had learned to write his name from the anti-illiteracy classes organized by our factory. "But look at him now," Master Lan continued, "he's so cultured that he practices calligraphy every day!" He opened his big red mouth to release a girlish giggle.

Everyone else laughed, too. I managed a smile, without understanding why.

Master Lan was in his late thirties, thin, hunchbacked, with a boyish hairstyle. His pale face was as smooth as a woman's. The moustache on his upper lip was so thin you could see each individual hair. His brownish eyes, unusual in a Chinese face, were clear and untroubled. There was something amiable and childlike about him. I decided immediately that I liked this man. He wore a green army uniform, minus insignia, and rubber army shoes. I soon came to know that he would wear blue when not in green; both sets were free gifts from his wife's work unit, an army uniform factory.

"Why so happy?" Master Lin said to Lan. "Eaten some bee droppings, haven't you?" There was no malice in his tone, but—bee droppings? Despite my curiosity, I stopped myself from interrupting my elders, and only later learned that was farmer's slang for honey. "A country bumpkin, I don't know nothing and you the wenhua man in our group, the general among us dwarfs," snorted Master Lin.

In his mid-forties and rather stocky, Master Lin's peasant upbringing was all apparent, especially from his earthy crew cut, the work of an amateur barber in his Anhui village—to save money, Lin had it cut when he visited home every few months. A homemade woolen jumper stretched over his thick waist, round and solid as a millstone. Below the jumper's V neck was the outfit's highlight—a starched collar attached to strings under his arm and over his holey undershirt. Since proper shirts were luxuries, most men wore cheap cotton jerseys under their jackets. My father wore a similar collar device to work, in the hope it resembled a proper white shirt when you buttoned up your jacket, or pulled on a jumper. But worn on its own, as Lin often had it, the collar resembled a silly bib.

"Old Lin, you would have become a good calligrapher, I say, if you just copied a decent copybook, in free style, or imitation Song Dynasty, anything," cut in Master Cheng. In a blue cloth coat, our uniform, he was cleaning a standard gauge with a blower. Similar in age to Master Lin, Cheng had a noble, handsome, but rather serious face topped with fine black hair scrupulously combed back, in the style of many top Chinese leaders. His sharp eyes, stern expression, and reserved manner left little doubt that he would be difficult to deal with.

"I don't know nothing. Unlike certain people, I don't want to be anybody, a calligrapher or whatever," said Master Lin, looking down at his own desk.

A slight uneasiness swept across Master Cheng's face, like a cloud casting brief shadows on a sunny day.

The masters asked some basic questions about me. I was

glad when they switched back to gossiping about people I didn't know and factory matters I couldn't follow. When that conversation dried up, they sipped tea from white enamel mugs, stained deep brown by strong, cheap tea leaves. In China, no work is done without tea.

They weren't busy, I noticed. The factory was preoccupied by next week's Spring Festival, the most important date on the Chinese calendar, the masters explained, and we only had work to do when people brought gauges to us for checking or fixing.

Putting on his glasses, Master Lin began to copy lines from the *People's Daily*. I threw a glance his way and spotted the headline: "Workers All Over the Country Enthusiastically Stick to Their Posts on the Production Line before Spring Festival." As the Party mouthpiece, the paper was so dull that people joked it worked quicker than sleeping pills. The fact that it held only two types of stories contributed to this soporific quality: the paper either reported good news or preached to China's one-billion-strong population on how they should behave.

Yet Master Lin copied pages at a time, and I suddenly understood why Master Lan mocked him as a calligrapher. One wouldn't copy *People's Daily* for the art of calligraphy, nor for its literary merits. But at least it served one purpose—he looked occupied.

Master Lan studied his tools for a while before dozing off in his chair, his head drooping sideways, spittle dripping from his open mouth.

"Are there books I can study, Master Lin?" I asked my master—Boss Wang had decided that I was to be the apprentice of Lin, the oldest member of the pressure-gauge section.

"Books?" My master raised a surprised look above his copying. "Oh, yes, I've got one somewhere. I'll look when I've got a moment, but no hurry, you've just arrived."

I was not used to idling. Even during school holidays, I had homework as well as embroidery. I thought about the class I left behind. My classmates must be very busy right now, preparing for the end-of-term exam. And very cold, too, came a selfishly comforting thought. In the winter, we were not allowed to stamp our numb feet even though the classroom was icy and broken windows sucked in the biting wind. The chilblains on my hands were already shrinking.

Settling into a chair and desk that belonged to a colleague on sick leave, I looked around. The workshop was roughly the size of my classroom, where fifty students squeezed into four neat rows. Here a large worktable with a greasy plastic surface dominated the room, its wooden legs dark and shiny from countless greasy hands—only close to the floor did the original color survive. Three devices for testing pressure gauges crouched on the corners of the table, in hibernation under transparent covers.

Despite the warmth and bright light, I couldn't feel at ease in the workshop. Perhaps it was the black iron window frames. Unlike the wooden frames at home, these were heavy and cold, almost hostile. I imagined prison windows would look like that.

So, this was to be my confinement.

What could I do? I longed to pop across the corridor for a chat with Rong Ling, another young apprentice assigned to the power-gauge section, in the room right opposite ours. But I wasn't supposed to. Our two sections, together with another that handled electric gauges, comprised the meter-and-gauge group, all under the leadership of Boss Wang.

The only "event" of note that day had come when the boss introduced Rong Ling and me to all of our colleagues. The head of electronics, Fatty Wang, squinted at us from top to toe, as if selecting a daughter-in-law. "How young you two are!" she said in a singsong voice. Mourning her lost youth already? Fatty Wang, short and fat, was only in her mid-thirties.

"You've got lots of hair!" she told Rong. My fellow apprentice's neatly braided plaits spread on her shoulders like broomsticks. Whenever bored, Rong would chew their tips, sucking for inspiration. Each feature on her goose-egg-shaped face was pretty enough, yet the whole combination somehow lacked vitality. Her well-formed body was buried under a yellow jacket that left her face more yellow.

"Eh, not bad looking," Fatty Wang's thick palm rested on my thin shoulder. "Quite tall, aren't you? Only a bit too skinny. Still, you are earning now, your mother will fatten you up." I smiled at her awkwardly, for I knew I wasn't pretty. A lumpy Chinese jacket covered my thin body. My old-fashioned, heavy-framed glasses made me look serious and my curly hair was a mess: just like my mother and grandma, I happened to be one of the few Chinese with naturally curly hair.

Doing nothing all day was surprisingly tiring.

That night, I dreamed I had become a steelworker. Dressed in the same canvas uniform and peaked cap as the worker on our clock, I gripped a shovel and fed fuel into an insatiable furnace of dancing fire. My face glowed scarlet and orange from the flames, as streams of sweat rolled down into the white towel around my neck. This was a worker's life, full of action, noise, and purpose!

But I woke up, only to face another empty day.

Luckily, Chinese New Year was fast approaching. On New Year's Eve, as was customary, the off-work horn blew two and a half hours early. No one did any work that day anyway. After a bit of cleaning up, workers chatted and waited in excited anticipation of four consecutive days' holiday, the longest of the year. We only had public holidays to look forward to; there was there was no personal holiday allowance at all.

I rode home, my bike laden with ham, fish, and fruits: as part of the welfare package, wealthier state-owned enterprises presented workers with gifts at festival time.

I had a rocket launch to thank for this year's generosity. In May 1980, China successfully blasted a carrier rocket into the Pacific. Meetings nationwide applauded this first launch from Chinese soil, a symbol of our ever-improving rocket technology. We had watched a documentary about the launch during our training session. From a top-secret location in Xinjiang, China's nuclear testing ground in the desert northwest, the white carrier rocket shot into the blue sky, its tail burning with flame. It landed, as planned, eight thousand kilometers away, near the Solomon Islands. We didn't know then that the launch would bring us practical benefits in addition to national pride. And only later did I learn the real significance of the launch: capable of carrying multimegaton warheads, the missile also enabled China, for the first time, to strike the continental United States.

I knew my factory had played some role, but not exactly what. Anyway, Beijing rewarded all factories under the Ministry of Aerospace.

Outside the factory walls, rationing was still in practice, though the quantity per person was steadily growing. Queues were common. Ma carried half a dozen colorful coupons with her—a little pig on the meat coupon, a cotton flower for cloth—so she could grab the shopping opportunity whenever it arose. You might wait years for a bicycle, an indispensable item still hard to buy. Years of following in Soviet footsteps meant China prioritized industrial goods over consumer products.

Arriving downstairs with the heavy load, I had to shout for help. Ma ran down like the wind.

"*Aiya*, mother of mine!" came her pet phrase, equally good for joy, surprise, or anger. "So many goodies!" she added with a smile and a poke of the ham. Ma examined each item like a soldier studying a war trophy. "Wonderful to have a work unit look after you, isn't it? I gave you a good rice bowl. Cherish it." She rarely missed an opportunity to remind me that she had supplied this lifeline. It had become her hobby and obsession. She could put it in many ways, depending on her mood. Today, she was in good spirits. Poverty had always made Spring Festival a stressful time for her, for all Chinese families felt obliged to produce good dishes, snacks for visitors, and new clothes for the children. This year's free supply eased the pressure.

In the communal kitchen, Nai was bustling over the annual feast. An excellent cook, she had been working around the clock. The evidence was piled up on different plates: cooked food, half-cooked food, and food still to be cooked. Bang! Bang! She crashed out a rhythm on the chopping board, mincing meat with a large chopper in each hand.

Our neighbors were also busy in the kitchen. There was an unspoken competition to see which family could produce more and better dishes. The chefs chatted and tasted each other's food. Living on top of each other, we got along well with our neighbors, borrowing rice and lending a hand whenever necessary. In a one-roomed flat at the far end was a young couple with a little girl. The other family was a middle-aged couple with their daughter Little Flower, who was still waiting for the government to assign her a job.

"Yesterday, an old colleague of mine came to see me. Moley Miao, the women with a big mole on her chin, remember? She said I could join her as an administrator at Confucius Temple Market," Ma revealed as I helped her clean the flat. "They need more administrators to collect management fees from *getihu* during the Spring Festival. If they like me, they may hire me as long term staff."

Getihu were the new breed of private businesspeople running the market stalls and changing the country. Many of them in Nanjing started their businesses in the Confucius Temple Market, the heart of a busy residential and tourist area about twenty minutes' bike ride from home, through Wuding Gate and toward the city center. Rows of stalls there sold anything and everything of use: cooking pots, padded trousers, straw brooms, pickled pig tails, dried persimmon, frogs on skewers, and crickets in tiny bamboo cages. With better service and cheaper prices than the state-run shops, such markets sprung up all over the city, like mushrooms after spring rain.

"Really? Are you going for it?" Good news, then. I knew that Ma, still young and active, would be dangerously bored at home.

"I'll start tomorrow," she said, "just to give it a try. The pay isn't bad, and the job itself doesn't sound too demanding. *Ai*," she let out a sigh while dusting the top most windows with a chicken-feather duster. "There are not a huge amount of choices for unskilled old bones like mine. It's just…getihu," she gave a disapproving tut-tut. "Not sure about them."

Confucius himself first placed the merchant class far down the social pecking order. In the 1950s, Chairman Mao went much further—abolishing the private sector in his failed bid to provide wealth for all. All private businesses were chopped off as "capitalist tails." My mother felt it was degrading for a retired worker from a state-owned enterprise to work with them. Yet she was pragmatic enough not to reject the opportunity.

Outside, kids started letting off firecrackers. Strings of explosives writhed in the air, deafening everyone nearby.

This year's supply of firecrackers was the best in years, thanks, in fact, to the getihu. Children in our village couldn't wait to get their hands on them. With earsplitting noise and squeals of joy, an old year was ending, and the new one was impatient to start.

Chapter 4

Raw Rice Has Been Cooked

Happiness glistened on our front door. Printed in gold on red shiny paper was the large character *fu*. Meaning happiness or good fortune, it shows a person knelt before an altar, praying for happiness. The character was stuck upside down, fu *dao*, in wordplaying tradition to ensure that fu would "arrive"—another meaning of "dao"—at our home. Behind the door, our whole family, dressed in our best outfits, gathered for the annual reunion dinner. I had a new cover, made of floral-patterned cotton, for my padded Chinese jacket, and a pair of leather shoes instead of cotton slippers.

In keeping with tradition, Nai first brought in a fish cooked in soy sauce and announced: "We have fish every year," then put it aside for later consumption. In Chinese, *yu*, or fish, sounds like the character for surplus or abundance—hope for a prosperous year ahead.

At Ma's insistence, Nai sat opposite the door, in the seat reserved for the most honorable person. Ordinarily she didn't even sit at the table but ate her tiny portion in the kitchen, like a servant. Ma then stood up, raising a little porcelain cup with teardrops engraved around the edge. "A lot has happened this year. I retired, Little Li took over my job, and I am trying to get another one."

"Yes, go for the Confucius Temple job," cut in my father, who had rushed back for the festival. "Deng Xiaoping said, 'Whether white or black, a cat is a good cat so long as it

catches the rat.' I say a job is a good job so long as it pays."
Pleased with his remarks, he voiced them loud enough for
the whole building to hear.

Ignoring her husband, Ma continued her speech.
"Sesame stalks put forth flowers notch by notch. I wish
for our lives to get better and better. Cheers!"

Our cups and glasses clinked in the air. I drank tea since
I was allergic to alcohol, while everyone else downed a type
of white liquor, the firewater that soon turned their faces
red. Even my brother Xiaoshi was helping himself. He
was tall for his age, but painfully skinny, as if forgetting
to grow horizontally. Some of his naughty friends were
already whistling for him outside our window. It was Nai
who made him sit down and eat.

"Eat, eat, I have loads more," Nai urged, with an ear-to-
ear smile that revealed her deep dimples.

With plenty of materials to work with, Nai and Ma had
cooked the best New Year banquet in years: chicken soup;
sweet-and-sour fish, traditionally shaped like a squirrel;
a "lucky reunion" stew in a clay pot; stir-fried green
vegetables; and Nai's specialty, the "lion's head"—a dish
of minced meatballs. Food is always the thread that binds
Chinese families close together. As our appetites rose with
the steam, our chopsticks seized their targets with speed
and precision. Spring Festival was the only time we could
enjoy food without limit.

"Delicious, Nai!" my sister Weijia praised. Wearing a
stripy woolen scarf, an expensive gift from her boyfriend,
she looked particularly attractive today. Her double-lidded
eyes were so lively they seemed to talk, and her fresh white
face resembled a young lily just rising above the water.
While I was the dreamer, and our brother the troublemaker,
Weijia was the sensible child among the siblings. She also
had a different surname, Huang, from our mother's side.
In China, children take their father's family names, but

since my mother was an only child, she had demanded that her first child, boy or girl, would continue the Huang family line.

"From now on, no more embroidery," Ma announced. "How long have we done this *tamade* embroidery, Nai? Ten years, mother of mine! I can't remember how many times the needles stabbed my hands. Enough is enough. I'd like to rest after my day's work. Nai, you can take things easy. Let me toast you," Ma touched her cup with Nai's.

"No, no, no," Nai protested, "I'm an old useless woman."

"Useless?" Ma arched her eyebrows yet higher. "Nai, you have slaved all your life for us. Without you, our family would have collapsed. Only because of you, we have survived, all survived." She lifted her head and tossed back the remaining liquor.

"I want to toast you, too," said Father. Towering over Nai's little figure, he touched her porcelain cup with his and slurped down a pickled duck's bottom. He made such noises as though, if he chewed quietly, we wouldn't know it was his favorite dish. Luckily, eating quietly is not required table manners in China. After a satisfied burp, he continued, in his usual loud voice: "I should really thank you, Nai. You've made a much greater contribution to this family than myself." His handsome, dark face filled with the red flush of alcohol.

Father, named Zhang Songshou ("pine tree," "longevity"), was blessed with a full forehead and a strong square jaw—auspicious features according to traditional Chinese physiognomy. He wore a buttoned-up navy tunic, a style popularized by Dr. Sun Yat-sen and worn by everyone from Mao down to the peasantry. Indeed, it had become a national uniform for Chinese men, the only difference being the material one could afford. Even my brother was clad in a blue cotton tunic.

The commonplace attire failed to dampen Father's dignified air. He was just a low-ranking clerk, though I didn't know exactly what that meant. In fact, I didn't know my father well at all. For us, he was more of a distant relative, never around. Since we called Ma's mother Nai, we had to call his mother Granny Zhang, a respectful but distant term.

Everyone else called her Granny Long Tits, after the pendulous breasts this formidable woman aired in public each sweaty Nanjing summer. Nobody in the neighborhood ever forgot the time she shocked the postman by flipping her breasts over her shoulder. The wife of an affluent merchant, she had money but few manners.

Her eldest and most spoiled child, Father graduated from senior middle school in 1951, two years after the Communist takeover. He was soon plunged into the harsh reality of New China as a prison officer in the *laogai*—the "reform through labor" system. Father was sent to a labor camp in neighboring Anhui province to help supervise thirty thousand inmates—landlords, Nationalist Party members, and other potential opponents detained without trial. The prisoners labored on the Huai River, whose lower reaches were plagued by floods. The project was gargantuan, broadening the river's passage and removing part of a mountain. Relying on the man-conquering-nature spirit of 1950s China but little food, hundreds dropped dead from exhaustion and hunger. Father told me about those days when I chanced on a yellowing photo of him in uniform, young, handsome, and slightly jaunty, looking forward to his future.

After that, Father's history became sketchy. In 1958, just a year after his marriage, he was labeled a "rightist," a crime he supposedly committed after heeding Chairman Mao's call to "let one hundred flowers bloom and one hundred schools of thought contend!" The Party invited intellectuals to offer suggestions and criticism. Though hardly an intellectual, my father offered enough critical words to fall into the Communist trap, along with half a million other victims across the country. Our Great Helmsman casually remarked that there were leftists, rightists, and those in the middle among the masses, but ninety-five percent were good. To root out that rotten five percent, however, work units everywhere compiled blacklists long enough to meet the quota. Father was publicly denounced, his salary cut in half. He kept his job but was stripped of his uniform.

I was ignorant of his disgrace until I failed to get into the Foreign Languages School. When rehabilitation finally came in 1978, his name was cleared, and he was paid a symbolic amount for his financial losses. Father was then transferred to work as a clerk at a casting factory manned by former laogai prisoners in a small city in Anhui province, closer to Nanjing than before. It was almost impossible to be transferred to another province, even one's home province, due to the draconian controls of *hukou*, the household registration system.

Hu means family, and *kou* member, but together they contain not a hint of domestic warmth. In reality, hukou was a cruel tool wielded by the government to bind people geographically and occupationally, with little consideration for the family. Residence permits tied China's citizens to where they were born or employed. When I was young, the police sometimes turned up in the dead of night to check our battered, palm-sized hukou book. Anyone not included could be arrested and repatriated to their original place of residence. Granny Long Tits's old maid, who had served her mistress all her life, was kicked back to her home village in this way. Hukou effectively chained peasants to their villages and kept millions of couples apart. Those who lived far from home were allowed twelve days every year to spend with their families. Twelve days! The emotional and sexual needs of the masses were of no concern to the leadership.

Food rations and other social welfare were issued according to each household's hukou book. Because my father wasn't in our hukou book, he was not counted when Liming allocated our family a flat. As a result, our flat was small even by the factory's standards. No wonder Ma was so bitter. Even in his absence there were too many daily reminders of the damage he had caused.

His long absence and short temper meant that none of us children were close to him. Even in a calm mood, he always spoke at the top of his voice. "It's partly a professional habit," he once explained. "At work, none of us talked to the prisoners, but barked orders. 'Get the bloody job done quickly. Otherwise, no supper for you tonight!'"

In his better moods, Father shouted jokes with little regard for taste or sensitivity. "You are not our natural daughter, you know," he used to tell me when I was little. "We picked you up from a coal dump. That's why you are so dark." Most Chinese consider dark skin ugly. His joke haunted me for years. As the middle child, I wasn't very confident anyway.

Spurred by the spirit and good food on our New Year's Eve table, Father was in the mood for fun. "Recently, a big fight broke out in our dining hall," he began. "The man who sold food there always asked '*Mo?*' which in Anhui dialect means 'What?' One day when he shouted 'Mo?' to the person next in line, the guy replied 'Mo,' meaning bread rolls in Shandong dialect. 'Mo?' the seller raised his voice. 'Mo!' came the same reply. 'What the fucking mo do you want?' 'I want the fucking mo!' After a few more rounds, the seller grew so angry he slapped the man with his soup ladle! 'Shut up your fucking mo!'"

We all burst out laughing. Father had a talent for mimicking different dialects and wearing different faces, skills he picked up from prisoners under his watch. He was pleased with our reaction, and his own laughter thundered across the room.

Firecrackers jolted me awake early on New Year's Day. Their explosions banished evil spirits, leaving the air heavy with gunpowder, mixing with the aroma of cooking food. When I was little, these sounds and smells used to excite me immensely. I would run around outside with my little friends, looking for firecrackers that had not exploded so that we could light them ourselves.

I kicked out the cold copper hot-water bottle and turned, my quilt tightly folded to keep in the warmth. On top of the cupboard, Chairman Mao's Little Red Book waved mechanically inside the hero clock. It didn't matter what time it was now. No plan. Nothing to look forward to.

I used to get together with school friends during the festival, visit them at home. But this year I was still too embarrassed to face my former classmates. Whenever I bumped into them, I would mumble a few courtesies, then run away as fast as possible. Maybe they thought I had become arrogant, now that I was a "salary woman." I found myself friendless and alone.

Spring Festival is the ideal time to work on one's *guanxi*, the connections or interpersonal relationships so vital to life in China. Packing plenty of gifts, you visit the home of whoever you wish to be on better terms with. People love to have guests during the festival, a sign of popularity. Apprentices pay respect to their masters, hoping they will teach them every skill and trick and hold nothing back. But my master went home to the countryside. If I were smart, I would pay a courtesy call on Boss Wang. But I felt too embarrassed to do even that.

After I got up, I decided to look at my textbooks, particularly Chinese literature and English. Yet to my horror, I could not find them anywhere. Had Ma thrown them out? It wouldn't be the first time. Once an older cousin from Shandong province came for the summer, bringing half a dozen wonderful novels as gifts, including *Ode to Youth,* a revolutionary hit in the 1950s, and a trio by literary giant Ba Jin, *Home, Spring,* and *Autumn.* I guessed her father, a ranking military officer, had confiscated them, for they were not available in shops. We devoured them until one day Ma sold them to a rubbish collector for a mere half a *yuan!*

While I was allergic to alcohol, Ma seemed allergic to books. There was no sight of them in our flat, which was why my sister and I called it a "cultural desert." I never had the chance to finish this last set, bought when I started the first year of senior middle school, little knowing my school days would soon end.

"Have you seen my textbooks, Ma?" I asked when she returned from her first day's work at Confucius Temple market.

"Our flat is so small. I've sold all the useless books lying around," she replied, not even looking at me. Before sitting down on her usual chair by the window, she folded up a newspaper on the table. "If I kept everything, our home would be as messy as a rubbish dump!"

"But those books are mine!" I protested, pouring out the tears and frustration that had been building for days.

"Yours?" she snapped, the two new moons dancing above her slanted eyes. I realized too late she was in a bad mood, and tired. "I paid for them! It's only been a matter of days since you began to work. Don't forget who put the rice bowl into your hands."

Forget? Did I have a chance to forget? "It was you who forced me out of school and forced me to take your rice bowl!"

"Zhang Lijia! How ungrateful you are!" Ma always used

my full name when I was in trouble. "Don't you see what a great sacrifice I made for you? Without this job, I am nothing, nobody! Would you be happy if you ended up like Little Flower?"

She lowered her voice for this insult, pointing next door. Our neighbor's daughter had always had difficulty with her studies. Fighting back tears, I said, as calmly as I could: "Who cares about your precious rice bowl? If you can, please return to your great job, as I would love to return to school."

"Aiya, mother of mine!" She sprang up. My mother usually spoke like southern rain dripping down from a curved roof, soft, clear, and unhurried. But when she was furious, the gentle raindrops gave way to a shrill attack. With one hand on her hip, she shot me an accusing finger. "You've grown up. Your wings are strong now, and you dare to argue back. What did I do to deserve this? Do you have any idea how hard it's been for me? I had three young mouths to feed, an old woman to look after, and I got no help from your dad. For thirteen years, I did acid pickling. Any idea how dangerous, how harmful that was? Now I'm retired, I didn't take one day's rest and went straight into another job. What was it for?"

She broke off. A trail of tears slid down her face, like a string of pearls reflecting the lamplight. She blew her nose and carried on. "You little beast! Do you know, I was out in the cold for nine hours today, collecting fees from stall owners and peddlers? They can't have proper jobs like yours, so they have to take up buying and selling in the street, to be looked down upon by people. While you…"

"Fuck!" shouted my father, barging his way into the flat and our argument. "You shameful, unfilial thing! Outrageous! You got my bike and a new watch from Ma. Still ungrateful? Get lost!" He pushed me hard on the chest, and sent me slamming into the door.

"Stop!" intervened my little grandma, who had stayed at the stove chanting a Buddhist mantra until the row escalated. "My left eyelid has been twitching for days." She bravely held back Father's big hand, though she trembled like a leaf in strong wind. "You aren't going to kill Little Li. She's only a child."

Turning to Ma, Nai went down on her knees. "Yufang, I beg you," she said, clasping her hands together in supplication. "For my sake, stop. What are you arguing for on New Year's Day? I thought our family was going to get better."

I fled into the darkness. Despite the cold, there were many people outside, mostly kids playing. The sounds of fireworks exploded back and forth. With a sharp whistle, golden chrysanthemums blossomed in the dark sky and then fell like shooting stars.

Where to go? My brother Xiaoshi was an old hand at expulsion. Whenever he drove Ma mad, she would bark at him to get lost. And he would calmly do so, reemerging the next day. As long as he went to school Ma stopped worrying about him. I guessed he spent the night with one of his naughty friends, or in some secret hiding place in the wilderness. But I didn't know any hiding place. I felt truly lost. There wasn't even a park in this densely populated village where I could sit and cry quietly for a while.

My legs automatically took me toward my old school: I used to walk four times a day along the route. Battered by the cold wind, I drew in my neck like a turtle and pushed my hands up the spacious sleeves of my old-style jacket. From time to time, fireworks illuminated the village. Through moody eyes, I focused for the first time on the ugliness of my world: the rows of block buildings projected little life. Everything was practical and functional. There was a vegetable market, a shop selling daily necessities, a clinic, and two schools.

In five minutes, I was standing between the primary school and the middle school, at the heart of the village. Fond memories of schooldays fermented in my mind like old liquor. Then, the future overflowed with possibilities; now, my fate was sealed.

"Aiya!" I screamed and jumped when a firecracker exploded on the ground in front of me—this new type exploded wherever you threw it. I looked around and saw a group of boys cackling wildly. Swallowing my anger, I moved quickly away: it was best to avoid those "waiting-for-jobs youth," a term coined by the newspapers. With nothing to occupy them, idle youths hung around, smoking, fighting, or falling into crime. Two months earlier, two of my neighbors had been executed—one nineteen and the other barely sixteen years old—for instigating a fight that killed another youngster in the village.

Their execution was a big day out for my school. The sixteen-year-old was a former classmate of mine named Roc. His old classmates and other children, as young as twelve, joined the excited crowds filling to the ten-thousand-seat Nanjing Stadium for the public sentencing rally. "Scare the monkey by killing a chicken"—the authorities invited the masses to witness the iron fist of proletarian dictatorship and to draw lessons from negative examples. The guilty verdicts were read out to loud applause. Then the condemned, wearing a placard stating their crimes, were paraded onto open-top army trucks, toward the execution ground in the western suburbs. I had been to this killing field several times, although in the crush of bodies I never got close enough to witness the spill of blood as, from behind, bullets ripped open the prisoners' heads. But the boys in my village had shared many vivid accounts. The Chinese seemed to take pleasure in this ghoulish spectator sport, watching soldiers kill the "rotten eggs," as local slang termed the baddies. No one doubted they were guilty. This time, however, I didn't follow the herd: Roc wasn't just a "rotten egg." He was a childhood friend who caught cicadas and swam in the Pig Pool with me.

The whole tragic drama, from the fight to the execution, took place so quickly: there were quotas to be met in the crackdown against soaring crime, regardless of whether suspects were under eighteen, technically the minimum age for capital punishment. The only way officials knew how to combat the rising crime was to punish some people swiftly and without mercy. No effort was made to tackle the social roots of the problem.

I too might have ended up as a "waiting-for-job youth." Maybe I ought to have been thankful to have any job at all. For me, Ma had given up the most important and cherished thing in her life, a job that provided self-esteem and identity along with income. I had not acknowledged her sacrifice, which must have hurt her.

Unlike Nai, my mother always liked to stress what she did for us. I never forgot the pair of red leather shoes she bought, the best I ever wore as a child. With poverty so familiar, Chinese were obsessed by price, so in my bliss I did not forget to ask. "Twelve yuan," she replied. That was a lot of money. For days, I stuck out my feet under the school desk to show off my beautiful shoes. Then a classmate wearing an identical pair declared that her mother paid only seven, and told everyone I was a liar—in those years, the same products had the same prices everywhere. Hurt and embarrassed, I confronted Ma, who defended her exaggeration: "I just wanted you to know that things don't come easily for us."

After I grew up, I began to wonder if Ma's stress on her own efforts reflected her jealousy. Three months after the birth of each of her children, Ma went back to her full-time job, like other women in the cities. It was Nai who fed and looked after us. As a result, we were all closer to our grandma. Ma was probably fighting for our affection.

The fact Ma had to fight for something she expected by right compounded the bitterness of her professional and personal life. Her marriage had been a disaster. When she was nineteen, a matchmaker entrusted with the job by Granny Long Tits introduced her to a tall, handsome man with a good job, although in another city. He invited Ma out to dance while on home leave in Nanjing. I imagined they made a wonderful pair, good-looking and good dancers, too. When he soon proposed, Nai urged Ma to accept—not only because she thought him a good candidate but also because she worried her daughter was getting old. In her view, an old maid hanging around the home would bring disgrace on the family.

After their marriage, Father went back to Anhui, leaving Ma a "widow to a live husband," in her own words. She had to function as both mother and father, fixing things at home and changing the heavy gas cylinders. When he came home, life wasn't any better. Under his good looks, he turned out to be selfish, incompetent, and bad-tempered, "rubbish coated in gold and jade," as Ma put it. Worse still, after his disgrace, Ma became politically vulnerable. If Father were not a "stinking rightist," Ma might not have fallen victim to the May Sixteenth Faction accusation either.

Wrapped up in reflection, I was oblivious to the cold. I began to feel more sorry for my mother, and less so for myself. She had been very disappointed in life and particularly in Father. I shouldn't let her down.

Tired and hungry, I decided to head home. I knew Nai was waiting for me, behind the happiness symbol that now looked so misplaced on our door. And after softening me up with some festival food, she would persuade me to apologize to Ma.

"Raw rice has been cooked," she would say.

Chapter 5

The Liming Empire

Two sentries stood at the factory gate, still as robots in the morning chill. Only the white fog of their breath betrayed them as human. When I passed, I stepped off my bike, right foot brushing the ground, like a dragonfly skimming water, before getting back in the saddle. At first, I had always halted completely at the gate, as the rules required, pulled out my pass and opened it up, but now I copied my more confident colleagues, who barely stopped and never opened their passes.

Beyond the back gate, the dark gray rectangle that housed my workshop came into sight. I was earlier than usual.

The first of any apprentice's morning duties was to fetch boiled water for the endless cups of tea to come. Clutching a battered metal thermos, I went downstairs to the massive workshop of Unit Twenty-one. Every day, when the portable hot-water tank was wheeled in, half a dozen apprentices swarmed around its steaming tap, like bees sensing nectar.

Lathing, milling, planning, and grinding, a dozen machines clashed around us in a metallic orchestra of noise and industry. Unit Twenty-one handled the design and manufacture of tools. Three shifts of workers kept its powerful symphony playing day and night. I was fascinated by the spectacular red and gold sparks that sprayed from spinning lathes, though I knew their beauty could be lethal, severing stray fingers.

The workers, all in blue canvas uniforms, worked downstairs. Engineers, union chiefs, family planners, and other cadres of Communist bureaucracy worked upstairs. Most work units shared the same arrangement. As Confucius said, "those who labor with their minds are destined to rule over those who labor with their hands." He would have been pleased to discover that two and a half thousand years later, the situation was unchanged. My gauges group was the only upstairs section to work with our hands.

Taking my turn at the tank, I carefully filled my thermos and returned upstairs, leaving the roar of the factory floor behind. This chore should have served as a daily reminder of my lucky position. Our room was clean and air-conditioned to keep the standard gauges stable.

At eight o'clock sharp, the "start work" horn shook the loudspeakers scattered throughout the walled compound. Only military factories used such horns—as if they were military camps. The sun had just risen, shining lazily without much warmth. Inside the workshop, I sat at my desk, young, energetic, ready to do something, without knowing what.

By eleven, my stomach started to rumble. Breakfast was always porridge, some leftover rice boiled in water that never satisfied me for long. Trying to fool my stomach, I drank more tea, but only felt hungrier.

At twelve, I rushed home for lunch and was back at quarter past one. I wished I could grind out four hours in the afternoon with my own reading. But it wasn't allowed.

I should have been able to trust my watch, but the hour hand never seemed to move from one plum blossom to the next. Made in Nanjing, the city of plum blossoms, it had cost sixty yuan, and was the most expensive gift I had ever received from Ma—apart from the job itself.

Finally, wonderfully, the off-work horn blew at five fifteen. Dashing out, I searched for my father's old Forever-brand bicycle among the hundreds parked in the large shed behind our building. With its large, solid frame, the Forever was a deservedly popular men's model, since it could carry heavy loads—a pig, a sofa, a small family—and lasted a long time, if not forever.

I pedaled fast through the back gate and down the slope right after it. When thousands of workers poured out at high speed, we resembled a flood running through a broken dike. The tide slowed to make its way through the market street where farmers from nearby villages hawked fresh vegetables. On the brick walls behind this resurgent capitalism, faded slogans whispered, "Never forget class struggle."

The flood recovered speed, sweeping toward Wuding New Village, where many of us workers lived. A surging tide again, bicycle bells resounding against the sky, each bobbing black head another faceless part of the Liming factory machine.

Work trickled in as people delivered gauges for repair or annual check-up. Fitted to pipelines or containers, each pressure gauge indicated the capacity of the line or the physical status of the substance inside. Faulty ones could be deadly. Shortly before I joined the factory, a boiler explosion ended two workers' lives. Though the incident was termed an accident, everyone knew a faulty gauge was to blame.

Faulty relations between colleagues could be dangerous, too. Although Master Cheng behaved with authority, no one was officially in charge of our pressure-gauge section, which caused tension among my colleagues.

One day, a large gauge was delivered, showing an unusually high pressure of six hundred kilograms. On a form, I registered its work unit and the specifications that placed it under Cheng's sphere of influence—he considered checking high-pressure gauges a grander task than checking ordinary gauges. Long ago, he had claimed as his domain the inner room that housed the standard gauges.

After several trials, Master Cheng decided to return the severely malfunctioning gauge to the manufacturer. Master Lin watched Cheng from the corner of his eyes.

After everyone went home, I saw my master pick up the gauge. "Little Zhang, stay if you like." Despite his large size, my master was a soft-spoken man. I gladly stayed, for working overtime meant almost half a yuan extra, and, more importantly, time off later. For the precious flexitime, people fought for each hour of overtime, authorized by Boss Wang. On that day, however, Wang was away, and Lin was taking the initiative. He rolled up his shirtsleeves and the legs of his trousers with the air of a soldier readying for battle.

First he opened the gauge's casing, cleaned inside, and checked if the dial was faulty, or the needle loose. Next, he screwed the gauge onto a two-pronged pressure-checking device with a standard gauge on the other side. Since high pressure required a better seal, Master Lin fitted washers inside the connectors and bound them with white tape like injured limbs. He gritted his teeth so hard the muscle in his square jaw shivered as he exerted all his strength to screw the gauge onto the connector using the largest set of wrenches. Helping him to push, I felt for once like a useful assistant. Since both gauges would experience the same pressure, a functioning gauge would read the same as the standard, or within an acceptable range. But the high-pressure gauge was still giving the wrong reading, indicating serious problems. Removing the dial, my master found the hairspring in a messy condition. He sat down to start surgery, twisting the right side of his face to hold a magnifier in his right eye. Patiently, and obviously enjoying himself, he rewound the twisted hairspring. As he worked, he hummed folk songs, something I had never heard him do before.

With he gauge closed back up, he ran the test again, shouting, "102.00, 201.50, 302.00!" and I recorded them on a chart. For the first four months, I was ordered not to check anything myself, only to assist Master Lin. "All within accepted allowance!" he announced proudly.

It was late when we stamped the new expiration date, six months away, on the glass.

The next morning, Master Cheng turned up only a few minutes after me. His stern face fell rock hard when he saw the work surface, an oily mess Master Lin had told me to leave the night before. Lin's untidy methods often irritated the fastidious Cheng. Worse still, Lin had fixed the very gauge he himself had failed to mend. I smelled a storm rising in the greasy air.

"Old Lin, what did you do last night?" Master Cheng shouted as soon as my master walked into the door.

"I fixed the high-pressure gauge," replied Lin, without any trace of boasting in his tone.

"Did you know you violated the rule?" barked Cheng, trying the old trick of gaining the initiative by striking the first blow. "Don't tell me 'you don't know nothing.' The standard gauge should be higher than the tested one. If we had a thousand-kilogram gauge, I would have fixed the gauge myself!"

Master Lin argued, still in his soft voice, that we could use a standard gauge of same specification in special circumstances. And he knew the gauge was needed back urgently. If we sent it outside, it would cost money and time.

"Oh, you sound so unselfish. Chinese peasants are famous for being unselfish." Master Cheng made a face and everyone laughed.

My master was gritting his teeth again. The muscle in his jaw quivered with suppressed anger.

Master Cheng went firmly on. "I know your little plan. You wanted to earn some extra money and flexitime. But did you get Boss Wang's permission?"

"No, I just wanted to give it a try. If I couldn't fix it, I wouldn't claim anything."

"Old Lin," Master Cheng raised his voice, "you wanted to embarrass me, didn't you? Why? You want to become head of the section! I know your little peasant trick. But I say: don't dream during the bright daytime!" Master Cheng struck again. His noble face became twisted with anger.

My master's square jaw quivered more markedly. He probably did want to earn extra money and flexitime. But I believed he was a conscientious worker, and I had seen the satisfaction the difficult work had given him. Failing to find words powerful enough to hit back, he picked up a wrench and threw it at his old enemy and colleague. He missed, but they attacked each other like two big bears. As the other men pulled them apart Cheng was still showering Lin with abuse. "Look at you, Old Lin, your tail went up to the sky ever since you took an apprentice. So what? I tell you, when I joined the army, you were still making mud pies with your piss!"

My master's verbal riposte was limited to "*Tamade!*" the national swearword, a shorter and slightly less brutal form of "*caotamade*"—literally, "fuck his mother."

After lunch, Master Cheng went out. "I am going to the clinic. I feel my blood pressure is a little high," he declared gravely.

"Secret agent!" hissed Master Lin as soon as Cheng walked out of the door. "He is going to report on me! If not, I'll change my surname." He didn't have to. Lin was soon called in by Boss Wang to explain what had happened.

Master Cheng had picked up his habit during the Cultural Revolution, when people were encouraged to spy and inform on their colleagues, friends, and relatives. Several people had already fallen victim to his reports. Limited by poor education and mediocrity, Cheng never got the promotions he coveted. But he carried on reporting, driven by a self-imposed responsibility to inform the leadership about the actions of the people—especially those he disliked. Once Lin fashioned a metal seat for his wife's bike with a piece of discarded metal from our workshop. In his report to the work unit boss, Cheng made it sound like frequent misbehavior. As punishment, Lin was openly criticized at a public meeting, humiliation for a down-to-earth man who cared so much for saving face.

The two men's strife made my life no easier, though the rare drama was a fairly welcome interruption of the monotony of work. I didn't understand why I had been assigned to this workshop when the workload was far from enough to keep everyone occupied. Later, I came to understand that surplus labor and low efficiency defined the state-owned enterprise. China had faithfully copied the Soviet Union's central planning in building up its industry. Each year, the state provided both raw materials and a production target for every factory. The Nanjing Wristwatch Factory, for example, churned out Plum Blossom watches without regard for the saturation of the watch market; we produced rockets with guaranteed orders from the People's Liberation Army. Just as enterprises good and bad received standard funds from the state, all workers received a standard salary, regardless of performance. "Work, slack or game, it's all the same," went a popular saying. That was what my mother meant by "rice bowl."

By the time I became a worker, a bonus system had been reintroduced, which was in theory performance-linked. In reality, the difference remained marginal, and it meant nothing to me, since first-year apprentices were not entitled to any bonus.

What I was entitled to was endless time. My Soviet hero, Pavel Korchaguin, what would he think about me? To strike for a goal, he would say. But what was my goal in life?

If I wanted to listen, there was plenty of advice on offer. As soon as the factory off-work horn sounded, loud broadcasts would screech to life: the factory had its own propaganda studio. Breathless announcers told moving stories of model workers like Master Wang, socialist-minded and professionally proficient, who continued to operate his turning machine despite serious illness. Loudspeakers were the most widespread propaganda tool the Chinese Communists used, installed in every factory, school, village, neighborhood committee hall, and army camp—even in moving trains and aboard ships.

I preferred books. The wall of propaganda faded into a background hum when I entered the factory library, located in the so-called "living quarters," together with the dining hall, dormitories, and cinema.

I read magazines, like monthly journal *China Youth*. Mixing innocent love stories and discussions on the meaning of life, it was a breath of fresh air after the stuffy *People's Daily*.

When I was too hungry to read on, I would borrow books, choosing at random: *100,000 Questions*, an encyclopedia of general knowledge; foreign mysteries like Sherlock Holmes; or Chinese classics such as *The Romance of the Three*

Kingdoms, or *Journey to the West*. There were few new titles of any type. A librarian would fetch the books, two at most each time, and hand them to me over a glass counter.

I turned to books not out of love for literature, but as an escape route from the Liming empire. A large state-owned enterprise like ours functioned like a small communist state. There were residential buildings for workers with families, and dormitories for single people from outside Nanjing; there were kindergartens, schools, shower houses, dining halls, a library for those who felt culture calling, and a cinema. If I suffered minor medical problems, I went to a clinic in the village, but for major problems, I could go to the factory-run hospital.

All my life was within fifteen minutes' cycle ride, all within the gray territory of the empire. I came to work through the back gate, known in the factory as Gate Three. The very front gate was called Gate One and the gate dividing the living quarters and production area was Gate Two. Why not call them directly "back gate" or "front gate"; or name them according to their location—"Tiger Street Gate," or "Scholar Road Gate"? I guessed that the authorities loved numbers as they loved orders. Our factory was given a code within the Ministry; within the factory, each unit was given a number; and within the unit, each group was numbered, too. A worker from the seventh group of Unit Twenty-three, Factory 105 under the Ministry of Aerospace, itself the seventh machine-building industry—I felt pinned down by these numbers.

One night, I was absorbed in *The Dream of the Red Chamber*, probably the most popular literary work in China. A romantic, I adored this Qing Dynasty classic of love and decline within a large noble family. When Jade, the heroine, died, and the man she loved married someone else,

I broke into uncontrollable sobs, as if my own lover had just deserted me. Nai was startled from her snores. "What happened? What's wrong?" she opened her sleepy eyes.

"Nothing, Jade just die, died…"

Nai sighed and lay down again. She knew this famous tale well. "No need to cry, it's not real," she said. "You cry too much, all because of your weeping mark. It's unlucky. Get rid of it."

If she had her way, Nai would have taken a needle to the black mole under my left eye. Once at school, my sister and I went to the cinema to watch a North Korean tearjerker, *The Fates of Two Korean Girls.* Twin sisters are separated by civil war—a believable fate—but little did I know how false was the fantasy that followed. The girl who ends up in North Korea enjoys a happy life of socialism and plenty while her sister in the south suffers the worst terrors of capitalism. I cried so hard over her bad luck that the man next to me complained he couldn't hear a word. Ever since, Weijia has called me "tear bag."

"You're so superstitious," I told Nai, refusing her offer.

Ma came out to see what was happening. "It's no good reading too many books, no good," she repeated with a disapproving tut-tut. "Your dad used to be a bookworm, you know. He comes home only twelve days a year. Does he help me with any housework? No, he reads these useless books. It all comes to nothing. He can't do big things like a real educated man; nor can he do small, practical things like a workman. He is just like Kong Yiji."

Ridiculous in his tattered long gown, a symbol of the gentry class that despised him, Kong Yiji lives in a novel by China's literary giant Lu Xun. After many years pursuing an academic career, Kong failed the imperial exam, yet he insists on wearing a gown and refuses to associate with working-class people who wear short jackets and trousers. I had recently enjoyed the full collection of Lu Xun's works, borrowed from the library. I had to admit Ma's comparison was apt.

Ma took obvious pleasure in criticizing her husband, no matter whether he was around or not. Shaking her head, she turned to the toilet. Then, as if talking to herself, she added, "He might not have got himself into trouble if not for these books."

There was one more reason she opposed my hobby. "Electricity costs money," she would shout from her dim room if I stayed up late. "This is not a hotel nor your workshop!"

I actually considered reading in the factory at night. Master Lin didn't mind, but Master Cheng did. A born conservative, Cheng opposed anything out of the ordinary.

Chapter 6

Spring Outing

In the balmy air, under the rain of Ma's watering can, the green garlic seedlings shot up from their white cloves. A few days ago they were just peeping out from the clay pot that balanced on the edge of the balcony, between the drying rails for clothes that clung to every home. With little space to spare, one had to learn to exploit every inch.

Both Ma and Nai loved flowers and plants. They crowded the balcony, a cherished space of just one cubic meter, with pots of jasmine, Chinese rose, ball cactus, and white-edged morning glory. In winter, they managed to keep a small pot of asparagus fern inside the room. Whenever Nai cracked an egg, she crumbled the shell to help the plants grow. In a couple of months, the balcony would erupt in a rainbow of color, defying its drab setting.

We grew garlic and scallions, too, to use in cooking. Ma liked to tend her pots when she returned home in the evening. In a small way, she was blossoming herself: when her employer realized she was reasonably educated, Ma had been given more complicated administrative tasks, rather than just collecting money from the stall owners and peddlers at Confucius Temple Market. In the company of her beloved plants, she looked content and relaxed. This was the moment I had been looking for.

"Ma, can I have some money, please?" I asked, standing gingerly behind her near the door. "I was invited to go out with some friends."

"Which friends?" She picked a tiny weed and dropped it casually over the railing.

"Those who joined the factory at the same time. Five yuan would be enough." She grimaced, and I compromised. "Four will do."

For the first year, my monthly income was thirty and a half yuan per month. Since I hadn't gotten the job myself, Ma insisted from the outset that I hand over thirty yuan, and keep just fifty fen for myself, the cost of one thin book or five sesame breads. Whenever I needed money to go out, or to buy books or clothes, I had to apply.

She thought about this application before reaching for her paper purse, folded from pages of a glossy film magazine. She pulled out four one-yuan notes. From the top note, a female tractor driver, creased and blackened by countless hands, smiled at me brightly.

Ma handed over a lecture first. "When I was your age, I didn't have any pocket money. I wore Nai's discarded clothes. I had to walk a long way to my school with a box lunch from home. What lunch? Cold rice with hot water, plus some pickle if I was lucky. You've got a half-new bike, a brand-new watch, and a great job."

I bit my tongue to force back the reply my heart begged me to make—"Well, fifty fen of pocket money isn't much better off!" Since the New Year, I had adopted a new non-confrontational policy.

When I took the notes, together with some grain coupons, I felt like a beggar.

Nai was cutting pork against the grain to ensure the meat stayed tender. Her left hand held the meat tight while her right chopped so fast I worried she would cut her fingers. But she never did. She had spent most of her life around the cooking stove. Things had become a little easier. Without embroidery to tie her down, Nai had started going out to play mah-jongg, her favorite pastime, which she hadn't enjoyed for many years. Still, she cooked and cleaned while every morning Ma bought vegetables, and occasionally meat, from the village market. Shopping was no small task. To treat a guest, Ma had to get up before dawn and queue for hours to buy a frozen fish. This scarcity was like torture to a people as obsessed with food as the Chinese, so much so that we always greeted each other with "Have you eaten yet?" rather than "How are you?"

I took the chopping board to slice shallots, ginger, and garlic cloves, three essential items for a good stir-fry.

After heating up the oil, Nai threw them into the wok. "Tsssss…" Steam and smells flashed upward.

"Any lads in your outing?" she asked, quickly stirring the garlic shoots.

"Several, I think."

"Anyone fancies you?" she nudged me. Nai was keen for me to go out so that I would get myself a boyfriend, like my sister.

I shook my head and smiled ruefully. Who would be interested in me, skinny and ugly, like an undernourished bean sprout? Nai slipped something in my trouser pocket. I pulled out a two-yuan note, soggy from her wet hands.

"Oh, Nai, you shouldn't."

"Shhh…" My mother didn't approve of Nai giving money to us children under the table. "Can't be short of cash in front of lads."

Somehow Nai always managed to save bits and pieces, from embroidery work or the New Year lucky money she received from my parents or my sister's wealthy boyfriend. She squirreled these savings away under her cotton mattress, or sewed them into a pocket of her underclothes. Once she aired her mattress on the clothesline. By the time she remembered, her secret stash of forty yuan, wrapped in rough toilet paper, had long been blown away. Poor Nai hit herself hard on the chest and cried the whole night.

"I'll give you lots of money when I make big, big money," I promised her.

"Will I see that day?" chuckled Nai, dimples smiling in her cheeks. "I'm so old half my body is already in the yellow earth!"

Her name, Yang Huizhen, "wisdom and treasure," was an identity that she earned only after she took up embroidery work. Before, she was known as Huang-Yang Si: Mrs. Huang, née Yang—before the Communist takeover, women were usually addressed by their husband's surname and their maiden name.

A very traditional woman, Nai rarely opened up her past to us. I knew precious little about her early life apart from the story of how her mother's death saved her from being crippled as badly as the lame grannies in our village. The painful process of foot binding started at six years old. Long cloth strips were used to bind the feet, viciously tight, stunting growth to the three inches of male sexual fantasy. At night, Nai sometimes dared to loosen the cloths and ease the pain. After her mother died, the distant relatives Nai slaved for never bothered to check her bindings. Any natural mother would have made sure her daughter's feet were properly bound—no decent man would marry a woman with big feet.

When Nai had suffered her stroke and was taken, unconscious, to the Liming hospital, my tearful mother had shared these well-kept secrets because she thought Nai was going to die.

Born in a small town outside Nanjing, Nai's unlucky start in life was just a foretaste of a tragic, and tragically typical, passage through modern Chinese history. It was little surprise she ended up a courtesan, a common fate for orphan girls. She met my grandpa, fifteen years her senior, on the job—at his local brothel. Married and running a small grain-trading business, he bought her out as his concubine and settled with his new family in Nanjing. When the new government banned bigamy in the early 1950s, he chose to stay with Nai instead of his wife, who stayed behind in their hometown.

Her shame might have remained hidden but for Granddad's suicide in 1968. Nai kindly informed his first wife, who came to Nanjing with a large gang, hoping to seize some inheritance. Failing to find anything, she snatched Granddad's ashes and shouted that my grandma, a mere "concubine," had no right to them. In those highly political years, who dared associate with a former prostitute? Shunned, my family was forced to move and settled in Wuding New Village where nobody knew us.

On that night in the bare, cold hospital, Ma and I hugged each other and our tears mingled. Although we were atheists, we prayed and prayed to Buddha that Nai would live. As if by a miracle, she recovered. Despite her small, frail frame, she was amazingly resilient. As China's Taoists say, water is the softest substance, yet over time it can wear down the hardest rock.

Knowing her past often made me wonder how Nai could be so calm and kind. When Father was away and Ma in trouble, Nai's never-failing smile was our safe haven. She meant home. And she was always there, laboring diligently without a single boast or complaint. As a Chinese grandma, she would never say "I love you" to us, but her love was as concrete as a sizzling dish. In order to allow the children to have few more bites, she often starved herself, claiming that she didn't like this or that dish. What a fussy eater!, I used to think.

I had been promising to give Nai "big money" since I was a child, the only way I knew how to repay her kindness.

I pedaled fast under a canopy of parasol trees. The freedom was intoxicating. Racing with the boys, I felt like a caged animal enjoying its first run in the wild. A tomboy at heart, I loved physical challenges. When we came down a slope at full speed, I let go of the handlebars. Our laughter resonated in the crisp spring air.

Nothing chained me to the cage of home but a shortage of friends and money. Every evening and weekend I crouched amid my books, in the company of my own shadow.

Sunlight flooded the world. Half a dozen of us were cycling all the way to Purple Mountain Park in the eastern outskirts of Nanjing, the city's most popular attraction. We were to conquer the peak, which at four hundred forty meters was the highest spot around. The eerie, beautiful purple halo it displayed at dawn and dusk, caused by a purple-colored shale, gave the mountain its name.

There was little traffic. Apart from a few cyclists, vehicles were rarely found on Liberation Road—every Chinese city has such a street, named to mark the victory of Mao's People's Liberation Army over General Chiang Kai-shek's Nationalists. The latter expected a long fight for Nanjing, their capital, secure behind the natural barrier of the Yangtze River, but the PLA made a heroic, almost suicidal, crossing under heavy gunfire and seized the city. Chiang and the surviving Nationalists escaped to Taiwan. Before settling into Zhongnanhai in Beijing, the imperial compound that became Communist headquarters, Mao captured the lightning victory in poetry:

On the Purple Mountains sweeps a storm headlong:
Our troops have crossed the great river, a million strong.
The Tiger girt with Dragon outshines days gone by;
Heaven and earth o'erturned, our spirits ne'er so high!

The Tiger meant Stone City, a section of ancient wall in western Nanjing; the Dragon was Purple Mountain, our destination. These were not Mao's creations, but traditional ways to reference a city that had served as the capital of six dynasties.

The ruins of the Ming Palace slipped by as we rode out of town. As children, we often came here to play on the marble column bases clustered near the still-imposing Meridian Gate. These bases were finely carved yet sad in their lost purpose; the bottoms of pensioners resting after early morning exercise had made them shiny and smooth.

Here, one could never go far before bumping into history. The man who ordered the construction of the Palace was Zhu Yuanzhang, the beggar who became first emperor of the Ming Dynasty. His legendary rise inspired many folktales. This "Beggar King" proclaimed himself the new emperor and chose Nanjing as his capital for its beauty, wealth, and strategic location. Now a city of nearly four million people, my hometown still serves as the capital of Jiangsu province.

As we approached Purple Mountain, the tunnel of parasol trees seemed to grow grander. Soaring into the sky, they arched splendidly over the tarmac roads, the exuberant branches and leaves joining intimately in the air. The new leaves were such a fresh, transparent green that the color threatened to drip down any moment. Imported from France back in the 1930s, the trees kept off the burning summer heat like parasols and lent a majestic air to the city.

After deserting our bikes at the foot of the mountain, we began to scramble up a mud track, often steep, worn by other climbers. Charging toward the peak, we rested at the old pavilions, watchtowers, and observatories along the way. Over an hour later, just when we thought we would never get there, another turn revealed the main peak.

The view justified our sweat and scraped knees. Down at the foot of the mountain, the Yangtze River wound its way past Nanjing, stretching into the horizon. From so high, the ships on the river looked like ornaments decorating a jade belt. On its banks, bright yellow canola grew luxuriantly for miles. Lighting up the slopes where we sat were pink peach flowers, white pear flowers, and many others I could not name, mixed with solemn pine trees. A deep, brilliant-blue backdrop of sky completed the oil-painting view.

Standing on the highest rock, stretching my arms into the clouds, I wished I could turn into a bird. "Mountain, here I come!" I shouted.

"Are you mad? Shouting like that?" said Chen Songling, who had organized the trip.

"Why not! It's so liberating here. Every day I feel just like a prisoner at my workshop." Closing my eyes, I soaked up the gentle comfort of sunshine and the scent of spring.

"Why have I never seen a purple halo around the peak?" asked Rong Ling, my colleague from the power-gauge section. On clear days, we could see the peak from our workshop, with no high rises blocking our view.

"Emperor Qinshihuang certainly saw the halo." I told my friends the legend about the ruthless first unifier of China: during a tour to Nanjing, the emperor spotted the purple haze, interpreting it as a portent that a new emperor would arise here. Fearful of rivals, Qinshihuang ordered earthworks to disturb the mountain's feng shui, and commanded a trench be dug to divert its streams into the Yangtze. The trench became the Qinhuai River that served as the city moat and ran beside the Confucius Temple in downtown Nanjing.

"Where did you learn that?" Chen asked. Squatting on a massive rock, his tiny body appeared even smaller than normal. His bright eyes were too close together, lending him a rather ratty look.

"My teacher told me once when we climbed the mountain." Our school outing each spring to Purple Mountain Park was the highlight of the year. My last teacher, Moon-Faced Xu, liked to tell me stories that were not in the textbooks. I still remembered her disappointed look when I told her I was going to the factory.

Talking about school reminded me of the compositions we were assigned after each spring outing and the cliché we used. "When I felt exhausted just before reaching the peak, Chairman Mao's quotation came to me—'First of all, don't be afraid of hardship; second, don't be afraid of death.' The Communists don't even fear death, so why should I fear this small obstacle? Suddenly, I felt reenergized and rushed to the top."

On top of our rock, my companions laughed out of recognition.

"Little Zhang, listen to me," said Chen, acting the caring older brother. "Just forget about school. The more you assimilate with your colleagues at the factory, the happier you'll become."

Whenever I bumped into Chen on the way to work, our chat always took the same direction. He thought I was foolish to cling to school, like a toddler clinging to her mother's dried-up breast. "Just move on," he often urged me.

"I haven't got much to do at work. I am bored to death!" I complained.

"Wish I could enjoy some idling," said a plump girl nicknamed Porky—her family name was Zhu, which had the same pronunciation as the word for "pig."

"Do whatever you want to do, Little Zhang, sleeping, bluffing, visiting your friends, or sneaking out to the cinema, whatever," Chen suggested.

"No kidding? How about the rules?"

"You don't violate any rule if you don't get caught."

"Don't listen to him," Rong stepped in. "My master told me always to behave myself. Why? You may get away with your naughty behavior once or twice, but wait, when there's a promotion or pay raise, you never know who might report you."

Rong was even-tempered and none too ambitious. She had settled into her new life far more smoothly than I had, helped by her protective Master Mei, a middle-aged divorcée who had taken the young girl under her wing. We got along fine, but we were not close.

"Well, I do get my job done. My master, a youngish guy, is a real *gemen'r,*" the local slang for brother. Cupping his hand to fend off the breeze, Chen lit a cigarette. The young fitter looked pleased with himself, drumming his legs on the ground. "He'll cover up for me if I want to snooze after lunch. Of course, he got enough goodies from me: cigarettes, spirits, and good meat, you name it. See, guanxi works wonders. Remember the saying, 'Have small losses to make bigger gains.'"

Guanxi again, the invisible net. After Spring Festival, I did visit my own master at his messy flat in the village, bearing gifts prepared by Ma. But even if we had been more generous, I doubted the gifts would have made much difference. There seemed so little to learn in my job. I couldn't imagine how I could form a close guanxi with my reserved master.

Not everyone was as happy as Chen. The prettiest girl in our group, Little Wang, an electrician, sat down on her very first day to find herself sitting not on her chair but a man's big hand! It gripped her bum, and she sprang up with a scream that made her young male colleagues laugh hysterically. This was her welcome to the noble proletariat! Every day they tried to touch her. "They're like flies, I have to drive them away all the time," she moaned, swatting the air with her pretty hands.

"Report it to your boss," Rong suggested.

"I did on the first day. But he said it was only friendliness among the comrades.'"

Chen threw a new round of cigarettes. "Hey, Little Chen," one guy asked, "How much money do you spend on cigarettes?"

"Don't know exactly, but my salary certainly doesn't see me through every month."

"I save all my salary in the bank. My mum arranged it," volunteered Rong. Her mother ran a business roasting ducks in her kitchen. Dripping with profit, she didn't need Rong's money.

Chen rolled his small eyes. "Aiya! By the time you marry, you'll have a sizeable dowry, then?"

Rong threw a twig at him in protest. I wondered if Chen was interested in Rong. From what I could gather, she would prefer to marry someone with a university degree.

One's salary and its arrangement was no secret. Most of my friends gave between five and fifteen yuan to their families to help with food. I confessed that that I gave most to my mother.

"If I had to give my salary away, I'd have no incentive to get out of bed," said Porky. She operated the milling machine, a job no one envied, and had to work in three different rotating shifts. "I hate night shift to death," she grumbled.

Many workers had to take irregular shifts, working from afternoon till midnight, or from midnight till morning. Some were the creation of inefficient bureaucracy, but others were necessary to meet deadlines or technical demand, such as the slow process of acid pickling large machinery parts. Electricity shortages explained some shifts. China was so power-poor that each factory was allocated specific amounts during certain hours—this was also why our one day off each week came every Tuesday rather than Sunday.

No unusual shifts for me, thankfully, but I didn't know how much more I enjoyed my job than Porky. "Well, we pay our parents to show our gratitude," I said, partly trying to convince myself.

"Gratitude, why?" Chen cut in. "They look after me now and I'll look after them in the future. No big deal."

"We are the lucky ones," Rong said thoughtfully. "I didn't choose to become a worker. Since I have, I just try to be content."

I wished I could echo her words. Like my mother, Rong's mother thought that our round of dingzhi would be the last. When her mother went to the school to pull her out, the teacher argued against it, since Rong would graduate and take the university entry exam in just half a year's time. Her mother asked, "Can you guarantee, a hundred percent, that she would go to a university?"

"No, not even with the best student," admitted her teacher.

"So, let her go!"

Rong had once revealed to me that she did not expect to enter university but hoped to score high enough to reach a polytechnic and later become a detective or policewoman. How could she just throw away her old dream and slip contentedly into her new world?

Before we left the peak Chen lined us up and peered into the top of his old Seagull box camera. We posed on the largest rock, smiling triumphantly and holding out V signs with our fingers—not just celebrating our ascent, but copying a trend picked up from visitors from Taiwan and Hong Kong, without understanding why. For years we were told how, tortured by the capitalist system, the poor people from both Taiwan and Hong Kong lived in "deep water and scorching fire." After China opened its door and overseas relatives returned to visit in the late 1970s with lavish presents, mainlanders had suddenly realized that we were the ones suffering. So we began to copy them blindly, from fashions and accents to the V signs they flashed at every camera.

On the way home, we lunched in a small restaurant. Before parting, someone suggested we meet every two weeks or at least once a month. I remained silent, lacking the money to make such plans.

Chapter 7

Seize the Moment

A percussive tap sounded from the corridor, and I instantly became more alert. The source soon turned up in the doorway. At over six-feet tall, Zhi Yong, my eighteen-year-old colleague from the electric-gauge section down the corridor, was a giant by local standards. Like most Chinese, we knew and routinely swapped vital statistics, from height to how shortsighted we were. I had no precise measurement for Zhi's limbs, but they looked extraordinarily long and thin, reminding me of a mantis. His eyes were long and thin, too. The moustache on his even-featured face looked as out of place as painted legs on a snake.

"Masters, have you all eaten?" Zhi offered the common greeting, which didn't necessarily require an answer. He settled in a chair, propping one leg on the opposite knee to show off his knee-length boots, specially made from the finest and shiniest leather by his friend at a shoe factory. They looked too hot for May, but were clearly too cool to be tucked away. The distinctive tapping came from a half-moon metal plate on the soles. The protective plates were popular, their percussive sound considered attractive— after all, not every one could afford leather shoes.

As the only son of the most-senior deputy director of the factory, and perhaps more importantly, the newfound nephew of a man living in Taiwan, Zhi could now afford many of life's luxuries.

"Don't work too hard. Have a cigarette," he said, tossing around a pack of Marlboros, an imported luxury. So many Chinese men smoked that it seemed the addiction was an additional criterion for being a man. Master Lin rarely smoked, but he took one, too. A freebie, why not? He sniffed its fragrance before poking the cigarette behind one of his ears beside a ballpoint pen.

"Can I have one?" protested Master Li Zhiming, a slight woman in her late thirties who had recently returned after a long absence. "I don't smoke, but my husband does. Thank you, that'll make his day."

"How about you, Little Zhang? Save one for your boyfriend?" Zhi turned to me, with a glint in his eye.

"Our Little Zhang has high standards, all right?" cut in Master Li. "No worries," she hissed at me. "Entrust me as your matchmaker, I'll guarantee to find you a perfect man. Or return the goods."

"An apprentice is not allowed to court," I reminded her sheepishly. I didn't like colleagues laughing at my expense, but I was getting used to it.

That spring, Master Li had risen from her sickbed, along with dozens of other workers. The miracle cure was a new regulation stipulating that anyone who took more than two months' sick leave a year would not receive his or her full salary. For years, Li and other workers had enjoyed a life of relative leisure.

Although officially back on full time, she often came to work late, with her shopping hidden in a cloth bag, then found an excuse to leave early. Using her poor health as a weapon, she usually managed to get away. If anyone dared challenge her, Li had another ready weapon—a tongue sharper than a knife. Relentless in digging for dirt, she could pick a bone from an egg.

On her first day back, she offered me sympathy. "Little Zhang, how unfortunate that you ended up Old Lin's apprentice." She and Master Cheng had long formed a clique. Factionalism was rife in the Chinese workplace as workers teamed up in small groups out of simple survival instinct: in fighting was so common you often needed other people to help defend your interests. She soon got into her stride. "He is such a peasant. Oh yes, Little Zhang, be careful with the newspaper after Old Lin reads it—he wipes his boogers on it!"

I had indeed noticed that the pages of *The People's Daily* often stuck together. Picking one's nose in public was socially acceptable in China, though perhaps not if one pasted the results onto state property like the media. Now I found myself noticing other "peasant" habits of Lin's, like wiping his shoes with the cotton curtain draped over the door to keep in the heat. Still, he was a kind and decent man, even if we had little in common.

After complaining about my master, Master Li patted my face with affection. "No worries, I'll look after you." It turned out that she wanted me as her personal servant. "Little Zhang, I feel so tired today," she would whimper. "Be so kind as to bring me some dishes from the dining hall." She knew I didn't need to go there—I always went home for lunch. But if I dared to refuse, she would somehow find a mistake in my recording of the readings, or a date not clearly marked on the glass. And she would make sure that everyone else knew about it. I was learning to put up with her, like the rest of my factory life. "Standing under low eaves, one has to lower one's head," as my grandma might say.

Master Li could even be sweet. "Did you go out to hunt recently?" she asked Zhi Yong.

"Oh yes, last week we went to the eastern mountains and shot lots of birds. The old woman stir-fried them. Tamade! So tasty!" The "old woman" was his mother, who would grant him anything he asked, even an air gun.

I listened attentively without saying much. I was attracted to the tall man, a totally new breed for me. He had long hair, nearly touching his shoulders. Extraordinary! On both little fingers he boasted fingernails five centimeters long! I was so impressed I insisted on measuring them. At my school, teachers inspected our nails, cut to the quick. Historically, wealthy and educated Chinese men, those from the south particularly, liked to keep their nails long—though not quite as long as Zhi's—to show their status, for men who labored with their hands had to cut their nails short. Zhi always gave me the same explanation for keeping his nails—"for convenience," which meant the convenience to pick his nose or ears. Still, I thought everything about him was cool.

When Zhi finished his hunting story, it was Master Li's turn to take center stage. While others used their fingers to point, she used her lips. Shifting them toward the inner room, she asked in a mysterious fashion, "Are they hiding in there again?"

Everyone knew whom she meant. Our inner room adjoined the inner room of Zhi Yong's electric section, the private haven of his two colleagues Little Wu, daughter of the factory's chief engineer, and Little Xu, son of another factory deputy director (there were six deputies in all). Wu and Xu were madly in love. When they arrived in the early morning, they'd head straight for their inner sanctum, toiling on gauges together until the off-work horn broke them apart.

Strangely, they would not admit they were a pair, even though they were allowed to court, for their years in countryside exile had reduced their apprenticeship from three years to one. But both were private, quiet people who had little so say to others. They lived in a secret world of their own, reluctant to give anyone else a glimpse inside. But their secrecy and aloofness, plus Wu's good looks, ignited greater interest in the affair.

Their boss Fatty Wang was a severe woman, which was why I never dared to visit the section. She used to be slim, I heard, but after giving birth to her son she swelled like yeast dough. Although she spread more stories than anyone about the Xu-Wu affair, she had to tolerate them, since both were diligent workers and factory princelings. Liming's leaders assigned their children to the electric-gauge section not for Fatty Wang's tender care, but for the clean and air-conditioned environment and work that required certain skills.

"What are they doing there all day long?" Master Li asked, widening her unusually round eyes.

"You asking me?" said Zhi. "Who should I ask?"

Master Li decided to enter our inner room to listen. "Take off your stinking shoes," said Master Cheng, always jealous of his territory.

"They are giggling!" Master Li reported on her return. She covered her mouth with a hand to suppress her own giggle. "I wonder if they have done it or not?" she asked aloud, thrusting her right index finger into her cupped left hand. The crude gesture won hysterical laughs from her audience. Other women, who also wondered how far the young lovers had gone, spied in a more subtle way than Li by staring at Wu's naked body in the shower house. But her belly stayed disappointingly flat.

Master Li paced up and down the center of the room, as if weighing up an important decision. Then, sitting down, she said in an unnecessarily hushed voice, "All right, let me give you something to bite. Someone told me personally that she spotted them together one night at Rain Flower Terrace!" She paused for dramatic effect. "They parked their bikes, then went deep inside the park. He had his arm around her waist!"

"Really!" the audience responded. Though Xu and Wu rarely took their eyes off one another, they never showed any physical intimacy at work or even touched hands.

As Master Li told her story, her eyebrows danced and her round face grew radiant. The larger her audience, the more animated she became. She loved nothing better than a good sex scandal and she had plenty to spill or invent. When a good-looking woman from Unit Twelve was promoted to deputy head, she concluded that woman had slept with a factory leader.

It was Li who provided my first "sex education." "Do you know why Old Mei is divorced?" Master Li had asked shortly after her return. Divorce, a rare event, was regarded with shame. "Her husband had an affair with his young apprentice! They were caught red-handed, you'll never guess where—that raid shelter on the way to Rain Flower Terrance!"

Fearful of Soviet attack in the early 1970s, the whole nation was mobilized to dig tens of thousands of shelters. Later abandoned, they served as playgrounds for adventurous children as well as desperate lovers.

The affair went on for a while, as did Li's breathless account. One day, a colleague became suspicious when Master Mei's husband didn't head home toward Wuding New Village but cycled in the other direction. He followed them, out of Gate One, then all the way to the shelter. After some hesitation, he entered the winding tunnel, braving pitch-darkness and foul odor, until, from a deep corner, he heard groans of pleasure rising and falling.

The story became even more colorful as it raced around the factory. Upon hearing the news, poor Mei felt so humiliated that she plunged straight into the Qinhuai River. Luckily, her colleagues from the casting unit dove in and saved her. After the incident, she requested a transfer to the power section, yet her story had arrived before she herself did.

"She's got herself to blame, such a nagging bitch!" Master Li twisted her lips in disapproval. "Her husband was sent off to labor camp for one year. Serves him right, criminal! His apprentice is finished, too, of course. Who'd dare marry a fox fairy, a worn-out shoe?"

I flushed red with embarrassment as Master Li elaborated on their "mating like wild dogs." Only later did I wonder where these juicy details came from. The informer could have seen nothing in the dark tunnel. No one in my family ever mentioned the word "sex" or even implied it. When I was little, I once asked my mother, "Where I born from?" She said it wasn't the sort of question for a child. I insisted, so she replied that I was born from her underarm, the same answer many of my young friends heard from their parents. Underarm? How bizarre! There did not seem to be a hole there. Ma never really explained periods either. Indeed, the word itself was too much, so we used "that unlucky thing" instead.

As Master Li entertained us with sex scandals, my colleagues sat there sipping tea and smoking, leaving some work open on the tabletop as if they were just taking a break. They spent a large proportion of their working hours *chuiniu*, "blowing bull"—bluffing or talking nonsense. They had recently decided I was trustworthy enough to work on my own, but my colleagues laughed at me when I tried to do as much as I could. "What will you do for the rest of the month?"

I soon grew tired of Master Li's gossip, racy or otherwise. I found myself anticipating the tap of metal on concrete. What else to look forward to? My job, simple and repetitive, taxed neither body nor brain. I screwed on the gauges, the left-hand side for the standard and right for the test; I checked them; I fixed them; I recorded the reading and stamped the new expiration date.

Sometimes the tapping would fade into the section opposite. Boss Wang, based in the power section, was often absent, attending meetings and nurturing guanxi by hanging around with his bosses. He was very ambitious. At other times, he took Master Mei and Rong Ling to test high-pressure electric cables. Master Qian, who usually stayed behind to test gauges used in the power system, always welcomed Zhi's visits. In his early thirties, Qian was quiet as a shadow. He avoided eye contact, and rarely spoke or expressed his opinion. "Live quietly with your tail between your legs, that's the only way to avoid trouble," his father was supposed to have told him as he lay dying from a knife stab, the result of faction fighting in the factory at the height of the Cultural Revolution. Following his father's lesson, Qian had diminished into an unnoticeable person.

Whenever possible I would sneak over the corridor to join Zhi. A smile would wrinkle his face. I was certainly a more enthusiastic listener than Master Qian. Apart from bird-hunting trips, Zhi would boast about his night outings to trap cats in the street. In theory, all cats were wild, since keeping pets was prohibited, but a small number of people managed to keep them secretly at home. Zhi's craving for cat meat, the best delicacy in the world in his view, must have saddened many households. "The snake and cat soup is, tamade! So tasty! Do you know what it's called? 'The battle between a dragon and a tiger,' tamade good!" I upset Nai by repeating this story, for she believed a cat was the reincarnation of nine monks.

Our conversations were limited. I had few out-of-work activities. I possessed no expensive toys like a TV set or a cassette player. I could talk about books, but Zhi lacked the slightest interest.

At least I could breathe more freely over there—I never feared Master Qian as much as I did my own masters. In fact, Zhi and I sometimes forgot his existence altogether and launched verbal wars, "Bamboo Stick" versus "Four Eyes." When the war escalated, we shot each other with eyedrops, some of the free medicine state workers enjoyed.

I had never taken serious interest in any boy before. This little spark of affection brightened up my life, otherwise still and stagnant.

While Rong worried that working in the sun would darken her skin, I envied her opportunities to get out. I would jump to complete trivial errands like fetching cotton yarn or industrial oil from the warehouse. That meant a trip to unit headquarters to get the signature of the administrator, then walking across half the factory to the warehouse. Up to an hour killed!

I found it hard to stay still. Nai joked that I wasn't bundled up properly when I was born, and that my restlessness was the result. All newborn babies in China are swaddled tightly in layers of cloth. It keeps them warm, stops them from scratching themselves, and starts the process of taming them into well-behaved children.

One guaranteed outing fell every payday, the twenty-fifth of each month, when I collected the salaries for our group of fourteen workers. Jostling other enthusiastic representatives, I cornered the young accountant who flicked the wooden beads of her abacus like a musician plucking strings. Nothing confidential. Each worker was paid according to his grade, earned through the working years providing you behaved yourself. There were eight grades, with a corresponding salary raging from thirty-four and a half for a first-grade worker to one hundred and ten yuan. Even bonuses rarely varied. Still, the job of touching real money, after a month's anticipation, was formidable.

My daily outings were usually limited to toilet trips through the long building, down to the basement to squat over one of five trenches cut without partitions into the concrete floor. On my return, I walked along the main road, inhaling the fresh air and singing lines from popular songs, something prohibited at the workshop. Sometimes I would visit the simple garden next to our building. In spring, I watched three magnolia trees come to life, blossoming with large flowers, gloriously white, and then wither within a fortnight. In the middle of the garden, there was a small pond where red goldfish darted like flames. For a few minutes, I would watch the fish swing their fat tails, darting from one end to the other, pushing their confinement to its limits. Then I would return to my own.

I waited, perpetually, for the tapping sound from the corridor, the music in my life.

Chapter 8

The Long Hair Drama

When Love the People was in full flow, only those keen to "pat the horse's bottom"—flatter—sat close to the stage.

"Since the reform and opening up, a handful of young people have become deluded by the prosperity in the West and have begun to worship capitalism," he preached, spittle flying over his notes and into the audience.

Political instructor Wang Aimin was the ideologue-in-chief of our unit. A bony man, he had a rectangular face the shape of the meeting hall itself. His cold eyes blinked involuntarily, lending a sinister look that belied his given name, Aimin, "Love the People." Wang loved to talk up the latest political movement: today, a campaign against bourgeois liberalism, symbolized by bell-bottoms, called "trumpet trousers" in Chinese.

"Unable to distinguish between fragrant flowers and poisonous weeds, these young people pick up capitalist trash like the 'trumpet trousers' and rotten music," Wang spat through a southern accent. "We must resolutely defend the 'four cardinal principles' of socialism and firmly oppose bourgeois liberalism!"

The colorful trash of capitalism was creeping into China's gray kingdom, though in all truth, it had not quite reached remote corners like our factory yet. Some high-up people were already worried that decadent Western ideas and lifestyles were corrupting young people's minds.

Newspapers warned that tight jeans would reduce fertility as the design hampered ventilation.

Wang shouted out the new rules the factory was enforcing. High-heeled shoes and bright red lips were not acceptable; trouser legs' width must be smaller than twenty-two centimeters but bigger than fifteen; men's hair could not be longer than their earlobes. The list went on.

But Karl Marx had longer hair than that! I swallowed this impossible retort and gazed at his gray locks, billowing to his shoulder in a giant poster on the wall behind Wang's head. The ceiling fans threw fast-changing shadows onto Marx and the other poster boys of Communism: Engels, Lenin, Stalin, and our very own Chairman Mao. Pushing the humid air around the dark hall, the fan over my head was making a small but disturbing noise. Just imagine the chaos if it suddenly span off the ceiling and into the dozing proletariat. Only recently, such an accident happened for real, nearly beheading two workers.

Outside, drizzle fell from a gray sky. It was plum-rain season: when the plums ripened in late spring, the rain reached the lower reaches of the Yangtze and could last until early June, where we were now. For weeks in a row, everything had grown damp and moldy. The atmosphere was suffocating.

Wang's speech, "long and rotten as an old granny's foot-binding cloth," was sending some to sleep. Master Qian sat with straight back and head—he had achieved such mastery that if he avoided snoring no one would realize he was not awake. Beside me, Master Lan was tending his fine moustache again: he never needed to shave properly but plucked a few hairs in idle moments; Rong was chewing her hair broom, looking vacantly ahead; Master Li was gossiping as usual, hardly moving her lips; Little Xu and Little Wu sat together, oblivious to the world around them.

There were more meetings than hairs on a cow. "Cleaner toilets for a stronger China!" a recent one had urged, pushing the political significance of better hygiene. The majority were far less comical, yet my peers and I were too young to appreciate the pleasures of boredom compared to the political terror our parents suffered. On top of meetings within our unit, we had meetings and weekly study sessions within our gauge group, and, once a month, we filled the assembly hall for a factory-wide meeting. After thirty years in power, the Chinese Communist Party was the focus of most meetings. Before the call to attack "trumpet trousers," we were told to copy Lei Feng, again.

This young soldier dreamed not about girls but Chairman Mao's quotations. According to his diary, Lei wanted merely to be the "rustless screw" of Mao's revolution, serving the Party and the people. Conveniently, he had died back in 1963, so his diary could be doctored into a manual of good socialist citizenship. Over the years since his Cultural Revolution heyday, Lei slipped effortlessly into every role the Party chose.

1981 saw a political tug-of-war between liberals and conservatives. The hard-liners were alarmed by bold economic policies like family farming and the reintroduction of bonuses, as well as some rather bold criticism of the Party emerging in the new scar literature. The screenplay *Unrequited Love* was about a distinguished intellectual who returns to China hoping to help with the socialist construction, but finds himself persecuted and begins to question whether his motherland loves him back. The propaganda tsars dusted off Lei Feng, hoping the martyr's hundred-percent loyalty to the Party would inspire the masses.

Posters of Lei Feng still covered the back wall of our meeting hall. The baby-faced solider smiled happily while reading Chairman Mao's works, cleaning his army truck, or penning his famous record, packed with Maoist sound bites. "People can't survive without food," he supposedly wrote, "and we can't make revolution without Chairman Mao's thought."

Sitting neatly on rows of wooden benches between the two sets of posters were over three hundred workers from our work unit, or *danwei*. Danwei generally meant employer. Within the factory, it also referred to a specific unit, like Unit Twenty-three. Just like hukou, the household registration system, danwei was a powerful word. On the one hand, it provided social welfare; on the other, it served as a controlling arm of the state. Without my danwei's permission, I couldn't get married or cremated. And it was through the danwei, at endless meetings like this, that the government relayed political messages, voiced by faithful Party servants like Political Instructor Wang.

"Today is your first warning. I shall not mention anyone's name." He shot a disapproving glance toward the corner where Zhi sat grooming his long nails. "You'd better go for a pee and take a good look at yourself." Wang often mixed earthy local sayings into his political hectoring. Few of the dozy audience appreciated his humor, so he finished his speech with a threat. "Sort yourself out quickly. I am not always so polite!"

After the meeting, Wang summoned Boss Wang (they were not related) to discuss Zhi's long hair. Boss Wang then had a private conversation with Zhi. The next day Zhi turned up at work wearing a green army cap despite the heat. His hair was shorter, but still exceeded the critical earlobe limit. "A wise man will not fight when the odds are obviously against him," Zhi's tolerant master tried folk wisdom. "Cut your hair now and grow it back when the campaign blows over." Zhi refused to listen. Everyone around him had a turn, but he stubbornly guarded his hair like a soldier protecting a besieged city.

Sundown left a trail of bloodred clouds in the west, yet evening offered no respite from the burning heat of early July. As soon as the plum-rain season ended, Nanjing had begun again to earn its reputation as one of China's four furnace cities. Everyone believed that the furnace was roaring over forty degrees, yet the government only reported thirty-eight or thirty-nine—the authorities controlled even the temperature. Once the official temperature exceeded thirty-seven degrees, factories and government organizations had to cut an hour off each worker's day. If it topped forty, we could all go home.

Gingerly, I was heading to Zhi Yong's flat in a small residential area a few minutes' walk from the factory's Gate One. I had not seen him for more than two weeks. Shortly after "capitalist trash" were denounced as the enemy of the People, Zhi was detained by plainclothes security personnel, commonly known as "the secret agents," who patrolled the factory. That morning, Zhi was told to get a proper haircut if he ever wanted to set foot in the factory again.

He hadn't since. When he failed to show up, Boss Wang called his home, one of few to boast a telephone. Zhi's anxious mother pleaded ignorance. He had come home to pick some money and clothes before storming out again. The poor mother, a retired teacher who had long lost the ability to control her only child, begged Boss Wang not to inform the father. Not yet.

The emptiness in the corridor, without his tapping walk, marked his absence. When rumor reported his return, I decided to visit him—I worried that he might lose his job. The labor law stated that any employee who failed to turn up for fifteen days was automatically considered to have left the position.

Tortured by the heat, people fled outside to escape their cramped rooms, peeling off their clothes and splashing the pavement with bucket after bucket of water. But the heat bounced back, like a Ping-Pong ball on a smooth table. The asphalt roads, baked soft by the sun, blackened the shoes of unwary pedestrians. The air hung heavily. The tips of the leaves lay still. Hidden high in the trees, cicadas chirped mechanically, on and on. The whole world felt like a bamboo steamer.

Sweat crawled along my skin like parades of little ants, even though I had just been to the factory's shower house. Somehow the little ants also made their way to my throat: I coughed as I knocked on his door. Zhi's mother, a benign, gray-haired woman, opened it.

"Aiya, please come in!" She was obviously surprised and delighted that a colleague had come. She led me into his room where Zhi was lying on a sofa, listening to songs by Teresa Deng, the pretty Taiwanese singer. As the music changed melody, colorful lights danced on a massive cassette player. How cool!, I thought enviously.

"Little Zhang, how come? Which wind brought you here?" He stood up. He wore "trumpet trousers" with large flares and a white singlet, rolled up to his stomach as if exposing some flesh could help reduce the heat. I could hardly avoid noticing what a bamboo stick he was, without the cover of his usual loose shirt.

"Er, I've just been to the shower house and just popped over to see how you're getting on." I pushed my glasses back up my nose, trying to sound causal.

"Sit, sit." He pointed at a sofa opposite him and was about to turn the music off.

"Please, just lower the volume." Being alone with Zhi in his room, I felt uncomfortable and hoped the singer's female voice would put me more at ease. I did enjoy the opportunity to listen to "decadent music," as her songs were labeled. Cantopop, increasingly popular among the young, was a target of the ongoing campaign against bourgeois liberalism. No public radio was allowed to play it. Yet millions fell under her spell. Her sweet voice, whispering soft words of love, felt like a gentle breeze after the violent gale of revolutionary songs.

As the diva's voice faded into the background, I sank deeper into the first sofa I had ever tried. So soft, so comfortable! A standard fan on the wooden floor blasted wind across the spacious, high-ceilinged room. These block buildings were designed in the 1950s by the "Old Hairy Ones," as we nicknamed the hirsute Soviet experts who helped our factory until political differences sent them home in the 1960s. Since most of the Old Hairy Ones came alone, beautiful girls from the factory had been selected to dance and swim with them. Now, these spacious blocks mostly housed factory dignitaries. Commoners were also found in such blocks, though their flats that had been split into several units.

"What a luxury to have your own room!" I said.

"*Couhe*," he grunted. His pet phrase meant "It's all right," "I make do," or "Passable." Typical of his unappreciative, unenthusiastic attitude. He rolled down his singlet and lit a cigarette, waiting for me to take the conversation on.

"Are you going to leave the factory?" I asked directly.

"Not sure yet," he said, brushing his hair with his long fingers.

Some friend had proposed setting up a business together, but he was yet to be convinced. As a lazybones, he was nervous of the hardship he might face. Also, deep in his heart, I reckoned that he looked down upon getihu.

"So why don't you go back to work before you have a mature plan?"

His mother, eavesdropping behind the door, stepped into our conversation with green tea and a plea. "Listen, listen to your colleague, please. I am worried to death. If you are really expelled by the factory, how about your father's reputation? You really could kill him. He's old...."

"Stop nagging, old woman!" He shouted at his mother. "I hate that fucking factory, and the fucking rules, caotamade! Do you know, on that day, that stupid 'secret agent' wanted to measure my hair with a ruler!"

"But you can't just hang around at home forever!" she snorted.

"I can if I want," He sounded like a spoiled child complaining about the food he was offered. He didn't look half as worried as his mother. I had been admiring his courage. Now I saw that his war of resistance was partly due to stubbornness and partly because he knew the problem would be solved for him one way or another.

His mother softened her tone. "Look, as long as you agree to go back to the factory, I'll arrange everything."

After a few days, Zhi Yong finally returned, with his hair cut above his earlobes, yet retaining its cool, longish style. Obviously his director father had been informed and arrangements had been made. He was given a mild punishment with the excuse that he had to look after his sick mother.

The midday sun was blazing down, turning the world white as an overexposed picture. I could hardly believe that I was in that picture, sitting on the backseat of a shining red motorbike, driven by Zhi Yong. It was only a locally made Golden City, but still, a luxury item. We raced down the street like a gush of wind, on our way to buy an electric fan. Zhi had offered to transport it as soon as I mentioned my family's decision to buy one, the hottest ticket in a city besieged by heat. The fan would be the first electrical household appliance we owned. I gladly took up his offer. I guessed that he was grateful for my visit, a secret never mentioned by either of us. He was ready to come back and just needed a little push.

Before shopping, Zhi took me for a joyride downtown between New Street and the Drum Tower. I loved the thrill of sitting on a fast-moving vehicle, overtaking the bicycle crowds. I had always envied trendy girls on the back of boys' motorbikes, with their long hair flying in the wind (wearing a helmet was not compulsory for the passenger, and even drivers rarely wore them). Were passersby now watching me with the same envy? I lacked the ease and grace of those long-haired girls. Terrified I might fall off, I squeezed tight behind him. So close I could pick up his smell, a mixture of cigarettes and his unique body odor. That smell was the closest I had come to the mysterious world of men.

Too embarrassed to clutch his thin body, my hands awkwardly grabbed a handle at the back of the bike. Several times, when he turned a corner, I nearly grabbed him, but resisted the temptation and steadied myself. Watching my every move in the large wing mirrors, he must have been amused by this display. I suspected that he deliberately kept his speed up before cornering. Still, I loved the sensation and the closeness.

These were the most joyful moments I had known since falling into the factory well.

Chapter 9

Weijia

Goose bumps swelled across our bodies as soon as we took off our clothes. Even with the crowds, the changing room was freezing. I teamed up with my sister Weijia for the battle: our village shower house was always awash with people.

It was a Saturday afternoon in November 1981. Weijia had returned home for the weekend and I was back early from a training course for the young workers, mostly unskilled and poorly educated. Despite the dull content, I was very much enjoying the course. Three months away from the workshop! I almost felt like I was back in my school days, which were quickly fading into distant memory.

With chattering teeth, we rolled our clothes into a bundle like a spring roll and stashed it on top of the other spring rolls balanced on the long wooden benches of the changing room. There was no privacy. It had never existed in our basic, crowded lives, but here, least of all. Concerned with getting a wash without catching a cold, we hardly bothered to notice whether the girls standing next to us had bigger breasts.

Washing was free for me, and half price for Weijia, as a family member of a Liming employee. The benefit was another small reminder of how lucky we state workers should feel. Those who had to pay the full price of ten fen fought extra hard to stand under one of the two dozen scalding-hot showers, installed along the walls without a single partition. Verbal abuse rose with the steam, and punches rained down daily. It was quite a sight to see women, naked and soapy, pulling hair or punching flesh as the slippery floor sent them tumbling over.

My sister never bothered with such fights. My parent didn't name her Weijia—"only and best"—for nothing. She narrowed her beautiful, shortsighted eyes, assessing the crowds. A blur of naked flesh.

"Aiya, is that Auntie Wang?" she warmly greeted her target, a skinny woman, scratching herself under a shower. "I went to school with your daughter Little Red. Remember? How is she doing anyway?" While talking, she pushed herself closer to the shower.

"Oh, oh," the woman hesitated for a moment, knitting her eyebrows in concentration. "I must be getting old. Little Red is fine, temping at a shop. Want to have a wash?" The ribs showed through her chest, resembling an overused washboard. To us, she was an angel.

After she left, we tightly guarded our newly won position. Using a tough sponge made from towel gourd, we rubbed each other's backs until little black rolls of dirt fell down like a fleeing colony of rice worms.

Weijia had a full-grown woman's body. When I rubbed, her soft, perfectly formed breasts moved up and down too. I was always jealous of my sister's beauty. When we went out together, people would often remark: "Why, your sister is so pretty and you are so ugly." Chinese tend to make public remarks about people's appearance, often with little subtlety.

I wondered if she had done that "clouds and rain" business with Changyong. Although he lived with his parents, like all unmarried Chinese, he had his own room, which offered plenty of opportunity, but my sister was a very sensible girl who, I guessed, would not violate a taboo to have sex before marriage.

The pair had begun to date during the troubled summer of 1976. We all camped outside in makeshift tents for fear of a repeat of the earthquake that took two hundred thousand lives in Tangshan, south of Beijing, that July. Major disasters were often viewed as omens of dynastic change. Sure enough, Chairman Mao, who had ruled and shaped "New China" since 1949, died shortly afterward. The earth did not shiver in Nanjing, but Weijia must have— they fell in love. Weijia spent so much time with Changyong that we had grown apart. Besides, our temperaments could not have been more different.

It was dark when we walked out of the shower house. "Are you still at war with Ma?" Weijia asked.

I nodded. One month earlier, Ma and I had had yet another argument when she joyfully reported a central government directive tightening control of dingzhi. I suspected Ma had secret doubts about dingzhi, which explained why she always looked for evidence to convince herself that she had done a wise thing for both of us. Instead of playing along, I questioned what benefits I had gained, with one yuan's pocket money every month. Ma was enraged. She threw me my one-month salary and ordered me to eat outside.

"How are you coping?" Weijia asked as we walked toward a restaurant. Her treat tonight.

"Not too badly." I admitted that I had been surviving on bread rolls and dumplings, the cheapest types, bought from street hawkers. But I enjoyed the freedom of controlling my own money. From what I saved on food, I spent on two books and a velveteen jacket with a leopard pattern.

"Very stylish, don't you think?" I was a little disappointed that my sister had not made any remarks on my new outfit.

Weijia shook her pretty head. "It's too *reyan*, a hundred percent too *reyan*," eye-catching, with a negative connotation in the verb *re*, inviting or causing. "I'm sure your bosses don't like this sort of thing. I told you many times before, if you want to get anywhere in China, simply don't try to be different!"

She had indeed warned me before that our society had no stomach for conspicuousness. Parents of left-handed children even tried to make them to use the "right" hand. One summer when the Nanjing furnace came early and intense, Weijia still wore a long-sleeved shirt. Why not swap it for short-sleeved comfort? "Everyone else is still in long sleeves," she replied. "No point being the first to change." Her answer echoed the wisdom of our ancestors: "The rafter that juts out rots first." But my sister's lectures entered my left ear, exited the right, and rarely stayed for long in between.

We sat down at a food stall on the road leading into Wuding New Village. More and more of these privately run eateries were opening, keeping prices low for noodles, dumplings, steamed rolls, and sesame breads. Our place didn't even have a door. To enter the simple concrete hut, we stepped past a steaming wok on top of a rusty oil drum. At its base, an air blower fanned the stove, shooting sparks into the night air, and fanning our appetites as well. We ordered noodles in a hot clay pot with ham, quail's eggs, and vegetables. Bones and other leftovers littered the phlegm-stained floor. The greasy tables were discarded desks from my school. Yet the food tasted heavenly.

Under the fluorescent bulb, Weijia, her face fresh and pink after the long shower, looked like a young lily just rising above the water. Her hair was almost like my own now, short and wavy. I used to envy her silky, straight hair, shoulder-length and pulled back in a ponytail, for I never liked my own hair, sticking out all over the place as if it had a mind of its own. But during the summer holiday, I watched with amazement as she got a perm, certainly a potentially controversial style, at her boyfriend's request. She was in love.

She had gone not long after the first private hair parlor in the village opened for business, just opposite our noodle shack. It attracted the most daring and fashionable young women, who were fed up with the only other barber in the village, a one-room affair attached to the shower house, and subsidized by the factory, that offered just one type of haircut: short and simple. Deeply curious, I accompanied Weijia inside. The young barber, proudly sporting a perm himself, rolled her hair into curlers, then strapped her into the electric chair. Hanging from the ceiling, the permanent-wave machine dangled a web of wires. The barber clipped a wire to each curler, and the picture of torture was complete! My poor sister nervously rolled her eyes upward. When a wisp of smoke curled from her head, she screamed and, I think, would have bolted out the door but for the tangle of wires. Luckily, her hair was not burnt. Plenty of other girls did suffer for their vanity.

Weijia looked perkier with shiny black waves. But now a slight ripple was all that remained of her daring adventure. She couldn't afford to destroy the good impression she had made on the school authorities who, after all, would assign her a job upon graduation next year, she explained.

My sister ate her noodles in a ladylike fashion, picking up a few strands each time, rolling them around her chopsticks, then slowly toward her mouth. Lacking her patience or grace, I wolfed down my noodles. As young children, all three of us, and Father, too, when he was around, would race to get the dishes, then shovel them into our mouths, storing some in our cheeks like monkeys, returning for more before the dish disappeared. In later years, Ma began to distribute the food, forbidding us from picking at the dishes ourselves. Still, I never got out of the habit of eating fast.

"Mm, nice and spicy!" I put some chili oil on my noodles. Unlike most Nanjing people, I loved spicy food.

"No wonder you've got such a temper!" joked Weijia. "Seriously, try to control it and don't upset our mother."

"It's Ma who upsets me. Look at her, where does her get her bad temper?"

"Menopause," Weijia said. The papers had just started using this new term, explaining how women going through it could experience anxiety and mood swings. "Ma also suffers from 'red-eye disease.' See, our mother thinks she is very clever, but in the end, she got nowhere: her husband is useless, her son a hooligan, and now even her favorite daughter is turning against her." My sister had always claimed that I was Ma's favorite. As the eldest child, Weijia won everyone's affection, especially from Father and his family. As the only boy and, therefore, heir to the Zhang family line, Xiaoshi was strongly favored by Nai, the traditionalist. Sandwiched between them, I received the least attention. I always felt that Father's joke about finding me in a coal dump reflected his disappointment in me. Probably out of maternal instinct, Ma took pity on me and usually scolded Weijia when quarrels broke out between us: I wasn't half as argumentative as she. And my sister would complain that Ma was unfair.

"Hao, I'll try to make peace with her." A puppy of hers, I never used to argue. Now, my unfulfilling life at the factory had triggered my rebellious side. I almost enjoyed annoying her, though I usually regretted it if she really became upset. "I shouldn't have been so rude the other day. But I was fed up with her telling me how much money she lost from retiring early. Fed up, really. Do you think Ma would have retired if she had foreseen the salary reform?"

Shortly after she passed down her "rice bowl," the salary that had remained more or less unchanged for many years began to rise, as did inflation. Using every new bit of information, Ma worked out again and again exactly how much she had lost by retiring early. Her newfound job satisfaction, something she hadn't experienced for many years, failed to compensate.

"She would have," my sister nodded, "but she will always talk about money and will always be tight about money."

Having been so poor all her life, stinginess became Ma's habit, Weijia reasoned. But it was Weija's wedding Ma was probably saving for. As someone who cared about appearances, our mother would want the wedding tricycle, decorated with double-happiness paper cutouts, and red ribbons to arrive laden with dowry at the front door of her son-in-law, in full view of the nosy neighborhood. That meant at least six duvets with silk covers, two pieces of finest brocade, one woolen coat, and one TV set—and better a twelve-inch screen than a nine.

I drained my noodle soup and waited for Weijia to finish.

"How is your long-haired colleague? What's his name, Little Zhi, right? You haven't talked much about him lately."

"Couhe," I borrowed Zhi's pet phrase. "All right, I suppose."

"Any chance of further development? He's well-off, right?"

He was, but wealth was low on my criteria for a boyfriend. After the motorbike ride, we had become quite close. Sometimes he would offer me advice. "You are so naïve. Let me teach you something. For starters, you shouldn't have helped up that granny the other day." An old woman who fell to the ground was like a tiger's bottom—untouchable, he said. If she broke a bone and blamed me, I would have to pay all her hospital bills and more.

I let out one of my hearty laughs at his exaggeration.

He found fault even in my laughter. "Look at you, opening your big mouth and 'Ha, ha, ha.' Ladies should only smile without showing their teeth! Only men can do whatever they like."

Once, when we talked about plans for the future, I revealed that I would like to study at Liming Technical School, if it recruited students among factory workers that year. He strongly opposed it.

"Study? Why bother? Let me tell you, Little Zhang, no man in the world wants to marry a clever woman." He sounded as if he thought the whole purpose of my life was to find a man to marry! His own grand plan was to have every available household electrical appliance when he got married. He would not let his old woman get away with anything less.

Was he trying to impress me with his plan? Or was a houseful of appliances really his goal?

"He was so boring," I confessed to my sister.

Weijia widened her big eyes. "Boring? With his long hair and all that?" Yes, boring, and deeply conservative, despite the hair, knee-length boots and "all that." I came to view his trendy image as an attention-seeking facade, an attempt to show off his superiority. Besides, I found his drinking and gambling off-putting. The training course lent me the space I needed to forget him.

The tapping had started to fade.

Chapter 10

Would-Be
Model Worker

Another meeting, but no one dozed or gossiped. We sat in the power-gauge section waiting for someone to respond to Boss Wang's call for opinions. Only the hiss of radiators disturbed the nervous silence before the "election" of model young workers. This was work assessment, Chinese communist–style. Anything you said or did not say could tip the balance between you and your colleagues.

Looking around, Master Mei raised her stick-like arm and stood up. "I recommend Little Rong. She's a keen learner, a hard worker, and she observes all the rules." As she talked, Mei shifted her weight from left leg to right. She hadn't been so tiny before, apparently. But since her divorce six years earlier, she had begun to wither and become increasingly withdrawn. She was bitter about most things, including her unfaithful former husband and their only son, who turned out a hooligan. But the few things she did love, she loved with a passion. She took her apprentice Rong Ling as the daughter she never had, a good, obedient, tinghua girl who listened to what she said.

Almost obliged, Master Lin followed. "Uh, Little Zhang works very hard, she's warmhearted and willing to help. She's, she's just good." My master was a man of few words. He turned to Master Li for support, for I had been her personal servant. It was always better if a recommendation came from someone who was not your own master. However, Li, a highly talkative woman, chose that moment to be silent.

Suddenly, I saw Little Zhi's long arm up in the air. "I also recommend Little Zhang. She often carries out Lei Feng Spirit. Once, she helped a granny who fell to the ground." While withdrawing his arm, he brushed his long hair on the way. I stared at him, moved and surprised: Zhi never uttered a word in our group meetings. Though friendly enough on the surface, I knew he sensed the distance I had tried to keep. Our playful fights were no more. I felt a little guilty for "dumping" him, despite the fact that we had never even held hands.

"Both Little Zhang and Little Rong deserve to be model workers," was the compromise offered by Master Lan, our Mr. Goody-Goody, who would avoid upsetting a fly if he could.

Thus, both names were handed over to the leaders for consideration as honorable model workers in our unit. The election was an exercise in democratic centralism, democracy under centralized guidance, with the leader having the final say—the way China was run.

A week later, a red honor roll was posted onto our unit's blackboard, with Rong Ling's name highlighted in glorious gold.

I used to take such honors for granted. I had always been a model student—a "three good" student, good in morals, intelligence, and sports. I responded almost religiously to calls to pick up scrap metal for our country's steel production; organizing students to clean the public bus every March during "Learn from Lei Feng" week.

After entering the factory, I tried to be a good worker too, almost out of habit, even though my Girl Guide enthusiasm was fading. I did my best with assigned tasks and even volunteered to donate blood. My weight, however, failed me—the minimum was 100 pounds, and I weighed just eighty-eight. Rong failed even to offer, since her mother considered it unhealthy for a virgin to give blood. But I was reluctant to throw dirt at her.

Would I be much happier if my name shone out from that red roll, I wondered? Not much. I hated my job, the workshop, and the factory, so why bother even trying to be a model worker? If I should try anything, it should be to get out of this bloody place!

Opportunity was knocking.

Jiangsu TV University, new type of college termed an "open university" and designed to popularize learning, announced it was enrolling students. As China's proper universities could take so few students, other suppliers of higher education were springing up and wealthier enterprises began to finance classes for their own talents. My factory promised to organize and sponsor a mechanical engineering class.

"How brave of you!" said Master Li on learning that I had signed up for the exam, set for the end of March, only three months away. Her emphasis on "brave" plainly meant "reckless." Even model worker Rong Ling decided to wait for another year—fearing ridicule if she failed. I knew she had still to recover from the shock that she had suffered when a former classmate killed herself by drinking pesticide after failing the university entrance exam. But my desire to break free burnt off the fear of other people's scorn. Mechanical engineering? During my school days, while my journalist dream was still alive, I would have dismissed the course as being boring as chewing wax, but now it beckoned as the only way to obtain some near-decent education, and the only way to escape.

For once I felt engaged in a worthwhile battle. After a long hibernation, I was finally coming to life.

I worked out my priorities first of all. I calculated that it would be easier to memorize the dates in the Party's glorious history than to master a new chemical formula. Invigorated, I grabbed every waking minute to review what I had learned at school. I dreamed about dates and facts in my sleep.

Nai, with her own pocket money, bought bowls of pickled duck heads—she believed the old wives' tale that duck brain would enhance my brain power, just as pig tongue could boost eloquence, and bull testicles could work wonders for impotent men.

Like a determined runner, I was making a spurt toward the tape.

The admission notice from the TV University shot me right to the ninth heaven—China's highest.

I was to start TV University on September 1, 1982.

"Hao, well done!" Ma raised her teardrop porcelain cup, full of fiery liquor, her high cheeks already red. The family was holding a banquet to celebrate my becoming a *daxuesheng*, meaning literally, big student, and in practical terms, meaning a better job, maybe a better life.

"Little Li, you think I don't care about education. But I do, I do! My teacher used to say: 'The worth of other pursuits is small and the study of books exceeds them all,'" Ma said, in a voice full of the gentleness of southern rain. She always became more talkative after a few shots. "But you see, in this country, it's no good reading too many books." My father was dragged out again as an example. "I'm sure that he wouldn't have got himself into trouble if he hadn't read all those books. He even wrote articles." Ma continued. "I began to hate books then. I thought I might save you some trouble if you didn't have much education. 'Once bitten by a snake, you'll be afraid of ropes for ten years,' you see."

My mother's words barely registered. I felt rather drunk on the sweet taste of my little success, even if I was only drinking tea.

"*Amituofu*," Nai borrowed her Buddhist mantra to express her joy. "I knew you would pass: my left eyelid has been twitching." My grandma believed the superstition that when the left eyelid twitches, it means good fortune, whereas the right eyelid forebodes misfortune. But she always felt her eyes twitching after the event. "Just think about those good-looking, clever lads, your eyes will be dazzled! Which one to choose?" Nai winked at me, dimples smiling on her cheeks.

"Congratulations!" Weijia also rose with a toast and a brief smile flickering across her pretty face. "Soon, I'll be a primary school teacher, with lots of work and little pay, no match to you, a technician at a big enterprise. Lucky you, being Ma's favorite."

My sister's tone deepened the sour feeling in my own mind. Look, I did well in the TV University exam. If I were allowed to stay at school, wouldn't I have passed the proper university exam?

But I soon dismissed it. For the first time since leaving school, I felt my future was bright. I saw myself rise to become a technician, and then an engineer, and later, even a senior engineer. I was working at an important enterprise in China where I could make my contribution. I might even get a chance to work on the real thing—the rocket that could reach America!

With a new life to look forward to, my remaining days at the workshop became more endurable.

On my last day, Li patted my cheeks. "Little Zhang, please don't forget your friend who shared sweetness and bitterness with you down here, all right?" And then, as if to prove her worth, she revealed a secret—why I failed to become a model worker. It was our Political Instructor Wang, she said, who crossed my name from the model worker list. He strongly disliked me because he suspected I wore a perm, and only "decadent bourgeois elements" curled their hair. In our highly politicized society, nothing was personal.

"Why didn't he ever bother to ask me if my hair is natural?" I did not always believe Master Li's information, but this rang true.

"Well, not just your hair." Master Li pursed her lips, her round eyes darting to my clothes. "All right, it's just that you left him with a impression as someone who likes a freewheeling lifestyle with your leopard-skin jacket and things." Her tight lips rearranged into a sweet smile. "How lucky that you'll be out of here in no time."

Chapter 11

Quiet, Please, Comrades

The curtains were drawn in the classroom. The tiny math professor scratched his complex formula onto the blackboard. Whenever he turned his back on us students, we watched his bald head, fringed with white hair like the wild grass on a neglected roof. Then our eyes followed his thin, blue-veined hand, as we struggled to copy what it wrote.

We could hardly ask him to slow down as he flickered before us on two large televisions. Taped lectures were the backbone of TV University. It took a lot of concentration, given the lack of interaction between professor and student. But we were luckier than most—as an organized class, we also attended afternoon tutorials with real teachers, while tens of thousands of other students relied on watching TV programs at home, and their own hard work.

Academically, all TV University students followed the same curriculum, taking the same exams and enjoying summer and winter holidays like proper university students. Administratively, we remained within the confines of our work units, which continued to pay our full salaries.

But I no longer dreaded Liming. Every day as I neared Gate Six, a side gate in the southern compound, the nondescript building housing Liming Education and Training Center would loom up. I raced to the third floor, where our class camped, energized by the feeling that I had come up a little in the world: my training course one year ago had been on the ground floor.

Every morning we watched three lectures. So intensive was the course that I would snatch a fifteen-minute nap when I went home for lunch. Advanced math became my favorite. Although the professor's spidery formulas looked intimidating, in time solving them proved surprisingly rewarding. I looked forward to watching the small professor and the wild grass on his bald head. During breaks, I chatted and laughed with my classmates. Once again I belonged to a place where I felt happy.

In the late afternoon, I stayed to play volleyball, a national fad as the Chinese women's volleyball team was storming to victory worldwide. It was a luxury, for few Chinese could enjoy sports once out of school. Even at school, our sports were limited to jogging, a sport that required no equipment, followed by skipping for girls, soccer for boys, or hand-grenade practice for both. Clutching mock grenades, made from wood topped with metal to resemble the real thing, we lined up to throw them against the wall that encircled the playground. On the wall stretched a vast red slogan with the reason for our militaristic "sport"—to exercise our bodies and protect our motherland.

No hand grenades now, but I was definitely protecting our motherland, if a little indirectly.

I spent most of my time, including evenings, in class, but never experienced boredom. By doing homework there rather than at home, I could also get help, especially with my worst subject—mechanical drawing. I struggled to imagine how machinery parts looked from this or that angle. Liu Weidong, the head of the class, made painstaking efforts to help me. While I was the youngest, mild-mannered Liu was the oldest, pushing thirty.

One day, he brought a pile of putty from his unit. "Look, I know how to solve your problem," he said excitedly.

Liu molded a rectangle, punched some holes, then cut it vertically with a knife. "See, a longitudinal section of this part looks like this." He made a sectional drawing on paper. My gaze alternated from putty to drawing to putty. Suddenly, the drawing lessons began to make sense.

"Yes, got it!" I exclaimed. "Oh, thank you. How do you know all these things?"

"Liming Technical School," he smiled, flashing his buckteeth.

"Quite a few of our class studied there, right? Ning did."

"Yes, we studied together," his smile disappeared. "You like to talk with him, but as a friend I warn you to be careful." He looked around and lowered his voice. "Do you know his nickname? Butterfly!"

The class Prince Charming, Ning certainly loved to flutter around the pretty girls. Though not particularly handsome, he carried an air of sophistication rarely brought into a factory, and was one of the few Chinese men who made an effort to flatter women. When I met him for the first time, he said: "I've heard a lot about you. You're the one who scored so high without even attending senior middle school!" I was immediately taken by him, just like the rest of the girls, though I knew I stood no chance. He was the son of a high-ranking government official, whose family lived in the faded elegance of a former foreign consulate, west of the Drum Tower, Nanjing's central landmark.

I thanked Liu for his warning but didn't comply. How could I refuse delightful company? More importantly, Ning had access to film shows, treats reserved for ranking cadres and their families. He always invited a group of us: his desk mate, who followed him everywhere like a shadow; Ping, the prettiest girl in the class; Jun, my desk mate, who would stare, lovelorn, at Ping's slender back without taking in a word from the TV lectures; and me.

Ning's first treat was Charlie Chaplin's *Modern Times*, shown at an assembly hall inside a military compound. In the past, politics dominated people's lives, and comedies had more or less vanished: maybe the government worried that laughing would blunt the masses' revolutionary zeal. We left the cinema, mimicking the Chaplin walk and roaring with laughter. But I loved the romantic movies, mostly from Hollywood, dubbed by professional actors. Romance was rarely featured in Chinese novels or films because romantic love—not a respectable concept—played little role in our daily life. Even the very word for romance, *luomantike*, was imported, a clumsy transliteration.

"Warmly Congratulate the Communist Party's Sixty-second Birthday!" The golden characters shone on the red banner high above the stage at our factory's assembly hall. The hall was another solid legacy left by the hairy Soviet experts. Modest from the outside, it was massive on the inside, stretched to capacity that day by almost the entire army of ten thousand Liming employees, squeezed together on wooden benches.

Except for any male comrade who sported long hair, or female comrades wearing high-heeled shoes. A large blackboard at the entrance prohibited their entry, the result of a recent campaign against spiritual pollution. Hidden in our classroom, we were sheltered from the political weather. The chalked-up restrictions reminded me of Zhi Yong. How was he getting on? Couhe, I bet. A man without any aspiration, he was suited to the stagnant life of the workshop. How could I have fancied him?

We filed into the assembly hall like a well-trained regiment and settled into our assigned seats, a blur of white shirts and navy trousers—the singing-contest outfit. Every year on the first of July, every danwei throughout the motherland organized a singing contest to honor the birthday of the Chinese Communist Party, born in Shanghai back in 1921.

At center stage stood a long table, covered in red cloth and bearing four porcelain teacups. There would be four speeches then, we knew, and no singing until the party secretary, the factory director, the propaganda chief, and the head of the labor union had each recalled the Party's glorious history and expressed their hope that these revolutionary songs would inspire the workers' enthusiasm in production. All four were men. The higher the rank in China, the fewer women could be found. Chairman Mao's saying "Women hold up half the sky" remained as elusive as the sky itself.

Our TV University class was fortunate to perform early, before the audience's patience fully expired. With hands tucked behind our backs, chests thrust outward, and heads held high, "like the proud masters of this socialist country," we opened our mouths and bellowed.

> Socialism is great, socialism is great!
> In socialist countries, the people enjoy high social standing.
> Counterrevolutionaries were overthrown
> And the imperialists ran away with their tails between their legs.
> People from the whole country unite together,
> Joining in the high tide of socialist construction, socialist construction!

The usually mild-mannered Liu Weidong was transformed into a passionate chorus master, leaping up and down on the stage. Liu was always a model student leader, readily complying with any task given by the Party. Even in rural exile, he had toiled in his commune's "Chairman Mao Thought Propaganda Team." His chorus worked well until half a dozen students on the back row suddenly toppled off their stools! While laughter from the congregation was threatening to lift the roof, the rest of us dithered between singing on or checking if our fallen comrades were injured. Liu saved us by continuing with renewed vigor.

As the contest dragged into the evening, the audience began to drown out the performers. "Comrades, quiet, please!" The head of propaganda shouted the order. "This is a serious political activity, not a circus!" Most workers were happy to enjoy free entertainment during work hours, while many participants had been motivated by the flexitime they earned from rehearsals after work. By now, only comic moments grabbed the audience's attention. A soprano shrieked the tune "I love you, China," her voice cutting the air like a machine plane shredding metal; another amateur tenor was overambitious with his early notes and had to lower them at a crucial moment. One chorus sang the Party's praises and dodged the Party's blows—a colleague waving the heavy flag got carried away with his role.

Slowly, some of my classmates formed pairs. Ping was throwing more tender glances at Jun, my deskmate, after she had realized that Prince Charming was not really interested in her after all, despite his lavish attention. He could not help being drawn to pretty girls, like a butterfly tempted by a field of flowers.

Even I attracted a suitor. Following a laboratory test at a university (we had no lab of our own), Liu Weidong asked if I would like to eat wonton soup with him. He had something to show me.

Liu took me to a small eatery and ordered two bowls. When his soup arrived, he counted the wontons in the bowl. "Master, how many wonton should one bowl have?" he asked politely. In private shops and restaurants, the Marxist term "comrade" was giving way to "master"— these entrepreneurs, the brave pioneers of China's return to capitalism, were hardly "comrades."

"Twelve," the master replied.

"I'm sure I haven't got enough."

The waiter took his bowl, counted them, then added two more wonton. "These getihu, so naughty, always try to rip you off."

I almost choked on my laughter, amazed that he cared about matters like this, as small as sesame seeds. I restrained myself, and picked on his remarks about getihu. "My mother works with getihu, you know. She didn't really like them at first. But as she got to know them, she became friends with some."

Last Chinese New Year, a man who made cane juice by crushing sugarcane came to visit my mother with a bundle of fruit, and a large bottle of cane juice. "Master Huang, I'm so grateful to you because you are the first person who treated me as a human, not just a getihu." It turned out that the man was a university graduate, sent to jail after running into trouble during the Cultural Revolution. When he was released in the early 1980s, his factory refused to take him back. He ended up at Confucius Temple Market.

"Eh, maybe," Liu said vaguely. He tended not to confront me as much as he did other classmates. He concentrated on his wonton, his prominent front teeth scraping the porcelain spoon with each mouthful.

"What do you want to show me?"

Carefully cleaning his hands, he produced a scroll. "For you!"

I opened it and saw a lovely painting of plum blossoms, in Chinese ink and wash. On one side was a poem, in beautiful calligraphy. "Dappled shadows hang aslant over clear shallow water; secret fragrance wafts in moonlit dusk." The words came from a Song dynasty poet, waxing lyrical. I once told Liu that plum blossom was my favorite flower because it blossomed first in spring. A flower of courage.

"Is the calligraphy yours?"

"Yes," he replied, his head jerking more obviously than usual. The painting was by a well-known painter and calligrapher, and Liu's teacher.

"Fantastic!" I praised wholeheartedly. "Thank you so much."

"My pleasure. Do, do you…" Suddenly, he started to stammer. "Do you think there's a chance, chance, we could develop our friendship further?"

My first proposal?! But it failed to thrill. Liu was a nice guy and good to me, yet I found him priggish and wet. I had high ideals for my would-be boyfriend, doubtless due to the foreign films I devoured. He had to be handsome, and highly intelligent, with a great vision for life, and a romantic with little regard for the number of wontons in his bowl.

"Well, I am still young," I blushed. "For the moment, I'd like to focus on my study, not personal matters." A common excuse, badly given.

Chapter 12

Sacred Mountain

"Eat, eat!" My auntie pushed another leg into my rice bowl. Roast chicken seasoned with soy sauce was the Jinan specialty. "How does it compare to salty Nanjing duck?" she asked.

"More delicious!" I mumbled, spitting rice onto her table.

In summer 1984, I was enjoying the second holiday of my life. It was hard on the heels of my first-ever holiday, an eye-opening trip to Yellow Mountain I had taken with my sister and her husband, Changyong, as soon as term ended at TV University. Changyong's state-owned electronic company subsidized the trip for employees, each of whom could bring a few friends or relatives. The pair had married a year and a half earlier, as soon as Weijia turned twenty-one, the minimum age for marriage under China's family-planning policy. She couldn't wait for the government's recommended marriage age for women, twenty-five.

Through hard bargaining, Ma had agreed to increase my pocket money—on condition that I would not demand any dowry from her when I got married. Marriage, even the thought of boyfriends, seemed too distant to matter.

The Yellow Mountain range, in neighboring Anhui province, drew countless poets and artists in search of inspiration. It was a natural playground, fringed with cloud, where perilous stone steps ascended toward peaks with fanciful names like "The Fairy Maiden Pointing the

Way"—a rock resembling a person with raised arms, or "Dreaming Pen"—for a stone pillar. Masses of tourists now crowded the artists' peaceful haven, but the views remained unchanged. I loved every minute, charging up daunting climbs like Fairy Capital and Lotus Peak that put off some girls.

Weijia was more or less pulled up the steps by her attentive husband. Changyong wore very fashionable sunglasses, not the old type with pitch-black lenses, but imported shades whose tint changed with the light. To emphasize their origin, he proudly left the "Made in USA" label right on the lens. My brother-in-law had also become a worker at a young age. But in the new environment of reforms, he was quickly learning how to navigate the maze of a Communist marketplace steadily turning capitalist.

After Yellow Mountain, my feet were too itchy to stay at home. I had been saving my full allowance, determined to go somewhere during my precious second summer holiday. It happened that my aunt, Father's younger sister, had invited me to visit out of gratitude for some fish that Ma waited for hours to get for her. "Let me go, Ma. Read ten thousand books and travel ten thousand li," I begged, quoting ancient advice for young scholars. Ma had agreed, partly to reward me for my TV University exams: I scored ninety-nine in Principles of Mechanics, a subject many found difficult.

After an overnight train ride, I reached a large flat in the center of Jinan where Auntie, her husband, and their three unmarried daughters lived a rather free and chaotic life. There were no family meals—they ate at different times and different things, usually cooking for themselves. The results were dreadful, without exception. But Auntie compensated with ready-made treats like sausages and roast chicken, delicacies my family could only hope for during festivals.

I relished this exciting and varied life, free from my nagging mother. I got on well with the youngest girl, who was simply called San'er, Number Three. Two years older than me, she was tall, with long, graceful legs. Her pretty face was shaped like a sunflower seed, lit up by her smiles and big double-lidded eyes, like my sister's. Her thick long hair cascaded over slender shoulders, yet she seemed totally unaware of her own beauty. San'er also possessed a raw sense of humor, singing out "A fine lady farts loudly," whenever Auntie let loose. Together, we giggled and shared a closeness I never enjoyed with my own, rather serious sister. As an accountant for a large state-owned factory, where her father was Party Secretary for years, San'er easily managed to get time off to show me around Jinan, a city with many springs but few remarkable sights.

At my suggestion, that evening, San'er and I were planning to climb Tai Mountain, only four hours by train from Jinan. It was one of China's five sacred Taoist peaks. The others were known as the Southern, Western, Northern, and Central Peaks, but Tai Mountain, the Eastern Peak, was the most significant: the ancient Chinese believed the sun-giving east was the direction from which all life sprang.

"Eat more," Auntie urged. "If you girls don't eat enough, your legs will go as soft as noodles, like this." She bent her knees and stumbled for a few steps. It was not that funny but she began to laugh, mildly at first, then hysterically. A contagion of laughter shook her fleshy body, and as always, once under way, she took a long time to stop. At other moments, she would gaze out of the window, talking to herself or an imaginary lover in a thin girlish voice. If someone called her, she responded in her normal high pitch, with the strong Nanjing accent that never left her. Despite these warning signs, she took no medication. Apart from two breakdowns, when she was hospitalized, she was never treated properly. The family never admitted in public that she suffered from mental illness, a byword for rejection in Chinese society.

Her pathetically tiny husband sat in a corner watching his goldfish, oblivious to his wife's fit. He always appeared on the verge of tears. Well into his seventies, he accentuated his baldness by carefully pasting the surviving hairs across his head. The slightest movement bared his shining pate, but he clung to those strands, the last memories of youth and vitality.

He was a typical cadre of his time: clean of corruption and blindly loyal to the Party. He named most of his five children after the politics and events of the day. Weiping, "maintain the peace," the son living in Nanjing, was born shortly after the Korean War ended in stalemate; and San'er's proper name was Qing, "cleanup," named after the "Four Cleanups Campaign," a forerunner of the Cultural Revolution. Parents often used children's names to show how politically correct they were. A classmate of mine was called Wenhua, "culture," and her brother Geming, "revolution." No prizes for guessing when they were born.

It was hard to imagine how my romantic aunt coped with her revolutionary husband; harder still to imagine that she was once a slim and beautiful actress in an army song-and-dance troupe. In the early 1950s, army actresses served as a pool of brides for officers who had missed their chance to marry in their years of battling the Japanese and the Nationalists. Her marriage to my uncle, a much older cadre who had spotted her during a performance at his camp, was arranged. It was a "political task" she had to comply with, willingly or not. After the wedding, she retired from the army to become a primary school teacher.

The marriage brought Auntie five children, born before family planning, when China still blindly followed the

Soviet belief that more births meant a stronger nation. Having failed to rise high in the army, her old soldier retired and ended up the Party Secretary of a wireless equipment factory in Jinan. The stagnation in his career deepened Auntie's unhappiness. I felt sorry for her. Women of that generation could do little to change their fate.

"Will you two girls be all right on your own?" asked Auntie after she calmed down. "What if you bump into some hooligans?"

"We'll be fine. We are strong independent women!" San'er replied, swinging her skinny arms. She was as excited as me about our adventure, for she had never traveled anywhere apart from a trip to Nanjing with her mother.

"Hooligans are rare," piped up a tiny voice. "Ninety-five percent of the masses are good." As a Communist Party worker, my uncle must have picked up this statistic from Chairman Mao during his many political movements. If it was true, it still left nearly five million hooligans out there waiting for us.

Auntie giggled as she packed another roast chicken for the journey.

A stone passage marked "The First Gate to Heaven" was the start of our climb: from its arch hung the last electric light before darkness swallowed the steps. We had not thought to bring a torch. Feeling our way along, we could hear other climbers in the distance. Summer was a popular time to visit Tai Mountain, and most visitors climbed at night to catch the sunrise, which ranked even higher in travelers' lore than the sunup over Yellow Mountain in southeast China.

Giggling and chatting, San'er and I made our way up the six thousand steps. After only five hundred, four young men approached from behind.

"Excuse me, female comrades, are you alone?"

"Yes, we are," I replied, looking at the spectacled young man in front of us, more curiously than cautiously.

"We are not bad people, we're students from Shandong University. Would you like to join us? We have a big torch. Look, this is my student card. Li Hongyan is my name."

In the torchlight, I glimpsed an earnest face. "Sure!" San'er and I quickly agreed, and introduced ourselves. They were history students on their last summer holiday before graduation. Before long, San'er and I mingled with them like old friends.

The students showed off their knowledge by explaining that emperors throughout the dynasties used to visit Tai Mountain, believing mountains to be the home of gods and spirits, especially those associated with rain. An emperor, believing himself the son of heaven, would commune with the gods and spirits on the peaks of sacred mountains; he would pray for propitious winds and rain, so that harvests would be guaranteed, the people content, and he could continue his reign.

The narrow stone steps zigzagged into the darkness like an endless snake. To keep us going, we took turns telling stories. Li, clearly their leader, began with the tale of Zhu Yuanzhang, beggar king turned founder of the Ming Dynasty. He chose this Nanjing-based story for my sake, I supposed.

After taking power, Zhu ordered a commemorative pavilion be built for those who rendered outstanding service. At the banquet inside the lavish building, one clever minister named Xu noticed it was made entirely of wood, with very thin walls. He recalled a friend, who had given up his title to go home, warning him to follow the emperor closely on the day of the banquet. In the middle of the meal, the emperor rose—ostensibly to relieve himself. Xu followed. "Why are you coming, too?" the emperor asked.

"To protect your highness," Xu replied.

"There is no need."

But Xu begged him: "Your highness, do you really want to keep not even one follower?" After they left, the pavilion collapsed in fire, killing all the other founders of the Dynasty—the emperor had ensured that no one would challenge his power.

Li told his tale eloquently, in perfect Mandarin. "All the emperors were the same," he concluded. "You can share hardships with them but not the fruits of victory. Chairman Mao was just like that. Didn't he kill all his loyal ministers, one by one?"

Our great leader? I was shocked. Although the process of demystifying Mao had begun, he was still greatly admired in China. But I started to admire Li more: in my small circle of friends, who could make such clever remarks?

"Yes, Chairman Mao was just another imperial emperor," agreed a short student. "Things might have been different if Mao had gone abroad for some Western education."

The conversation grew more lighthearted as we trotted up the steps. The students sang a popular song of the time, "Where the peach tree blossoms you'll find my lovely hometown," it went. I challenged Li on his lack of a hometown Tianjin accent, so he laid it on thick to tell a local joke. Our laughter echoed into the dark gullies below.

"What's Nanjing dialect like?" the short student asked.

"*Youtiao a you a? Mu de le!*" I blurted out.

"What did you say?" they all asked.

"'Do you still have any doughsticks? Not one!' But Nanjing dialect is so ugly that you don't need to know." I had been trying to hide my accent and speak standard Mandarin with the students.

"It's not ugly at all, at least when you say it," Li flattered me. "I like accents. It would be dull if everyone talked like newsreaders."

The Gate in the Middle of the Sky, halfway up the mountain, offered a well-lit break. I noticed that Li had a scholarly charm. Behind horn-rimmed spectacles lay a pair of deep-set, thoughtful eyes. The high bridge of his nose lent him a definite dignity, and his lips were full and sensual. His slim form was clad in jeans and a simple T-shirt. Li smiled at me and I blushed when I realized I was staring.

After a while, we set off with renewed energy for the peak, 5,068 feet above sea level. As we ascended into thinner air I had to stop more often to catch my breath. By the Archway to the Celestial Beings, I was exhausted, my legs the noodles of Auntie's prediction. The last leg of the journey lay up a perilously steep stairway. When Li offered a hand, I took it gladly, surprised by its strength.

Soft rain fell on the stone steps under the peak while we sat and waited for the day to break. The climate amid the mountain mists was unstable. Li arranged his three friends to share one of the two raincoats they brought along, while he shared the other with my cousin and me—me between them. Under this small shelter, we squashed together. I could feel his breath. Several times, our bare arms touched. Except for that joyride with Zhi Yong, I had never been so close to a man. We hardly spoke, but sat listening to the falling rain and the wind chasing through the treetops. The short student fell asleep and began to snore mildly. Wide awake, my heart was racing faster than the rain—all because of this stranger beside me.

As it grew colder on the peak, Li went to borrow some padded army coats. I suddenly remembered the roast chicken, to everyone's delight. "It was on this peak that the imperial offering to heaven used to take place, and the offering to the earth was made at the base," explained Li. "But I doubt any of the sacrifices could be as good as this chicken!"

At sunrise, the early morning cloud was too thick for a postcard scene. Then the new day turned quickly, blindingly bright, full of promise and hope.

We had no excuse to stay longer with our escorts, who had gallantly and safely taken us to the top. I boldly looked into Li's eyes when I shook his hand to bid farewell. Did I imagine a few sparks there?

Back down the path lay temples and cultural relics celebrated through China's many centuries, which had been hidden under the thick veil of darkness. But I had lost all interest. I knew it was not just fatigue. Several times, I thought I saw the smiling faces of the students among the crowds, but at a closer look, they turned into strangers.

Chapter 13

Red Rock

"What's this Li chap like?" asked Auntie.

"He's a little thin, almost good-looking," reported San'er to her mother, "but too scholarly for my liking."

We had just returned from Tai Mountain. After supper, Auntie listened attentively and responded with lengthy laughter. "Any chance of you and the Li chap getting together?" she asked, placing her two index fingers together, her eyes gleaming with a smile.

"No!" I shook my head violently, "No way! We don't even live in the same city."

"'Because of fate, people thousands of li apart can tie the knot,'" replied Auntie, quoting a Chinese saying. What an old romantic!

In bed that night, images of Li Hongyan filled my head.

The following afternoon, I cycled to my uncle's factory to shower. When I passed the gate of Shandong University, I realized it was just around the corner from the factory. Standing under the hot shower, a wild idea sprang to mind.

Li was lying in his upper bunk bed, reading a book, when I turned up at his dormitory with wet hair and a plastic net bag holding my soap and face towel. He looked surprised, but a warm smile soon blossomed on his face. "Please come in!"

"Er, I happened to be nearby," I said, pushing my glasses up my nose. "So, I suddenly thought of coming to see you, just to thank you properly. I was also curious what life is like for a proper university student."

"You are a proper university student, too," he said kindly while climbing down from his top bunk.

"Proper university students stay at campus, but we stay at home." My sense of inferiority was never far below the surface.

There were six bunk beds in the room, and two other students, but they nodded at me politely and quickly found some excuse to leave.

He sat on the lower bunk, opposite me. With his deep-set eyes, he looked straight into mine. I could not meet this daring gaze.

"You seem to have recovered?" he said.

"Almost."

"Every inch of my body is aching. How pathetic! You know, all the boys were so impressed by you two girls, so brave and so energetic."

"Really?" I smiled, briefly meeting his searching eyes. My heart started to pound again. "We had sensible shoes. San'er and I saw some girls climbing in their high heels!"

My eyes scanned the room nervously and caught sight of his half-opened book, in Japanese script. "Are you studying?"

"Oh, no. How can I study in my state? It's a novel. It's much more interesting to read works in the original language, don't you agree?"

"I don't know. I guess so." My heart filled with admiration: the idea of reading a book in a foreign language was as foreign as the language itself.

"Do you study English at TV University?"

"Only for a few terms. How about you?"

"We learned a little as well as our second foreign language, but mostly I picked it up myself. My English isn't quite as good as my Japanese, but good enough to read novels. I don't understand why some students choose to focus in foreign languages," he continued as I flipped through the pages. "It should only be a tool, in my view, not a subject of study—unless you want to be a linguist."

He sounded rather arrogant, but I did not know the subject well enough to argue.

Footsteps and the clink of metal spoons on enamel bowls sounded in the corridor—the students were walking to the dining hall. I rose. "I'll have to go now. Otherwise, my auntie would get worried."

He walked with me to the gate while I pushed the bike. The setting sun cast long shadows. Ours looked good together, I thought.

We shook hands to say good-bye. A sadness struck me: how easily just walk away from him, and never see him again. But why accept the passive role of a shy girl? "Maybe we can meet up again sometime?"

"Absolutely, how about tomorrow?" His face lit up with a smile, as if he had been awaiting such an invitation. "Term has not started yet. I'll take you to see the Yellow River."

The next morning, we cycled out of the city on our Flying Pigeons. The sun shone with a special brightness. In childish high spirits, I burst out singing.

"You are so lively," he said, "I truly envy you. I often feel like an old man already. Many of my classmates are the same."

"You history students have been under the spell of Old Confucius for too long."

He soon joined in my singing. After crossing the Great Yellow River Iron Bridge, Li led the way toward a mud path along the riverbank. Poplars stood in a line, straight and tall, like soldiers on guard. Beyond the path, red sorghum—taller than a man—formed a long stretch of green curtain.

At a quiet spot, we parked our bikes.

"Let's sit here." Walking halfway down the slope, I found a weeping willow tree. I sat down on my handkerchief and he placed himself right next to me, too closely, I thought. We hardly knew each other. But I didn't move.

"Hot today, isn't it?" I said absentmindedly.

"When your heart is at ease, coolness will come."

I turned to look at him. His lips were full and sensual. Under his horn-rimmed spectacles, there seemed to be two little flames dancing. I looked straight ahead.

In front of us, the Yellow River ran swiftly east. The water literally looked yellow, as the river carried and churned the dark yellow mud of the soft loess plateau far upstream. Jinan stood on the last leg of its five-thousand-kilometer journey from Tibet to the Gulf of Bohai.

At school, we learned to love this "Mother River" that suckled the people of ancient China. But it proved an enigmatic water dragon, earning its other name, "River of Sorrow": centuries of flooding and changes of course had caused much destruction and death.

Pressured by the intimate silence, I began to sweat. As I toyed with a stone, my mind raced, looking for something impersonal to say. "Was the Yellow River really the 'cradle of Chinese civilization'?"

"Yes, it certainly was. Ever since prehistoric times, the river brought fertile soil from the upper reaches down to the plains in central China. It helped to form an economic base there." His own words gurgled out like a flowing stream. I knew I had pressed the right button.

Li said that he was fascinated by the way that efforts to tame this "dragon" had led to China's centralized, autocratic system. He visibly relaxed as he talked, explaining how the need to organize large numbers of laborers in water projects provided the base for despotic states. The group who proved most successful in harnessing a major watercourse invariably became the ruling class.

"So clever, you are. But where do you get all your daring ideas, not from your textbooks, surely?"

"Well, I'm a history student, but I don't just listen to what I'm fed. Besides, I have foreign friends." He looked at the river, a sour look on his face. "Yes, it's a great river, but it only bred an autocratic state. All that praise, songs like 'Ode to the Yellow River'—over the top! The Great Wall, too!" he snorted.

That July the government had launched a campaign to raise funds to renovate parts of the Wall, which were crumbling after centuries of neglect.

"Pathetic! To build a wall to keep off the invading nomads?" Li scoffed, twisting his full lips. "It shows how inward-thinking we were! It's pathetic, don't you think? We Chinese seem so desperate to grab something we can feel proud of: the Great Wall, the Yellow River." He took the stone from my hand and threw it with force into the river.

"You're so cynical and critical!" My criticism was sugarcoated.

"I guess I am cynical," he grinned, flashing his white teeth. I liked his smile, boyish and shy, unlike his arrogant talk. "But I'm not always critical. I do think you look lovely today."

I reddened. I secretly agreed with him—I had grown a little from the undernourished bean sprout I was. I wore the same outfit as the day we climbed Tai Mountain—a flowery blouse and a pair of white, tight trousers that ended below the knees. Not the most practical outfit, but I liked to look my best on my few outings.

The atmosphere became intimate again. I took a pear from my bag and concentrated on peeling it with a small knife I brought along: in the sleepless hours of the previous night, I had anticipated every detail. When I turned to offer the half of the pear to him, he took not the fruit but my lips! He kissed me gently at first, but determinedly, with one hand pressing my head, as if to prevent me from running away. I was surprised but I played along, hesitantly at first, then more passionately as I got the hang of it. I felt dizzy; my heart was melting, and I melted in his arms. I was twenty and had never been kissed, save in my dreams. Never did I expect this moment would come so quickly!

"God, you are sweet!" He exclaimed upon releasing my mouth. Then, he took the bashed half pear from my hand. "Why did you buy pear?" he asked with a solemn look on his face.

Too late I realized the word for "pear" sounded like the Chinese character for "separate." Couples were not supposed to share pears. Dazed for a brief moment, I smiled brightly.

"You sound like my grandma! You're not superstitious, are you?" I was suddenly in love. Nothing else mattered.

He smiled, too. He confessed that on the day we met he had spotted me earlier, with my reyan outfit. When he realized that we had no companions, he had decided to approach us with a gallant excuse.

The Yellow River brought a gentle, comforting breeze to the happy hours we spent in the shadow of that dancing willow tree. We missed lunch. Yet, my stomach, which usually reported hunger like clockwork, forgot to rumble. "Beauty is edible," he said. Li did most of the talking. I found interest in his every word.

His name, Hongyan, meant Red Rock, the title of a famous novel. It was the tale of revolutionaries martyred in a prison uprising against the Nationalist regime. Li's father, a Communist Party worker, had hoped his son would grow up red and tough as a rock, to carry on the revolutionary cause. To his father's dismay, Li had turned his back on the faith. When the university authorities invited him as a freshman to apply for Party membership, thanks to his distinguished academic record, he firmly refused. "I live for myself, not for some ridiculous ideas," he scoffed. Nevertheless, I took an immediate liking to his name, so romantic yet so manly.

I also talked about my family and my dream of studying at university.

"Stop feeling sorry for yourself," he said, printing a kiss on my forehead. "In my view, university offers students the skill to learn and a system that forces them to learn, that's why we have exams. But if you have the will to learn, then you can be equally successful. Many great people never went to proper university, including your beloved Chairman Mao."

"I used to love him more than I loved my father. But I am not sure anymore."

"Talking about love, I must confess I was surprised that a pretty girl like you didn't have boyfriends before. You didn't know how to kiss." He winked at me.

Color rose in my cheeks. "Yes, I need more practice." I sought his lips again.

I had only one week left in Jinan. In that short time, we managed to see each other daily. I made all kinds of excuses to sneak out. Before leaving, I would stare at myself in the mirror, wondering if I looked pretty. I wore no makeup— few girls had any then—but I made sure to comb my unruly long hair and tease a curl out onto my forehead, just as my mother used to do. Finally I had found love! I was in a constant state of ecstasy.

Sometimes, we were obliged to include San'er in our outings. Once, in a crowded public bus, Red Rock began to caress my hair. I pushed him away, pointing to San'er, who was standing only a few steps away from us. "I am in love with you, I can't help myself. Even the most stupid person in the world can see that. Why don't you tell her?"

Later on that day, I confessed to my cousin. I asked her not only to keep my secret but also cover up for me, which she readily agreed. "I knew. I figured it out from the very beginning! Look at you, glowing as if you've taken some magic pill." She flashed a mischievous grin, "And I've done my research. Your guy is one of the four most talented scholars in Shandong University. Did you know that?" It turned out that the mother of San'er's sister-in-law was a professor at the University.

Madly in love, I would sometimes sneak out at night to see Red Rock even when we had not agreed a meeting. It was easy to locate him, either at his dormitory or the library. And he always knew where to go—privacy existed wherever you could find it.

One night, as soon as we found the quiet corner of a park, we threw ourselves into each other's arms. Standing so closely together I could feel his arousal through our thin summer clothes.

"Is every man like this?" I was taught to believe that only indecent men had dirty desires for women.

"Yes, absolutely every man. A man can't be called a man if he has no reaction while holding a beautiful girl in his arms."

His hands, under my shirt, began to venture down my body. "Have you really not done it?" he whispered.

"No," I replied, feeling almost apologetic for my inexperience. There was no sex education at school, nor any literature that could substitute for it. Master Li's sex scandals were too sketchy to fill the gap. I had never even touched myself. We were led to believe that masturbation was not only disgusting but also damaging to your health, especially for men: the traditional belief held that one drop of semen equaled ten drops of blood.

His exploring hands stopped their descent. "In that case, I'll spare you," he withdrew from under my skirt, spanking my behind.

"How many girls have you not spared?"

"About half a dozen."

"My heaven, you've been busy."

"I can't help myself. I am hopelessly romantic."

"But the university students are not supposed to court, let alone to have sex."

"Rules cannot change human nature. And forbidden fruit is more tasty."

"But where do you do it?" My curiosity got the better of me.

"Where there's a will, there's a way." The most common place was the most obvious, the student dormitory, he explained. There was an unspoken rule among students that everyone tried to provide privacy for whoever needed it. "When you came to see me, my roommates thought you were my girlfriend, or you might become my girlfriend, so they left us alone. Otherwise, we do it behind trees in a park, like here for instance, if my little princess consents," he said playfully.

Dying to know every detail about his life, I asked him to describe his romantic liaisons.

Red Rock had a girlfriend from his school back in Tianjin, though they never slept together. His first sexual partner was a girl from the English department who chased him after he won a speech competition. "I didn't really love her, but she offered herself to me and I found it hard to resist. It was fun for a while, then I got tired of her since she was too vain." Li's last girlfriend was an American student who came to Shandong University to study Chinese. He was one of the few selected to share a room with the foreign students. This was a perk, not only for the better conditions at the foreign students' dormitory, but also for the chance to speak English with native speakers, or, in Li's case, even to sleep with them.

Li's connection with foreign students helped explain why he was so Westernized, using expressions like "My

God," which I had never heard before. His American girlfriend, a solid girl with dirty-blond hair, christened him Walter. After she returned home, the relationship automatically terminated.

"So who seduced who?"

"She seduced me, definitely. She was keen to try out a Chinese fellow."

"You weren't in love, then?"

"Well, I was attracted by her. So when she took off her top to show her full bosom, I was willing prey. In the future, when you fall in love with some man, chase him, and I can guarantee a hundred percent success. Mentally, men are much weaker creatures than women."

"Thanks for the tip. Hope I'll have a chance to apply it in the near future. If I'm desperate, I can always offer my body—a virgin's body."

Detecting my bitter tone, he gently stroked my face. "You know I can't promise you anything."

Yes, I did know, but I was too happy to worry about the future or throw away this unexpected love.

I was leaving in two days and still had one request. We had done two of the three "must-sees" in Shandong province: Tai Mountain and the Yellow River. I wanted to see the third on my way home.

The Confucius Temple, the Bethlehem of ancient China, was a haven. Hand in hand, we strolled through a series of courtyards, stealing a kiss under the pine trees, in defiance of Confucian teaching.

Similar in style to the Forbidden City in Beijing, the temple complex at Qufu dominated the small town, birthplace of China's top sage, Confucius, or Kong Zi. Started as a simple memorial hall by his disciples, it was expanded, reconstructed, and renovated over the years by rulers seeking to legitimize their right to rule.

Only a humble teacher in his lifetime, Confucius had the most profound impact on Chinese culture. Confucianism, a code of behavior rather than a religion, stresses high moral standards for government and strictly defined hierarchical relationships. Its essence is obedience, respect, selflessness, and working for the common good.

As a history student, Red Rock proved a perfect guide, explaining the background. Then he launched his attack. "It's so outdated. Of course we need respect, but we must respect everyone, not just the wife her husband, low-ranking people those of high rank, and officials their rulers. It's ridiculous that the government often launches anti–bourgeois liberalism campaigns. We don't have enough liberalism; we need anti-feudalism campaigns!"

I often felt like his student. But his lectures were eye-opening.

In a central courtyard, we saw a group of Japanese tourists examining some stelae: the temple housed thousands of stelae with inscriptions from several dynasties.

"What do Nanjing people think of the Japanese?" he asked.

"'Most still hate the Japanese devils. The blood debt is too huge to forget.'"

These tourists looked so polite and harmless. It was hard to imagine how the soldiers from their fathers' generation had massacred over three hundred thousand people in my hometown, back in 1937.

"It's understandable that you lot hate the Japanese. But the Chinese Communists shouldn't. In fact, they should be grateful."

This was heretical stuff!

"The Party would almost certainly have been annihilated by the Nationalists but for the Sino-Japanese War," he argued. "In 1936, a year after the Long March, when the Communists were still weak, Chiang Kai-Shek was kidnapped and forced to work with the Communists to fight against the invading foreign enemy."

"Really?" Our history textbooks taught a different version. Yet I preferred to believe Li, for I knew our history books sometimes lied about facts.

Since I could take the matter no further, I changed the subject by asking him why he chose Japanese as his first foreign language.

"Because Japanese research into Chinese history has far surpassed ours. They are free from the guidance of any ideology. Independent thinking has never been encouraged here." He turned to me. "It's good that you are not as cynical as me. But for God's sake, don't believe everything our government tells you."

We took our last supper at a small restaurant near the railway station west of Qufu. The train tracks would have run straight through Confucius's birthplace but for his descendants' fight to protect the feng shui of their ancestral graveyard. Their petition forced a detour. The station had a threadbare feel. Only slow trains stopped, including a night train to Nanjing.

"Eat something. You have a hard night ahead of you." Red Rock put some food into my bowl.

"I am not hungry."

"Come on." Gently, he wiped tears off my cheeks. "This isn't the end of the world."

"It is, it is for me!" I sobbed. Something beautiful and unbelievable had happened. But now it was ending. He held my hands in his, trying to console me. Public affection was still unacceptable in China. A heated discussion raged in the Nanjing press after a man complained to a paper about a young couple on his local bus. "In our socialist country, we have our moral standards," he reminded readers. "These two shameless young people can do whatever they like, but not kiss on a public bus!" Desperate, we kissed and cared nothing for what others might say.

We nestled in a corner at the back, away from the noisy eaters in the front. Through the open back door, I could see a courtyard and tile-roofed farmhouse. In the middle of the yard, a blindfolded donkey was grinding soaked soy beans into white foamy milk for the next day's bean curd. The aroma of crushed beans floated in the air.

"Why is the donkey wearing a blindfold?" I asked.

"It will refuse to move forward if it knows the he is only going in circles."

"The donkey has tearful eyes."

"How do you know?"

"All donkeys have sad eyes."

When we paid the bill, the restaurant owner approached us. "We have rooms at back if you're interested," she pointed to the rear of the house, a knowing smile on her face. "And no bother with the marriage certificate, if you know what I mean."

He turned to me expectantly. I had a good long look at the back. The gray donkey continued to walk in circles, and the farmhouse looked alluring. But I shook my head. My conservative ideal remained to court, fall in love, and present myself as a virgin to my husband on our wedding day.

Chapter 14

Fortress Besieged

When Ma returned home from work, I was locked in *Fortress Besieged*. My Red Rock had given me his favorite book to commemorate our love, just before the tearful farewell at the run-down station.

I had resumed the swing of life, TV lectures in the morning, tutorial classes in the afternoon, and more study in the evening. What happened in Jinan, the secret dating and kisses in quiet park corners, seemed a century away. In the dead of night, when I played back some of those moments in my mind, I wondered if it was only a dream.

The book was the only solid proof. Written in the 1940s by Qian Zhongshu, one of China's greatest contemporary scholars, *Fortress Besieged* is a love story about a scholar returned from Europe and his romantic liaisons. He constantly looks for kindred spirits but each time he finds a new love, he feels shackled. In the end, miserably married, he concludes that marriage is like a fortress, with those outside trying to get in and those already in trying to leave.

While reading, I took notes: Red Rock had instructed me to study the story like a textbook and then write a review.

Suddenly, a coarse hand closed its pages. I looked up and saw Ma's two new moons knitted together.

"We need to talk," she ordered.

What for, this time? She shut the door, her slanted eyes stabbing in my direction. "Zhang Lijia, are you grateful that I let you to go to Jinan?"

Full name? I must be in trouble. "Very grateful, Ma. What did I do wrong?"

"Ask yourself! I let you go because I trusted that you are a girl with self-respect. But now, confess to me the shameful things you did there."

"I have nothing to confess. I don't understand...."

After falling back to reality, I had told my family the details of my trip, covering the meeting with Li and his friends, but not what had followed, naturally.

Ma pulled out a letter and held it high with the air of a policeman and his prize evidence. "What about the university student Li Hongyan? What's this about?"

"Is it for me? Give it here!" I raised my voice, eyes flaring. I sent Li a letter as soon as I got home, saying how much I missed him and thanking him for the "happiest and most memorable time in my life." I had been looking forward to his reply.

"Give it to you? I want you to confess first, though I know everything." Despite myself, I almost wanted to laugh: my mother was aping the tricks used by Chinese police to interrogate criminals.

My faint smile provoked her. "Confess! I've made a phone call to Jinan already."

San'er! I was sold out by my cousin. Anger stirred with the feeling of betrayal. I could picture now what happened: when Li's letter arrived on that day, Ma, who arrived home for lunch before I did, had become suspicious, for I had never received any personal letters before. She had then opened and read it—most Chinese parents saw nothing wrong in reading their children's letters. Alarmed by the content, Ma had gone to the post office to call my aunt, who had then revealed all, doubtless adding some color from her own imagination.

I had become a laughingstock among my relatives!

"All right, I did go out to see him. He is so intelligent and interesting to talk to."

"Just talk?" she grabbed my shoulders. "You are so young and naïve. How could you go out with this guy you hardly know? He is a university student, so what? He could still be a hooligan who dallies with women. Tell me he didn't take advantage of you."

"He didn't!" I replied impatiently, trying to shake off her hands.

But her fingers dug deeper into my shoulder blades. "Can you swear?"

"I swear to our ancestors that he didn't! If you don't trust me, take me to a gynecologist to have a test. Now, give me my letter." I snatched it from her hand. The letter was torn and stained with grease in one corner. "You have no right to open *my* letter!" I had to release the anger bursting my lungs.

"Mother of mine!" she shouted back. "Right? I have every right because I gave you your life. Don't ever use that tone to me again. As a mother, I deserve some respect."

"Respect?" I snorted. "If you want respect, you have to respect me as well!" I could hear Li's voice joining the argument.

As predicted, Ma dragged in the dingzhi issue. But her old lamentation on self-sacrifice had long ceased to excite me. I turned to go.

She dragged me back. The anger in her eyes had given way to pleading. "Listen, for once just listen to a more experienced woman. You have to be careful with men. One false step, you'll regret it for a thousand years. I regret I married your dad in such a hurry that I didn't know him or his family well enough."

It was almost political suicide to marry into such a family. Her father-in-law was a member of the Green Gang triad, while her mother-in-law, Granny Long Tits, was a former drug dealer. But my mother only learned about their backgrounds during the Cultural Revolution.

"Later I accused him of cheating me," Ma recalled, "but he said that his parents' past wasn't important in our relationship. What a joke!" She continued to hold my arms, fighting hard to control her shivering. "Don't even dream to marry a man from another city. I have gone through that. I can't begin to tell you the pain a living widow has to endure!" She spat out these words, as if they were fish bones choking her throat.

In the lamplight, I glimpsed once again the tear pearls on her face. I wanted to wipe them for her, but I didn't. She had opened and stained my sacred letter.

"Don't worry. I am not going to marry him yet."

I rushed to the toilet, my private sanctuary. Shutting myself in the stuffy room, I took out the letter. It only took one line for the tears to start. *Lijia, my darling, I am missing you*, he wrote, in English. My vision was blurred and the light was so dim. Mopping tears with my sleeve, I brought the letter closer to my face. The rest of the letter was in Chinese. He talked about how empty he felt after my departure and how he sometimes half expected me to turn up at his dormitory, with my long wet hair. At the end of the letter, he asked if I liked *Fortress Besieged* and encouraged me to read more books. *P.S.*, he added in English, *You stole my heart, Walter.*

I held the letter to my heart and somehow felt connected with him. The stinking smell subsided: in its place rose the inviting aroma of crushed soybeans. At a dark corner outside the railway station, we had hugged and kissed good-bye. I let him put a hand on my chest to feel my dancing heart. Then he held my naked breast in his hand and caressed it....

Darling Red Rock,

My mother has found out about you. At first I was very

angry with San'er for betraying me. When I calmed down, I realized that no one could believe the excuses I made for sneaking out so frequently.

Here are my thoughts on Fortress Besieged. *I have never written any book review before. Please don't laugh at me.*

It's tremendously interesting. The writing style is very witty and dramatically different from books by more recent writers. Not an easy read, though, for the author has peppered his text with references to names and events that I found difficult to follow. I detected a strong flavor of sarcasm. Is it one of the reasons that you are so fond of the book?

I don't think I agree with his theme—surely not everyone in the fortress of marriage wants to get out? Not my sister and her husband anyway. Last night, they came home for dinner. Afterward, she lay down in a bed, reading a magazine while he massaged her feet—after standing in class teaching the whole day, she often suffers from aching legs. I envy their happy marriage. It's a matter of finding the right person.

Sorry, I should be talking about the book. I don't really like the hero Fang Hongjian. He isn't a bad or unkind man, just sad and weak. I don't like weak men (among them my own father). Anyway, Fang lacks the courage to go for what he really wants, giving up his true love Miss Tang too easily and always giving in under pressure from society or family. He is a man with a "soft spine."

Some people say Chinese intellectuals have soft spines—do you agree?

One reason that I don't like Fang is that he just can't resist temptation. On a full moon night, he kisses a girl he doesn't even like; he has a one-night stand with a woman he despises only because she offers her sexy body to him. Personally, I found that rather disgusting. Animals mate to satisfy their desires. We humans should be above that. If I ever make love to a man, it's because I love him physically and spiritually.

Also, I simply don't understand why he doesn't study properly when he is abroad. What an amazing opportunity! But he wastes away his time in Europe. I would cherish the opportunity and study very hard.

I miss you every day and I'll write more soon.

Yours Forever,
Lijia

Soon, writing to Red Rock—I couldn't really think of him as Walter—became part of my life. I spent hours composing the letters, applying fancy words and flowery expressions or four-character idioms, like a student trying too hard to impress her teacher. Since TV University, I had kept a weekly journal instead of the diary that I started back at school. Now, letters to him replaced the journal as I confided everything about my family, my study, my loneliness, and my dreams. He became the focus in my quiet life.

I longed for his letters like a plum blossom longing for spring. They were not as frequent as mine, but enough to keep me happy. Since the letter incident, I told him to use the TV University address to circumvent my mother. I waited excitedly for the petite and pretty clerk to approach with a white envelope in her slim hands. To portion out the pleasure, I would often delay opening the letters. On my way home, I would stop at a quiet spot on the riverbank where I could relish his wisdom without being disturbed.

From time to time he enclosed clips of his articles, published in student magazines, academic journals, or local newspapers. The topics were impressively varied, from dry research to the colorful legend of Princess Zhaojun, a beautiful concubine in the Han Dynasty dispatched to marry a barbarian chieftain. Another piece linked mentality and language to argue that Chinese was not a good language for logical thinking, whereas German helped its speakers produce some of the world's greatest philosophers. We had a few, like Confucius and Zhuang Zi, the Taoist sage, but their work resembled the teaching of life experience rather than true philosophy, in his view. I did not always understand his articles but kept them carefully in an album.

I no longer spent much time with Prince Charming Ning or the group. He was a shallow butterfly after all. I even lost enthusiasm for the films. I was after a higher form of art: my Red Rock had raised my standard.

The winter and spring both may come, and pass by,
The summer days may fade, and the year may die:
But surely you will come back one day to me,
And I shall still be waiting, as once I vowed to be.

She wore a blond wig, and her face was caked in makeup; still, the Chinese actress didn't look very Western. She sang in Chinese, too, and beautifully. Outside her hut, Solveig tended her spinning wheel, patiently waiting for her beloved Peer Gynt to return.

Sitting in the dark among the packed audience, my eyes fixed on Solveig. Performed by an opera troupe from Beijing, *Peer Gynt* was one of few decent cultural events to grace our city. But no one was interested in coming along. Liu Weidong would have, but I dared not ask, given his continued interest in me. Being alone, I was doubly nervous since this was my first "high culture" event, and the audience was full of well-dressed, sophisticated-looking people. Red Rock would have blended into the crowd like a fish in water. Oh, how I missed him!

Once taboo, Western art saw the light of the day again in the reform era. I would usually regard opera as too much "Spring Snow"—a melody of the elite in the state of Chu that had become a byword for highbrow art. But the urge to cultivate myself and narrow the gap between Red Rock and myself, propelled me to aim high.

I was fascinated by the restless, free-spirited hero and his many adventures. In our Communist literature, a "rotten egg" like Peer Gynt could never be a hero. But what really moved me to tears was Peer's devoted wife Solveig. In her dreamlike melody, I could sense her inner strength and hope. I, too, was waiting for my man.

When I opened the front door, still feeling high and enlightened, I found that my brother-in-law had come by for a visit, bringing fresh crabs.

Changyong was dressed in a fine suit, its label proudly attached to his sleeve—"Pierre Cardin," it boasted. He refused to cut it off, for fear people wouldn't know what a good brand his suit was. Western suits became fashionable, thanks to leaders such as the Party Secretary Hu Yaobang, who had started receiving state guests in fine suits, probably in an effort to be accepted by the West.

"So good of Changyong, giving us so many crabs," Ma said merrily, pointing to the straw bag where a dozen freshwater crabs clawed desperately for freedom, foam spotting their mouths.

"Aiya, so big and still alive!" I said with a watery mouth. The Southerners' obsession with crabs seemed to have grown from the celebration of the downfall of the "Gang of Four" in the golden October of 1976, when crab stocks were exhausted in feasting that played on the nickname of the wicked quartet. As prices steadily rose, crabs became the symbol of good living. Without my brother-in-law, no crabs would ever have crawled their way onto our dinner table. "Thank you so much, Changyong," I said.

"No problem. I know Ma loves crabs. They gave me loads," Changyong replied casually.

We knew who "they" were: peasant entrepreneurs, who, responding to Deng Xiaoping's call, had set up workshops and factories in towns and villages, producing toys, paper, spirits of all kinds, or any marketable products.

Changyong sold his state-owned factory's products aboveboard and know-how under the table to these peasant entrepreneurs, who in return rewarded him with not only local specialties but also money, discreetly packed in little red paper bags. Not exactly legal. But so many ranking officials and their children were making huge profits by trading power for money, why not a salesman who knew something about in-demand technology?

"If you buy these crabs, how much would you have to pay? A hundred yuan, or even one-fifty?" Ma enjoyed her gifts more if they were converted into cash terms.

"No less than that," Changyong said matter-of-factly. "And you never see such good crabs at shops—they disappear through the back door."

"Exactly," Ma seized the chance to complain. "Nowadays, there's hardly anything good in the market. In Chairman Mao's time, the government liked to say 'the price is stable and the market is prosperous.' Now, everyone says 'the market is stable and the price is prosperous!'"

It was a popular saying, but not necessarily true. People just felt uneasy about rising prices, which had been kept artificially stable for many years at great cost to the economy. Supplies were more abundant thanks to the growing role of the free market. Ma must have forgotten the days when she had to get up at four in the morning to queue up for a frozen fish. Nevertheless, people's expectations had climbed, like prices themselves.

"Where did you go tonight with Weijia's coat?" Changyong asked.

"To see a foreign opera," Ma answered for me. "What's the name?"

"Just by yourself?" He shook his small head. Changyong's nickname was "Fish Head"— his family name "Yu" sounded like "fish," and his head was small, even in proportion to his lean frame. Indeed, he was a fish, thriving in the murky waters of China's marketplace. But he was pleasant-looking and smiled a great deal. "Did you understand the foreign opera, whatever the name is?"

"*Peer Gynt,*" I tried to sound as foreign as possible.

"Did you say 'fart'?" asked Nai, walking in from the kitchen. "Peer" sounded very much like *pi,* or "fart," in Chinese. My family split their sides with laughter. Nai, whose hearing was not at its best, often confused what she heard.

"In my view, foreign operas sound like wails and moans for someone who just died," Changyong gave a chuckle of delight.

"Yes, exactly, Changyong, just like wails!" Ma agreed eagerly. She was very fond of her son-in-law. My father, on the other hand, was less sure about this not-so-educated man. And not even handsome, unlike himself. "A beautiful flower wasted on a pile of cow dung!" Father commented once.

"Dog fart!" Ma told him off immediately. "Even if we search the whole world with bright lanterns, we can't necessarily find anyone better! He not only knows how to treat his wife but also how to make money, unlike you."

Changyong's influence over Ma was growing. He had even persuaded her to give up stealing water. "Too much hassle, Ma, dripping water like that. Here, take this." He had generously handed her some money from his wallet, which was always full of big notes.

Ma turned to me. "I worry about what to feed the family; and you went to see an opera that no one understands! Fifteen yuan for the ticket, what a waste!"

"Somehow, you are just different from the rest of us philistines," concluded my brother-in-law.

As Changyong's giant motorbike melted into the darkness, I said to myself: why shouldn't a daughter of philistines hear the high note of Spring Snow?

One winter night, the wind was wailing outside like a desperate wolf. I sat in the single bed, clutching my hot-water bottle, studying.

Suddenly, the door swung open, bringing in cold air, the strong smell of alcohol, and my brother. Xiaoshi was all hard lines and sharp edges.

"You, get out of MY fucking bed!" he roared. These days, he stained his every breath with a swearword, as if his tough-guy image relied on them.

"Hao, hao, I'm going." After my sister's marriage, Xiaoshi claimed the single bed because his friends laughed at him for sleeping with his granny. Fair enough. But I still used it whenever he was not around.

"Light off. I need my fucking sleep." He took off his leather jacket to get ready for bed. Stylish as it was, the jacket hardly kept him warm, but while off work, he made a point of not wearing the big green army coat, its collar and sleeves black and shiny from constant use.

It wasn't late. But there was no point in arguing with him. He could explode like fireworks over the slightest provocation, especially after he had become a boatman. More than a year before, he had given up his schooling altogether, before finishing junior middle school. "What's the fucking point of study?" He took piecemeal jobs for a while, then found a permanent job with the collectively owned Yangtze Shipping Company. Traveling on a filthy boat, he and other workers, usually roughnecks who couldn't find any better employment, loaded coal, sand, or other goods at one town along the Yangtze River, then unloaded them at another downstream. Before long, he learned that his job ranked as one of the three hardest professions in China, together with blacksmith and bean curd maker. I could imagine his long night on the boat in the company of oil lamps, which danced and flicked in the melancholic darkness like a ghost's shifting eyes.

On his off-duty days, he would hang around with other "rotten eggs" in the village, drinking, fighting, or causing pointless misery, such as letting the air out of bicycle tires. Somehow he felt his hardship earned him the right to misbehave.

Avoiding him like a thorn, I moved to the big bed. As I slowly undressed myself, I began to read the last pages of the textbook. I had an exam the next day.

"Turn the fucking light off!" Suddenly, Xiaoshi jumped out of his bed and turned off the light. He used such force, the cord snapped.

"You are my destined foe!" he growled in my direction in the darkness. "The old woman let you take over her job, because you are her favorite. But what's the fucking point? Dirty water gets chucked out and you stinky girls get married off!" He always felt that he, as the "heir" to the Zhang family line, was entitled to take over our mother's "decent job."

"Shush, if you have to fart, fart tomorrow." I was so accustomed to his insults they were rarely insulting.

Nai sat up, clasping her hands together in supplication, "I beg you, Xiaoshi, go to bed. Don't disturb your Ma."

Ma was disturbed. "What's happening here? Turn the light on." But the string was broken. She staggered in darkness to the desk lamp. "Mother of mine! What wrong medicine did you take to get this bad? You have no money to give your family, but you have money to drink, right?" She resented the fact that Xiaoshi refused to pay a penny to the family, despite his high income.

"I hate you and you," Xiaoshi thrust a finger at Ma and then me. "Because of you two, I ended up like a fucking vagrant." In his long johns, the silhouette of his thin body resembled a pathetic cartoon. In an excited state, he began to crack his finger joints, one after another, faster and faster. I hated the sound and always worried he would break a joint. When the cracking ceased, he walked toward the window and punched it. "I hate this fucking home!"

The shattered window let in the wailing wolf. We shivered.

Putting on his leather jacket, Xiaoshi walked out.

"Go as far as possible! What sin did my ancestors commit that I produced a nasty beast like you?" Ma shouted at his shadow. "Go and never return!"

Chapter 15

Journey to the North

Under the fat woman's tight grip, the tiny youth resembled a little chick under the iron claw of an eagle. "One yuan fine for spitting, right now!" she demanded, waving a dimpled hand. A red banner with the characters "on duty" encircled her trunk-like arm.

"I didn't do nothing, I…I just coughed it up…" The young peasant protested with an earthy accent.

A gale of laughter swept over the gathering audience in the massive waiting hall of Nanjing railway station. Crowds formed easily in the most populous nation on earth, whenever something slightly unusual—a traffic accident or an argument, for example—took place.

"Explain this to the police." The fat lady let out a great roar. "They won't be as gentle as me, I tell you!" She began to drag him forcefully toward the exit. "So dirty here, all because of you stinking migrants!"

Standing in my queue, I watched the drama in good humor. I had come early, to ensure I would not miss my night train to Beijing—I was going to see Li Hongyan, my Red Rock, for the first time in a year. Exactly a year!

We could have met up during Spring Festival, but he had to visit his family in Tianjin. Also, he felt very unsettled at the time, torn between pursuing an academic career and finding a job. He was more tempted by the academic option, although he hated the atmosphere at his university as well as the teaching itself. In the end, he was assigned a job in Beijing in the summer.

As soon as I had passed the defense of my graduation project, I set off for this long-anticipated reunion trip.

Everyone was dripping with sweat. At the back, where the queues lost their shape, travelers squatted on the ground, playing cards in the dim light, a piece of newspaper for a table. Others flopped over their luggage on the filthy floor, which was stained by phlegm, litter, and urine. The whole place stank worse than a pigsty.

Never mind. I would be in the arms of my beloved man soon, very soon.

After much pushing, shoving, and running, like a refugee chasing the last train to safety, I settled into my hard seat. How lucky I was! Most of my fellow passengers, squeezed together like flesh pancakes, would have to stand up for the next eighteen hours. The train was heavily overloaded, partly thanks to the so-called "floating population"—the migrants. With freedom newly granted by Deng Xiaoping, millions of farmers who had been chained to their land by Chairman Mao were flocking to cities all over the country. With sun-darkened skin and shabby clothing, they sat on their rolled-up bedding, or stood, being jostled by crowds, without a word of complaint.

Traveling by train offered insights into equality, Chinese style. There were three types of seats: soft sleepers, hard sleepers, and the hard seats that accommodated over ninety-five percent of passengers. Hard sleepers were for people traveling on official business. I had not yet enjoyed the luxury on a work trip. Sleepers were so scarce one had to queue up all night to buy one; more importantly, I could keep half the price difference between a sleeper and hard seat if I chose the latter. Soft sleepers were only for people of a certain rank, who swept through to a separate waiting lounge with air-conditioning and no queues; once safely aboard, their carriage windows carried white lace curtains to hide the privileges of the elite from the prying eyes of "Old Hundred Names," the commoners. Few would consider such a privilege in any way contradictory to the egalitarianism the government promoted. Deep down inside, we were as fond of hierarchy as our forefathers. I would make this point to Red Rock and he would surely agree and say: "Another hangover of feudalism."

Even hard seats did not come easily, especially in early August when homebound students overwhelmed the transport lines. I had to ask a tax officer friend for help. Jiang He was a classmate from junior middle school, and we'd hit it off at our reunion party earlier in the spring. In five years, the snotty-nosed, quiet boy had grown into an earnest youth, handsome, and very tall. Upon his graduation from vocational school, he had been assigned to the Nanjing tax bureau. Though the position was highly desirable, he did not find it fulfilling enough. He had embarked on a course in finance and management at Teach-Yourself University. I identified with Jiang and his uphill battle to improve his fate. None of the rest of our classmates, mostly workers and shop assistants, seemed to pursue a life that could be described as inspiring. Red Rock was the source of my snobbery.

Jiang was also a useful friend to have. Anyone in possession of any kind of power, such as charging tax, could trade it for any favor—securing a train ticket, for instance.

Once the train started moving, the unbearable heat shrank with the breeze from open windows. I was sandwiched between a bulky old man who panted heavily like a steam engine and a smelly, middle-aged businessman. Whenever he moved, "fox odor," regarded as a physical shortcoming, crept out from his underarms. As soon as we sat down, Smelly offered a round of cigarettes and started to chat. "I'm a purchasing agent for my plastic factory," he introduced himself. "Old master, where are you going?" he turned to Steam Engine.

"To treat my asthma. My son works in Beijing." After spitting on the floor, he ground the sticky discharge with his heel, as if it would disappear into the hard floor. To calm himself down, he drank hot green tea from an empty pickle jar.

"How about you, young comrade?" Smelly turned to me, drinking from a beer bottle.

"I am going to Beijing to visit…"

"I've been to Beijing many times. A lot to see, Tiananmen, the Great Wall…" before I could finish the sentence, the man began to give me a long list of sights. But I had seen them already when I went there for work with Master Lan, shortly before I started at TV University. This time I was traveling to see someone, someone special.

In the opposite seat sat a young couple and their baby boy. The chubby baby kept grabbing at the glasses of a student sitting next to them. So thin and short with only faint hair on his lip, he looked like a boy rather than a grown-up. His studious manner reminded me of Red Rock.

How was he doing, I wondered. Did he like his new job? In less than twenty-four hours, we would be together again. I decided if he still wanted me, I would give myself to him, whatever the outcome of our relationship. Over the previous year, I frequently returned in my thoughts to the little restaurant by the Confucius Temple. Maybe I should have said yes. What would it be like? I could just smell the crushed soybeans and feel his hand on my breast.

Crashing glass shattered my dreamworld. Smelly had just tossed his beer bottle out of the window. A dangerous act—the papers had recently reported that a flying bottle killed a peasant in her field—but people continued just the same. There were too many rules in China. As a result, people tended to break them whenever they could, ignoring traffic lights, jumping queues, evading tax, or throwing a bottle out of the train window: what a convenient way to get rid of it.

My neighbor let out a satisfied burp. I turned to look out the window. Darkness enveloped China's hinterlands. Street lamps on the road parallel to the railway line flew by so fast, glistening in the dark like shooting stars fallen from the night sky.

In the small hours of the morning, I grew tired and sleepy. Turning the pages of my magazine, I spotted the woman opposite putting her sleeping baby under the seat. Yes, why not? Spreading a newspaper under my seat, I did the same, curling up to sleep like the baby until the loudspeaker started to spit propaganda again at six sharp: the morning news from the Central People's Broadcasting Corporation reached every moving train across this vast country. There could be no escape from our masters' voice—it was piped into every carriage

As the train pulled into Beijing railway station, the clock struck two, followed by the first few notes from "The East is Red." I had known the song since childhood. "The east is red, the sun has risen. China has produced Mao Zedong." After an eighteen-hour journey, we had finally reached our destination, the heart of the nation, and the home of my beloved. A wave of emotion washed over me as I walked into the capital's dry dust.

After three bus transfers, I reached Li's work unit—the Chinese Sports History Research Institute up in the north of Beijing. I had not asked to be met at the station, for it was difficult to predict when I would secure the ticket. Li emerged at reception, in a smart short-sleeved shirt, looking exactly the same. "Glad you've made it. Was it difficult to find?" He smiled politely, but there were no sparks from his eyes.

My tears welled up at the sight of him. I suddenly became conscious of my filthy state, my salt-stained T-shirt and urine-scented hair. I felt like a lost pup that had just found its owner, desperate for a pat.

But there was no pat on my head. Instead, he took my hand and shook it, formally and briefly. He didn't want his new colleagues to know he had a girlfriend, of course. So I tried to sound impersonal, too. "No, not bad. Your instructions were pretty good."

"You're going to stay with a friend of mine, Little Bi, if you don't mind. I'll take you there by bike. Not far from here."

When I perched on the back of his bike, I touched his body lightly to steady myself. Then, I held tightly to the cold metal bar. I longed to rest my head on his back, just as I did once back in Jinan. But I didn't dare, for his tone remained polite and distant, a tone for a friend, not a girlfriend.

"Come on in, I'm Little Bi." A young woman opened the door to a flat in a block building, and held out her hand warmly. Judging from her dark skin, high cheekbones, and accent, I guessed she was from the south coast.

"I am Lijia. Thank you so much for letting me stay." I kept my greeting short because I had no clue how Li had introduced me.

"You can use this bed. My colleague is away on a trip," she pointed at one of the two beds in the room. "You must be so tired, why don't you make yourself comfortable?"

"I'd better go back to work. See you later." Red Rock excused himself and disappeared.

I went to sleep after a good wash, too tired to think about anything.

When I woke in the evening, I heard some low voices. It was Bi and my Red Rock, cuddled together in the opposite bed, one step away from mine. For a brief moment, the world went pitch black in front of me as the cruel, obvious truth sank in—she was his girlfriend, his current girlfriend.

We went out to eat dumplings at a back-street shop. As soon as our bottoms settled onto the greasy benches, Little Bi started to demonstrate ownership, feeding him a dumpling one moment and playfully planting a kiss on his cheek the next, despite the disapproving glances of other diners.

In an attempt to behave normally, I asked Little Bi about her life. She had studied Chinese literature at Shandong University and had recently been assigned a job as an editor at China's *Aviation News*.

"Why take up a job in a marginal publication?" I heard myself firing the question in a dismissive tone.

"It's a great job!" she boasted. "The pay is not bad, plus some free flights. Best of all, I don't have to be at my office from eight to five and I have plenty of time to write." She began to talk about a short story she was working on. "Oh, I love my writing so much," she said, her plain face animated and her eyes shining.

As the evening went by, I shrank further and further into myself. No point in trying to belittle Bi or her job. She was witty, lively, and well educated. I was no match for her.

Red Rock looked a little tired and quieter than usual, but was otherwise perfectly at ease with himself.

Sitting with the pair, I felt perched on a bed of needles. They stabbed right through my heart. I was grateful to get back to Little Bi's place with her.

When she washed herself from a basin I noticed she had a full-figured body despite her slender form. I observed my rival with curiosity and intense jealousy. She was a passionate girl, no doubt. Did they do it here when her colleague was away on business trips, I wondered? I remembered now he had indeed mentioned her in his letters, an editor at the university publication for which he contributed some pieces. Bi was clearly the reason that he had given up an academic life. And she was better suited for him, I had to admit.

The next morning, Little Bi kindly showed me a map, telling me where we were and how to get to the famous sights. In no mood for sightseeing, I lingered and wandered through Beijing streets for the whole day like an aimless ghost.

In the late afternoon, upon returning to Bi's flat, I stumbled into a bitter row.

"So, you're the tart!" she screamed as I darkened the doorway. "Get out of here. I don't ever want to see you again, you bitch, you fox fairy, you worn-out shoe!"

A string of dirty words flew out of her little cherry mouth. A worn-out shoe? Not a chance, thanks to you.

"I honestly didn't know you were together already." I protested feebly. My tears poured out like a gushing spring.

She replied by pushing me out. I would have fallen downstairs, if not for him grabbing me.

No sooner had Red Rock settled me at a cheap guesthouse nearby than he shot out again. "Don't worry, I'll punish her for what she did to you," he assured me, wearing his sour look, as if it would give me some comfort.

"No, don't," I said. "I understand her."

But he had left before the end of my sentence.

Deserted in the sparse room and bewildered, I wailed like an injured animal. "What am I doing here?" I asked again and again. I could not make sense of the nightmare. Sure, in the last months, his letters had grown less frequent. But I just presumed he was too busy. When I told him I was going to Beijing to see him, I thought his response was not too enthusiastic. But I brushed it away as one of his mood swings.

Why didn't he tell me? Why not? I would have accepted it, however disappointed I might feel. And I could have gone traveling with friends from TV University, instead of enduring this humiliation. Why didn't he tell me? It was hardly because he wanted to keep sleeping with me, while nursing a new romance. Or did he keep me in the dark to retain me as an admirer? Hardly worthwhile. Was he only dallying with me, as my mother suggested? Whatever the case, I felt wronged. Because of the time and distance between us, I had built up a perfect image of Red Rock. Now, all of a sudden, that image collapsed in a landslide.

We sat apart, each clinging to our own arm of the bench. Red Rock had granted me a solo audience early the next morning in Purple Bamboo Park, a peaceful grove around the corner from my guesthouse. At our feet, in place of the Yellow River running swiftly, lay a still pond, bereft of a single ripple. His face was shadowed by weeping willows.

"I am sorry about yesterday," he began.

"It's okay. Not your fault." I mumbled automatically.

"Don't worry. I'll teach her a lesson," he said in a judge's solemn and righteous tone. "Ridiculous! She was so uncivilized. She can get extremely jealous and possessive, you know. My God, she doesn't own me!"

While he went on about how Little Bi liked to "drink vinegar"—a Chinese euphemism for conjugal jealousy—I looked vacantly around, barely registering anything. The park bustled with life. Old men "walked" their caged birds, then hung them from trees, uncovering the bamboo cages to give the illusion of freedom and spark their pets into song. Peddlers screamed in the woods, in the belief that it trained their voices for the selling and haggling to come. In the central square, young people danced disco to a loud cassette player while a group of older people enjoyed the more graceful moves of ballroom dancing.

Many more practiced traditional tai chi. Our corner must be the quietest in the park, I thought. He always knew where to go.

When Red Rock, at long last, stopped talking, I said: "Don't you think you owe me an explanation?"

"What explanation?" he asked curtly, twisting his full lips, then added, "Okay, you know I am a romantic. I fell in love with her and I couldn't help it."

"Why didn't you tell me, then?"

"I never registered you as my girlfriend. So, I never felt I needed to explain."

I starred at him wild-eyed, lost for words. I had to admit that our relationship was a little vague. Apart from the time we were together, we didn't really say "I love you" so clearly. I sensed it would make him uncomfortable, for once he had laughed at the stock phrase "I'll never change my heart even if the sea dries up and rocks turn rotten." "Never say never," he asserted. But in his letters, he said things like "with lots of love," which I interpreted as "I love you." Anyway, in my view, when a boy kissed a girl, that was a physical declaration of love.

"I was under the impression that you loved me," I said, my voice thick with tears.

"I am not sure I can use the word love. All right, I had a crush on you, I admit."

"But only recently you called me 'darling' in your letter." Again, all of his intimate terms were expressed in English.

"If you knew English better, you would have known 'darling' or 'dear' is a common term of address. A shop owner calls all his customers 'darling' or 'love,' my English friends told me. It doesn't mean much."

It didn't mean much!

Now, I knew why he always hid in English to say "darling." I had been fooled by a false sense of intimacy.

"You are a terrific girl and I am very fond of you," he continued in a much softer tone, "but did you really expect such a long-distance relationship to work?" He turned to look at me, but I couldn't reply. The embankment holding back my tears had given way.

It would be too difficult for us to end up together, even if we hadn't shared the pear, the li—separation—when we first kissed. We would work for different danwei in different cities. There was a great wall that existed between a university student and a factory worker from another province. Just as migrants could now come to work in the cities, that didn't mean they could officially become urbanites—the wall between town and country was too high. But I couldn't see our situation clearly. I was in love, and his sweet words had blinded me.

Then Little Bi had walked into his life and he couldn't resist her, he said. He didn't even like the job he was assigned. But that was the only way to be together with her in Beijing. If he had known how infatuated I was, he would have said no when I wanted to come to Beijing. He let me come because he had promised that we would meet up again.

What a decent gentleman! It was no fault of his if he didn't sense that I was still in love with him.

"You always cry." He pulled out of his handkerchief and was about to wipe off my tears. I pushed his hands away.

He got up from the bench. "Look, I'll have to go back to work. I trust you can find your way back home."

I rose, too. Despite myself, I was a little surprised to see that we were almost the same height, with the help of my high heels—I had always thought him much taller.

"Yes, I can." I managed to say. Unable to bring myself to look into his eyes, I looked at the pool. In it, I saw the donkey's tearful eyes.

"Mother of mine, Beijing sounds wonderful!" Ma sighed. "Maybe I can go there too, one day, when I've got enough money."

The worst part of the whole drama was the happy, fictional version I had to invent upon my return. Compared to many other girls, I enjoyed freedom to do what I wanted, as long as it didn't cost my mother anything.

I poured the sad truth of my trip onto the pages of my diary, splashed by streams of tears. My tear ducts worked overtime to accompany this drama-queen performance, before an audience of one. I even had a perfect stage—my sister's empty flat as she accompanied her husband on a business trip. Broken heart, lost love, misery, and pain—I soon found that self-pity, indulgently applied, was an excellent way to nurse emotional wounds. So much so that when my words were spent and my performance over, I felt almost grateful to Li. At least I had loved!

I decided to end this chapter of my life by destroying the letters I had hoarded like treasure. One night, I took the whole bundle to the riverside, the very spot where I once secretly relished each letter. All were dated, numbered, and worn, read so many times.

I lit the letters, one after another. Touching the fire, the paper flashed gold, a last spark of the joy it had once delivered, before fraying into ash. In a minute, they were gone in the wind.

Chapter 16

Falling Back into the Well

"Daxuesheng, you are back!" Master Lan, still in his green army tunic, hailed me from a distance. Having reregistered at my old work unit, this daxuesheng—student—was waiting to return to the very pressure-gauge workshop I had left behind three years earlier. Opening his big red mouth, Lan was set to release one of his high-pitched giggles, until he saw tears in the corner of my eyes. "Don't be sad," he suggested, in a more somber tone. "There will surely be other opportunities for you."

After my Beijing misadventure, I had waited impatiently to be assigned a job within the factory. I had hoped for Unit 215, where I worked as an intern. Many of the factory's "brains" gathered there to design and test new products. By the end of my six-month internship, I had grown fond of its civilized atmosphere, lively conversations, and demanding but satisfying work.

As if to confirm the old saying "misfortune never comes singly," a provincial government directive dropped a bolt from the blue: all the TV University graduates of 1985 had to return to their original units; their expected promotion to cadre status would be up to each individual enterprise to decide.

I tailed behind Master Lan, my head hung low, like a woman returning to her mother's house after being cast off by her in-laws. I discovered, to my surprise, that Lan had risen to head the pressure-gauge section after it was made an independent group. "When the snipe and the clam grapple, it's the fisherman who stands to benefit." Lan became the lucky fisherman, the winner of the battle between Master Cheng and Master Lin, both older and more experienced. Lan still walked with his back hunched, yet the newly gained power seemed to have lent him some assertiveness. Master Cheng wasn't a total loser, Lan said: he had secured the whole old workshop for himself as the place to test standard gauges, while the rest of the group moved to the room that used to belong to the power-gauge section, which had recently been absorbed by the energy unit.

The door of the workshop opened into a makeshift hallway formed by the wall and a tall wooden cabinet. What a strange entrance! As I walked in, I was greeted by the clattering of a battered air conditioner that clung to the window like a mechanical tumor.

"Welcome to our new workshop!" Lan said cheerfully. Sitting on a wooden plank placed against the end of the cabinet, he swapped his rubber army shoes for a pair of white slippers. "Only slippers are allowed beyond this line," he said, "Everything has to conform to certain standards now."

"Oh, Little Zhang, hao, hao, hao, welcome back," Master Lin rose to greet me with a warm smile, tearing himself away from copying *The People's Daily*. "Some tea?" He was rounder now, his potbelly more protruding. Behind his ears nestled a pen and a cigarette.

"Sit down," said Boss Lan, pointing to one corner.

I sat down in my old chair, opposite Master Lin.

Although the new room was bigger, the layout was the same, with the big worktable in the middle, its wooden legs caked with grease. The unusual feature was that massive cabinet by the door, looming over Boss Lan's rusty swivel chair. I soon figured out why he'd chosen that spot. Since the workshop lay far from headquarters, our unit leader sometimes turned up unannounced to check if we were behaving ourselves. Without the wall, they would catch Lan dozing in his chair, dribble coating his chin, as he often did when nothing occupied him. Unlike most of us, he had a long way to travel to work. At noon he always went to eat with his mother, who lived alone near the factory. As a filial son he felt guilty that he couldn't look after her in his own home, since his wife and mother could not stand each other. So instead, he visited her every day at noon, forgoing his chance for a lunchtime nap.

As I was staring at the wall, two men in white coats emerged from behind it.

"Let me introduce our new colleagues," said Boss Lan. "This is Little Ma, Ma Guozhi, who was transferred from another factory. And this is Little Zhang, Zhang Xinmin, who got here through guanxi."

I stood up to meet my new colleagues, both not so little, in their early thirties. Ma was short, with a thick moustache and messy sideburns. His surname meant horse, a third tone "ma," falling and rising, while "ma," as in mother, is first tone, flat).

"I am a bit of a bore," Ma said, cigarette bouncing between his yellow lips, like a child clinging to a seesaw. He bowed. "But how delightful to work together with such an educated person." Amused by his own dramatic bow, he began to laugh. His smoker's laugh, coarse and throaty, died only when phlegm choked his throat. He moved to the window to cough it up. "Pah!" he shot the yellowish phlegm forcefully out of the window. It would land on the top of the bicycle shed, catch on a tree, or, on one infamous occasion, coat the head of a pedestrian, who sprinted upstairs to find the culprit!

As Ma turned away, Zhang shook my hand.

"Zhang Xinmin is also a university student, you know," said Boss Lan. "What are you studying?"

"I'm taking a correspondence course in Chinese literature," Zhang replied. "Well, my wife is forcing me to study, indeed, indeed. She feels I should achieve something. But achieve what? I believe in Taoism's nonaction."

He was no picture. The dark yellowish skin on his square face looked as rough as sandpaper. His top eyelids drooped slightly over his dull eyes where more white showed than black pupil. I felt sleepy just looking at him.

"Don't take the directive too personally," Zhang said kindly. "Indeed, this fucked-up country has no future, because it doesn't know how to treat intellectuals." He had reason to complain, I soon learned. His grandfather Zhang Bojun was a well-known scholar who for years acted as head of one of the eight "democratic" parties: they existed to demonstrate that China followed a multiparty system. Grandpa Zhang enjoyed a spell of close friendship with Chairman Mao. Yet in the anti-rightist movement of 1957, Mao named his friend the "biggest rightist" in China, confirming the old saying that "accompanying an emperor is as dangerous as accompanying a tiger." The same movement felled my father, a small potato. Zhang had been working at a collective factory until his grandmother, recently rehabilitated and again a member of the "democratic" personnel in Beijing, demanded some authority to arrange a better job for him.

I thanked Zhang for his sympathy and sank back into my chair. The greasy smell made my heart heavy. I had thought I would be free forever from those fumes.

With a small screwdriver, I expertly prized up the metal ring that kept the gauge's glass cover in place. I screwed the gauge onto the connectors, left-hand side for the standard gauge and the right-hand side for the tested one. I tested it; I fixed it; I recorded the reading, then stamped on a new expiration date. I should not have been surprised that I resumed the routine easily. Like riding a bicycle or any basic physical movement, once you know how, you can do it all your life.

The work was assigned by Boss Lan, who had been nicknamed "the sesame seed boss" because he was head of the smallest organization in the factory bureaucracy, but the position had more power and responsibility than before, due to the management's new policy of delegating power to the lower levels. At the end of each month, the boss now rated our performance according to the number of gauges we tested and fixed, the degree of difficulty, and our working attitude. The rating decided our bonus, an increasingly larger part of our income. He couldn't rate everyone the same, but significant variations would upset people. Our Mr. Goody-Goody surprised me by handling the matter with fairness and firmness.

An Industrial Responsibility System had been introduced, whereby our factory signed a "profit-and-loss contract" with its supervisory body—the Ministry of Aerospace—which allowed the enterprise to keep profits once a certain quota was met. With the profit retained, Liming was constructing more buildings in our village, to the delight of families like ours living in cramped flats.

Our workload was heavier, since workers now faced a penalty if they didn't bring gauges for testing before the expiration date. The new measure granted us new power, which we learned to abuse. Workers who turned up with expired gauges often offered small bribes to avoid being reported. Master Lin's ears carried more free cigarettes than ever before.

But even this increased workload failed to keep us busy all the time. One afternoon, as soon as Boss Lan left for a meeting, testing work stopped altogether. Little Ma jumped up. "Guys, quickly, time to play. Big Zhang, go get Zhi Yong." Since there were now two Zhangs at the workshop—hardly surprising, as Zhang was the most common family name in China and, therefore, the world—the male one became Big Zhang and I stayed Little.

Topped by his usual longish hair, Zhi Yong's head soon appeared over the cabinet. His electric-gauge section had also become independent, but remained a neighbor. "Aha, our daxuesheng is back!" he greeted me. "How are things? Couhe? Come on, join us. We need a fourth player for a good card game." Zhi's thin moustache was gone from his even-featured face. So too was the youthful innocence that once attracted me. Instead, there was a sordid air about him.

"No, I never liked playing cards," I replied flatly.

"Don't just sit there like a Buddha, Little Zhang," Little Ma joined in the persuasion. I shook my head.

"Oh, I see, I see," Zhi walked in. "Now our daxuesheng cannot lower herself to sit together with us." I fully expected such remarks. Anything I did differently, deviating even slightly from the norm, would now be explained by the useless degree I had earned.

"I don't like playing cards, either, but they force me," grumbled Big Zhang. "I should study. If I fail my exam, my wife will be very angry indeed!"

"Force you?" Little Ma threw a throaty laugh. "Smelly dog fart! Confess, can you sit still if we start to play?"

True, Zhang could never resist the temptation. His belief in nonaction, a concept of Taoism, a naturalistic philosophy, and China's only native religion, was just an excuse for being lazy.

"All right, little Zhang, you don't have to play," said Little Zhi, "but do us a favor, keep an eye out for that tamade secret agent."

Master Cheng retained his old habit of spying on colleagues. From time to time, he would emerge from his nest to check on us, especially when Boss Lan was out.

Cheng also eavesdropped on telephone conversations—our workshop and his shared the same number. Borrowing a standard gauge from his room, I once caught him listening on the extension as Boss Lan was talking to his supervisor. Cheng quickly pretended to be cleaning the mouthpiece.

The guys hid themselves behind the large cabinet, a Chinese wall of protection. Swearwords and cards showered Boss Lan's table. "Turtle egg!" "Dog fart!" "I'll give you the nine of hearts, tamade!" The loser had to clip clothespins to his lips, where they quivered grotesquely as the player mumbled through the pain. But the worst part of the torture, they claimed, was that a pinned person couldn't suck his cigarette satisfactorily. When Master Cheng later caught sight of the spectacle and made a big fuss, the punishment became crawling under the table, amid the butts and ashes.

After the game disbanded, I hardly had time to enjoy some peace before Fatty Wang, the head of the electric group, waddled in. She slumped into a chair and squinted at me. "Good, you've put on some weight." Since Master Li, the number-one gossip, was now permanently sick, Wang felt it was her responsibility to keep me updated. She claimed that Li was pocketing good commissions by selling scientific research equipment produced by her husband's work unit. "She bribed a factory doctor to get long-term sick leave, you know. And now, she's earning double income!" Fatty Wang held out two thick fingers. But her most shocking news was the split of Wu and Xu, the lovebirds. A year earlier, just as everyone was expecting their engagement, Wu was transferred to another work unit, with the apparent help of her father, and a week later, she married the son of a municipal leader. Xu, kept in the dark till the last moment, tried to commit suicide.

"I heard Little Wu got a diamond from her mother-in-law."

"She was no good," another colleague cut in. "She never intended to marry Little Xu. That's why she forbade him to tell anyone about their affair."

"Hey, guys, let's give Little Wu's husband some credit. He was so open-minded that he didn't mind that his wife was secondhand."

"Or maybe he was so thick that he couldn't tell the difference between a virgin and secondhand!" That set everyone into convulsions: sex scandals were still the best entertainment one could hope for.

My colleagues still spent much of their working hours blowing bull as they sat around Boss Lan's tables smoking and sipping tea. Ever since the arrival of the new guys, new games had come on the scene too, such as armpit-farting contests or cricket fights—the three guys each kept a cricket in a clay jar, a popular pastime for schoolboys.

Big Zhang provided new ingredients by relaying "small-road information." Since the government jealously guarded all information—as if its very survival depended on secrecy—ordinary Chinese had to rely on the small-road option, political gossip circulated by word of mouth. One source was Zhang's father's *Reference News*, a newspaper accessible only to those of a certain rank, which actually carried some real news, both international and domestic, in the form of reprints from the foreign press. In vivid detail he described how a princeling, the son of a high-ranking leader, with a fortune made from buying and selling steel, stayed at the presidential suite of the five-star Sheraton Hotel with his jewelry-laden mistress. The fact that Big Zhang himself could have been among the princelings, if not for Chairman Mao's disloyalty, doubled his hatred.

Wrapped in my own misery, I cared little for such tales.

Chapter 17

Home at War

A war was breaking out. Against Ma's wishes, my father had retired at fifty-six, nine years before the standard age, arguing that he could no longer take life as a homeless wanderer.

Father brought his single person's routine into our crowded flat, which felt smaller with his loud presence. If public concern for others is not a great virtue of Chinese people, my father was a worst-case scenario. He rose at dawn, a labor-camp habit he'd gained from years of waking to the sharp whistle that, at four, ordered prisoners out of bed and to work. Now he woke us instead, turning on the bright light and leaving the door wide open, crashing about in the communal kitchen where he washed. While brushing his teeth, he lifted his head, gargling loudly for minutes before spitting out forcefully. The whole family would lie awake in bed, impatient for the final bang of the front door.

He jogged through the dawn to White Egret Park. Clutching a little radio, he listened closely to the Central People's Broadcasting Corporation. For people of his generation, understanding the political weather was vital to their survival. At the park, he would walk backward around the lakeshore several times, an exercise that he believed had all sorts of mental and physical benefits, as long as you avoided the open manholes.

The first month was the worst—Father didn't know how to fill his empty days. He had no interests or hobbies whatsoever, having given up reading, withdrawing from the habit that plunged him into trouble. Persuaded by a neighbor, Father had briefly joined a *qigong* group in the park, who, oddly, claimed their breathing regime could generate a fragrant smell. But he soon gave up, detecting no new scents radiating from his body. Then, at the park, he met an amateur Beijing Opera group who invited him to join. At long last, he had found somewhere to make good use of his loud voice, and he was delighted. When he came back from morning exercise, he would sing all the way home. "Standing on top of the watchtower, I look down at the fine scenery, feather fan in my hand…" When he sang the high notes, he would half shut his eyes, moving his lower jaw strangely from one side to the other.

Ma had been swept along by the new ballroom-dancing craze filling dancehalls throughout the country, going out two or three nights a week, usually with Moley Miao, a colleague and a friend. Father did not approve. Once I accompanied them to an inexpensive dance run by a local "Cultural Hall for the Masses." Here, against the backdrop of a photo exhibition of the district's model workers and bright red posters with slogans like "Resolutely following the road of Socialism," drab-clothed dancers—some still in their canvas uniforms—moved to classic ballroom tunes on a concrete floor, under bright, intrusive lights. One after another, men went up to Ma, who danced with an old-fashioned grace that the young people couldn't master. Still in her usual gray jacket, she wore a pair of black leather shoes with a little bit of heel, not as high as the younger women risked, but high enough to lend an extra spring to her step. They were magic shoes. Having stepped into them, she couldn't stop spinning, waltz, foxtrot, tango… She swung around the dance hall, swift and elegant like a happy swallow dancing in the spring sky, her high cheeks red, her eyes glittering, and her expression dreamy.

Ma had invited her husband to come along, but he maintained that his steps had become rusty. Moreover, he tried to stop her, saying it wasn't appropriate for a married woman to go out dancing. Ma ignored him until one night, when Father made a huge fuss when a younger man escorted her home.

"Did you go dancing with that bowlegged man?" Father barked at Ma as soon as she entered the room. He had been standing at our tiny balcony, watching and waiting.

"Hush, quiet!" Ma tried to reason with him in a hushed voice. "Do you mean Little Liang? We just bumped into him on our way back. What are you so worked up about?"

"How can I not get worked up, seeing my fucking wife fooling around with other men?"

Little Liang lived in our building. He was not a dancer, and thus a most unlikely suspect.

"Mother of mine! Did you take the wrong medicine or what?" Ma slapped.

Sensing another storm coming, Nai sat up in bed, trembling and murmuring her mantra.

For the first time in twenty-eight years, my parents were living under the same roof. They could hardly stand each other. Ma had her own social circle, her own way of dealing with things, and her own space. Now, her husband had barged in, invading that space, interfering in her life, without providing any benefits. His low pension was just enough to feed himself.

"Dad!" I cut in, "Could you talk tomorrow? The neighbors are sleeping."

"Shut up!" he turned to me, "I want all of our neighbors to know what a flirty woman your ma is." Turning back to Ma, he raised his voice: "Listen, you cheap bone, you are my wife. From now on, I forbid you to go out dancing. It makes me fucking mad to know you are in another man's arms!" The veins on his full forehead bulged to busting and his eyes were wild and round like two Ping-Pong balls.

"You bastard, you thirteen o'clock!" Ma started her counterattack with the slang term for crazy person. "What a useless man you are! The only thing you can do is to insult your wife." Ma kicked off her high heels, fuming. "Look at you, so tall yet so useless. Why can't you take on a job like a decent man? No, you just won't."

My father's unwillingness to take on a job had been a constant cause of argument. As economic growth charged ahead, prices began to shoot up, rising together with urban discontent and frustration. Working-class families like ours, without extra sources of income, found themselves struggling. Just about every day, Ma reminded Father that our neighbor Teacher Zhang was taking on private students, her husband was moonlighting at another factory, and Old Li polished shoes in the street. But he wouldn't listen. After Ma threatened to throw him out of the house, he tried, half-heartedly, several jobs Changyong had fixed for him. But he found a night watchman's job degrading and too hard; a clerk's position too far away; and an accountancy post too complicated after just a few days. The problem was that Father regarded manual labor as beneath him, but he wasn't skilled or educated enough to take on intellectual work.

"A dog is more useful than you are!" Ma shouted, wagging an accusing finger at him, her other hand firmly propped on her hip for emphasis. "Marrying you is the worst thing that ever happened to me!"

"Useless? I am still a man!" He wasn't shouting but roaring, the two Ping-Pong balls in danger of rocketing across the room. As if to demonstrate a man's power, he grabbed for Ma's collar. "Confess, what's the relationship between you and the ugly man? If you dare to make me a cuckold, I'll take your life. Stingy whore!"

Immobilized by Father, Ma desperately tried to kick herself free.

I rushed up, prying at his hands. I loved my mother even when we argued, but I had never held much affection or respect for the man who fathered me. What he was doing now was not out of love but small-minded possessiveness.

His grip was too tight. My blood boiling, I sank my teeth into his hand until he screamed and let go.

Ma gathered her strength and slapped his face. "Shame on you. You sling mud at me!"

He slapped back, hard, leaving fingerprints on her face. For a moment, she was too stunned to speak but held her burning face.

"Help, quickly, quickly!" Nai managed to shout. Her Buddhist chanting had had little effect.

Of course, many of our neighbors had been listening attentively. Domestic arguments, interesting as they were, rarely offered interactive entertainment: it was generally best not to get involved. But Nai's open invitation brought several people inside to pull my parents apart. The rest stood outside, watching, gossiping, and laughing secretly, I was sure—middle-aged couples were not supposed to "drink vinegar."

Inside, my parents were still spurting insults through the wall between our rooms. "Fine! A gentleman doesn't degrade himself by arguing with a woman." Father attempted a lofty stance.

"Pah!" Mother spat in his direction. "Gentleman, you? Don't let our neighbors laugh their teeth out!"

"Caotamade!" She was interrupted by her husband's favorite swear.

"Whose mother do you want to fuck? Fuck eight generations of your ancestors!"

Ma put away her dancing shoes, not for fear of her husband, but for the peace of the family. Love, if it had ever existed between my parents, had long been worn away by hardship and many years' separation. But divorce, generally regarded as disgraceful, if not immoral, was out of the question. People simply didn't get divorced unless they were in some extraordinary circumstance like Master Mei and her adulterous husband. Marriage, like a job with a state-owned factory, was for life. "Marry a rooster, follow a rooster; marry a dog, follow a dog." The old saying still held for China's women.

"Oh, no!" Ma put down her porcelain cup on the table. Whenever the whole family gathered, she liked to have a few shots of the firewater. But tonight, my bad news spoiled her enjoyment: I had just failed to be promoted to cadre.

There were no words of reproach, but my mother's disappointment fell so heavily on me I had trouble breathing. I focused my eyes on the concrete floor, willing it to split and allow me underground. What a great loss of face! It wouldn't be so bad if I were not one of only three to miss out. One was the worst student at our class, and another was a troublemaker who had missed many lessons for her own side business. Everyone else rose to be a cadre, even Jun, my desk mate, who only graduated after re-sitting several exams.

Why? I wasn't a bad student at all.

My instinct was not to tell my family. But how could one hide a fire by wrapping it in paper? Ma knew too many people in the factory. So I chose to reveal the news at a Sunday dinner when Weijia was present, to avoid telling my humiliating tale twice.

"I thought you were the Zhang family's first daxue-sheng."

"Shut your big mouth!" Ma hit her husband with her chopsticks. "She still is. No one has taken her degree away."

"You must have offended your leaders, I bet, a hundred percent," concluded my sister.

I replied with a wan smile—my usual defense against embarrassment. "Yes, our Political Instructor Wang strongly opposed my promotion."

"See," said Weijia. I almost detected a brief smile, an "I told you so!" flickering through her lips. "'A fly doesn't buzz around an egg without a crack.' You must have left some 'little pigtail' at his hand." A "little pigtail" was a weakness, shortcoming, or misbehavior.

Liu Weidong, now the secretary to the factory's propaganda chief, who had spotted his talent in conducting "Socialism is Great," had investigated for me. It was the factory leaders' original intention to keep behind a small number of TV University graduates as workers, to ensure that future graduates would behave themselves, instead of taking their cadreship for granted. Our Political Instructor Wang made sure that I was among that minority. My little pigtail? I could only think of prejudice, which was probably enhanced by Master Cheng's secret reports on my illegal reading of "irrelevant books" and covering up for my colleagues' card playing. But even with my pigtail, how did I deserve such severe punishment?

My family knew the implication of the news. People in a factory were divided into two categories—workers and cadres. It would be a great leap to rise from worker to cadre, who enjoyed higher social standing, better welfare, and higher pay across the board. The news of old Boss Wang's recent death reminded me again the cruelty of the system. He had lost favor with his new boss after being transferred to the energy unit, and had therefore failed to secure the cadre status he had painstakingly worked toward for years. Angry and depressed, he had taken up drinking and died a slow death.

There was at least one advantage of being a worker—our grain ration was higher than that of the cadres, whose jobs were less physically demanding. All cadres were issued twenty-eight jin, or about fourteen kilograms, of grain per month, while workers' grain coupons depended on how taxing their jobs were. The more they sweated, the more they could eat. My ration was thirty-two jin. A lightweight.

On our dining table, Nai placed a chunk of meat into my bowl. "Eat, eat. One has to eat even if heaven collapses." She looked at me. "Not your fault. It's the weeping mark that brought you bad luck."

"Has your right eye been twitching again, Nai?" Weijia said, barely disguising her glee.

"It has indeed! Superstition or not, you can't ignore physiognomy. Get rid of your weeping mark, Little Li!"

"Nai," Ma retorted gently, "many years ago, you told me that my husband had an auspicious look. Look at him, rubbish coated in gold and jade!"

"He was born in unlucky times," Nai defended herself in her thin voice.

"But our Little Li does cry a great deal," said Weijia.

As my family discussed my unlucky signs, I left the room to stand on the tiny balcony.

Night had fallen on Wuding New Village. Lights flickered on in the identical gray buildings around me, as other families ate, argued, and watched identical TV programs.

Had I just missed the last opportunity? I knew some people already mocked me behind my back as "neo–white collar"—a white coat, like a doctor's, was our new uniform, yet I had the status of a manual worker. Even my colleagues didn't really consider me one of them because I was a daxuesheng with a degree. Like my father, I was another "Kong Yiji," a misfit who belonged neither to the long-gowned intellectuals nor the short-sleeved coolies.

I could easily picture my future, mechanically testing pressure gauges with greasy hands and an empty brain. With luck, I would marry one of the factory hands (most of my fellow workers intermarried) and live in one of those tiny flats in a gray building. Our child, born at Liming Hospital, would then go to the Liming kindergarten, then primary school, all within the formidable gray empire. I shivered at the thought.

Below me, withered leaves swirled in midair, round and round.

Chapter 18

Missiles and Misty Poems

At long last, I was within reach of our factory's biggest secret. A dozen meters of metal, twenty kilotons of nuclear warhead, and the iron will of a billion people. The missile lay on its side, the head a circular cone and the body a long, silver cylinder that gave off a cold gleam in the echoing warehouse. Tail fins clung to the end, to balance the rocket as it soared toward its destiny.

This was why armed guards patrolled the high walls and why new recruits swore to obey strict security rules. The full-range, intercontinental missile, capable of striking the United States, was partly produced and assembled right here at this workshop, and now I was in on the secret.

I tensed up at the silent force the missile presented. I had seen film footage, but it only showed distant launches and trails of smoke across the sky. To view the "first product" of our factory at such close quarters inside the high-security workshop of the general assembly section was a privilege specially granted by the director himself, one that most Chenguang workers never enjoyed. I stood among a group of students undergoing a two-week "patriotic education" course.

"The body is made up of the engine, the control and guidance system, and the bomb itself. When approaching the target, the warhead will separate from the main body," explained our host, a spectacled rocket scientist. We all wore white cloth coats, hats to cover our hair, and white slippers. He went on to explain the missile family, including ballistic missiles and cruise missiles, different classes of missiles defined by shooting range...

How ironic, I thought: one minute, the factory rejected me as a cadre; and the next, I was being educated as an intellectual, or *zhishifenzi*—literally a "knowledge element"—a loose Chinese term embracing people with any kind of higher education, even myself. Our leaders hoped some "patriotic education" would revive young intellectuals' faith in the Party, which had been lapsing fast in an ever more money-oriented society.

My curiosity was satisfied by the power on display, yet it stirred little patriotic feeling. We had been told too many times how far China had traveled since its days as the "sick man of Asia." When the rocket scientist finally finished, our teacher, the same Parrot who once trained us new arrivals, launched into a long speech.

"This is what we are capable of producing," Parrot gloated, shooting an affectionate glance at the missile. "We Chinese are peace lovers, but it is vital for a large nation like ours to have powerful weapons so that we will never be bullied by foreign powers again."

Since the Sino-Soviet split in the early 1960s, Chinese scientists, some of them US-trained, had been having some success on their own—most notably the successful launch of an ICBM in May 1980. In the reform era, the leaders in Beijing had decided to modernize the giant but poorly equipped army. In particular, they wanted a nuclear arsenal and the missiles to deliver it. Research on the solid-fueled, multistaged new generation of missiles was well under way.

I was not the first to escape into the gentle sunshine of early winter. One guy was already standing outside, smoking a cigarette. "Finished yet?" he asked. "I can't stand such talks. Why do we always have to portray ourselves as victims?" His Mandarin was accented, but refined.

"To make us feel grateful to the Party," I guessed. This quiet, thin man was in my course, but I had never spoken to him properly. I introduced myself.

"Pan Hai, every one calls me Old Pan," he replied. It usually took many years before someone was raised from "Little" to "Old." Pan was clearly an exception. He must be young, like any other trainee, yet there were already deep lines on his face, especially between his eyebrows, as if he had tasted bitterness in life. His eyes were sad and thoughtful, below a disheveled crop of hair that suggested he had just got up. His jacket was as crumpled as an old person's frown.

"I actually studied guided missiles at university," he revealed.

"Really?"

"I was so bored that I spent a lot of the time reading my own books. Do you like literature? I saw you reading books at class under the table."

"Yes, well, 'literature' sounds too serious, but I do enjoy reading." In the deep shadow cast by my failed promotion, I had taken solace in books.

"If you are interested, come have a look at my little library." He issued his invitation warmly.

What a luxury to have the whole workshop to myself! I could still hear the noise of spinning machines from the massive workshop downstairs. But by now I barely noticed their constant whir.

To escape from the family warfare, I had asked Boss Lan if I could use the workshop at night. "Sure, as long as you don't bring your boyfriend here!" He knew there was no danger of that.

In my sanctuary, there was no smoke, nor the wasted breath of blowing bull. Under the orange lamp on my desk, I read books, wrote in my diary, or wept freely in self-pity;

I sang Teresa Deng's songs emotionally as if facing a large audience; and I danced in the arms of an imaginary lover to music from a little radio.

I also beautified my soul—reading poetry. I had taken up Old Pan's invitation to see his large collection of books and borrowed a newly published *Collection of Misty Poems.* "Good for your soul," he said.

The movement those poems sprang from had seemed good for China's soul, too, until the Communist Party smashed the Democracy Wall. In late 1978, a poster-strewn wall in central Beijing was a public canvas for personal suffering and political demands. Young activists formed groups based around underground publications—politics and literature were always bedfellows in China. In *Exploration*, the electrician-turned-dissident Wei Jingsheng argued that China could never achieve its much-touted Four Modernizations without introducing a fifth—democracy. Less political was *Today*, China's first underground literary journal, which saw the debut of Misty Poetry, a very modern style named for its ambiguity.

Through the mist, I saw a world of rich imagination, vivid symbols, feelings, and emotions that had never been explored before in China. I felt a poem entitled "Assembly Line," by a fellow factory worker Shu Ting, was written just for me:

> On the assembly line of time
> night is nestled with night
> we retreat from the assembly line in the factory
> and file home
> above our heads
> an assembly line of stars stretches across the firmament
> beside us
> dazed young trees stand in a row

what is strange, though
is that I cannot feel
my own existence
the way I feel the trees and the stars
perhaps out of habit
perhaps out of sadness
I no longer have the strength to care
about the fixed position I am in.

With one hundred times the words, I could not have expressed the sense of ennui, something I knew too well, better than these simple verses.

I could see why the establishment tried so hard to suppress Misty Poetry—this art did not serve the masses, as Chairman Mao had instructed, for the masses could barely understand it. Only recently, as the political atmosphere has relaxed, were these poems unveiled in the public domain.

At night, Old Pan would often turn up at my workshop unannounced. With a cup of tea, I welcomed him and the books he brought along. They were his old favorites: Kafka's *The Trial*, *Snow Country* by Japanese Nobel laureate Kawabata Yasunari, or new exciting titles. The mid-1980s saw the blossoming of a hundred flowers in the garden of literature. With some breathing space granted by the government, writers sprang to life, applying Western techniques such as stream-of-consciousness narration, or returning to the roots of traditional literature.

In the gentle glow of my desk lamp, we would discuss and devour those books. I had always read here and there, as a passing pleasure. Only now, guided by Old Pan, did I really discover the golden palace of literature.

My literary friend had come a long way from his impoverished village in Anhui. Fully aware that education was the only way out, his strict father used to slap the children's hands with a ruler if they wrote the wrong character. Pan honored his ancestors by becoming the first villager to go to university. At Harbin Industrial University, a prestigious place specializing in military industry, he fell under the spell of the muse. Since being assigned to the factory a few months earlier, he had been teaching at Liming Technical School while pursuing his literary interests.

A melancholy air and a strong tobacco smell would fill the workshop whenever Pan descended into Master Lin's seat, opposite me. A reading would follow, while his messy crop of hair cast an eccentric shadow on the floor. Beyond the circle illuminated by my lamp, nothing existed but Pan's inflamed recital. I would hang on every word he uttered: something in those lyrics made me alive.

The Answer

Baseness is the password of the base,
Honor is the epitaph of the honorable.
Look how the gilded sky is covered
With the drifting, crooked shadows of the dead.

The Ice Age is over now,
Why is there still ice everywhere?
The Cape of Good Hope has been discovered,
Why do a thousand sails contest the Dead Sea?

Let me tell you, world,
I—do—not—believe!
If a thousand challengers lie beneath your feet,
Count me as number one thousand and one.

I don't believe the sky is blue;
I don't believe in the sound of thunder;

I don't believe that dreams are false;
I don't believe that death has no revenge.

If the sea is destined to breach the dikes,
Let the brackish water pour into my heart;
If the land is destined to rise,
Let humanity choose anew a peak for our existence.

A new juncture and glimmering stars
Adorn the unobstructed sky,
They are five-thousand-year-old pictographs,
The staring eyes of future generations.

"Don't you just love the defiant voice?" Pan once exclaimed after reciting this poem by Bei Dao, a leading Misty poet.

The poem was one of my favorites, too, written to commemorate the 1976 Tiananmen Incident, when hundreds of people disobeyed the authorities and publicly mourned the death of their beloved Premier Zhou Enlai. I adored the fresh, vivid imagery that turned China's ancient script into its people's future vision. Pan saw deeper significance in the poem.

"You can hear Bei Dao's cry for individualism. That's what poetry is always about—the personal and the marginal. Not the mouthpiece of politics." For the first time, a true sense of self was appearing in Chinese poetry, Pan declared. In Chinese culture, a person was defined by his relationship with others: traditional Confucianism emphasizes *keji*, self-restraint. Mao's Communist revolution went even further, attempting to destroy "self" and "individuality." We were required to think as one, to be unselfish, like the rustless screw Lei Feng, totally devoted to the Party. Between the hazy lines of the Misty poems, the dignity of individualism and self-expression were clearly being restored.

As he talked, Old Pan's face, usually passive and sad, became animated. The patriotic education course had organized several social outings, the most enjoyable part of the experience for its bored participants. But Pan always appeared shy, silent, and even awkward in a group of people.

Old Pan gradually introduced his own poems, on condition that I burnt them after reading. As I lit up his beautiful lyrics, reflections of his sensitive and anguished soul, I felt like a mourner for a short-lived flower. Why not publish them? "I am rarely pleased with my work," he replied with a weary smile. For him, poetry was simply a mirror for reflection, a place to search for private truth, he stressed. And a shell to retreat into, I wanted to add.

"He who stays near vermilion gets stained red; and he who stays near ink gets stained black," went an old saying. Old Pan's passion for literature was so infectious that I started to write little poems and some bits of prose. No flowers blossomed under my pen, but I was impressed with myself nonetheless. Like an eager student, I showed my writings to Pan, who would brighten them up with his magic touch.

Unlike him, I was vain enough to demand an audience. I sent a piece to *Liming News*, our factory's biweekly newsletter, now run by my friend Liu Weidong. My first published prose, a description of the beautiful sunset at Rain Flower Terrace, the nearby park, implored people not to ignore daily beauty. It proved a morale booster. "Our daxuesheng is different after all," praised Boss Lan with a string of girlish giggles. "I'll take one copy home to show my daughters."

I thought about Red Rock. How I wished he could read my piece, even if it was only in my factory newspaper! But there was little sense in opening old wounds. As for Political Instructor Wang, I could almost feel the sweet taste of revenge: my published article should show him that I wasn't as unworthy as he believed.

Carried away by this little success, I decided to try my luck with some proper literary magazines.

One day after work, I biked to the main post office at Confucius Temple to send off my writing. With both hands, I pushed my white envelope into the mouth of the green postbox. I almost felt that the letterbox returned my brief smile.

Chapter 19

A Tool of Struggle

"For…for…for…rin." I stretched my mouth into the alien sounds. "Foreign language is a tool of class struggle," Marx said, according to our schoolteacher, who then made our class parrot the words back to him. It was the second English sentence I ever learned. "Long live Chairman Mao!" was the first. But Mao was nine years dead, I was five years out of school, and Mao's successors were courting the capitalist world Marx despised. Newly fashionable after years under suspicion, foreign language was going to be my tool of struggle, too.

The idea had come from Zhou Fang, another trainee in the patriotic education course. Once we started talking, I poured out my life story. Fang suggested I join her English degree course at "Teach-Yourself University," a sort of open university. It made perfect sense. With language skills, I could hope to land a decent job outside the factory walls, as foreign investors were starting to set up shop in the city.

"A thousand-li journey begins with the first step." I took mine immediately, writing an application to Political Instructor Wang: I needed an introduction letter from my work unit to register for classes. To my dismay, there was a long silence. What could be the problem? The government was urging young people to study hard and strive for the Four Modernizations that were China's hope of catching up with the world.

I would miss the deadline if I waited any longer. Gathering my courage, I decided to inquire in person. I found him in his spacious but bare office, sitting at his desk, under a big portrait of Chairman Mao, reading *The People's Daily* and sipping tea—as he usually did when he wasn't at a meeting somewhere.

"Yes, I have," he answered coldly, staring through that frequent and disconcerting blink. "What use would it be if you mastered English? It's not relevant to your work, so the answer is no!" He spoke with a curt finality.

I swallowed my anger, to deny him the pleasure of seeing the misery he caused me. Wang was one of those cadres who never wasted any opportunity, however little, to exercise their power.

Tears in my eyes, I telephoned Fang. "Don't worry. There must be a way," she said. Fang's personal motto promised a solution for everything: "When a flood comes, build a dam to stop it; when invaders come, send soldiers to fight!"

The next day, she called me to her office at Work Unit Number Five, in the southern compound beyond the railway line, where my mother had toiled most of her life. To give myself an official excuse, I offered to collect pressure gauges from the units based there.

When I turned up, Fang was sitting behind her desk, smiling triumphantly, her eyes narrowing into two lines behind her glasses. In front of her lay an introduction letter, in her own handwriting, on a sheet of official Liming letterhead secured from her unit administrator, a friend. Its red seal beamed like a sun.

"You'll be fine with it," Fang predicted. "No one is going to bother to look at it carefully. All they need is your name and an official seal."

I held it to my chest. "How can I thank you enough?" I knew she was running a risk for me, even if it was a small one.

"Not at all."

Fang was a typical Southern girl, small and slender, with features as delicate as silk embroidery, cherry-like lips and pretty eyes. With her simple haircut, and glasses that like mine were ever reluctant to stay on her nose, she still looked like a young student. Only two years my senior, she was mature and resourceful, but beneath her serenity ran a live wire. She reminded me of a famous piece of Chinese flute music called "Spring River, Flowery Moon Night": on a peaceful spring night, the music suggests, when flowers are in full blossom, a river, shining under the silver moonlight, runs swiftly, full of life-affirming energy.

As I was about to leave, a middle-aged man with a cadre's air walked into the office. After peering at me through protruding eyes, he bellowed: "Is that Little Li?"

There was no mistaking that goldfish look. "Uncle Gao!" He was an engineer, a friend of my mother's who used to pay us visits years ago and help fix things at home. "You've grown so tall! You only came up to my waist last time I saw you." He grinned, shaking my hand and eyeing me up and down.

"Oh, very modern and fashionable. Like mother, like daughter," he commented.

"Lijia is very clever, too. She can speak pretty good English!" My friend Fang said.

While I protested her exaggeration, Uncle Gao was delighted at the news. "Good for you, good for you, little Li!" He paused for a moment, then issued an invitation: "Since you are here, would you like to see where your mother worked?"

"Sure."

"Your mother is a very capable woman," gushed Uncle Gao as we walked into the workshop. "When she was assistant to the foreman, she wrote the best annual reports we ever had. Then she was demoted to work on the acid-pickling floor. Really, a phoenix wasting away in a chicken coop." He shook his head. Without his colleagues standing by, he seemed freer to praise her. "She was a great dancer, too!" he added heartily.

He lit up with memories of weekend dance parties in the mid-fifties. Live music transformed the factory's simple basketball court into a ballroom of dreams, where young men fought for the hands of the liveliest and most attractive partners.

"That was so long ago," Uncle Gao let out a laugh, shaking off the sentimental memories. He turned to me. "Is your mother well?"

I updated him about Ma and the growing role she was playing at the Confucius Market. He listened attentively. A question occurred to me: why had he stopped visiting us all these years ago? I knew Father wouldn't like Ma to be friendly with any man, but she did need a man's help from time to time. Maybe their attention, too.

"I'm happy that your mother has found a use for her talents. This way, please."

You could follow your nose to this job. The stench of chemicals grew thicker with every step. Inside the workshop, I fought to control my churning stomach. Half a dozen huge tanks built into the ground bubbled with liquid the color of soy sauce. "Please don't touch anything!" shouted Uncle Gao through the roar of air pumps, as if the warning was necessary. The tanks seemed to me like dangerous monsters, salivating for their prey.

"Acid pickling is an anticorrosive treatment for machinery parts," he explained loudly. "First, we put the parts into that tank," he pointed as we walked, "to get rid of the surface grease. Then, we put them into hydrochloric acid, followed by the alkali tank to... Am I boring you?"

"Oh, no." Some nearby workers were going through the steps Gao described, the pattern of Ma's life for years.

Dull and dangerous. "Would my mother have got another job if she tried, do you think?" I asked.

"Yes, surely. I did suggest she try talking to the leaders when things calmed down. If she had gotten an administrative job, she might have earned a higher salary in time as she climbed the ranks. But I guess she cared too much about the extra money and food the acid picklers received, rib soup and eggs."

Images of those soups flashed in my mind, and a vague taste memory played on my tongue. I tried to remember Nai's thin voice, reminding us of Mother's sacrifice, but she was drowned out by the cries that greeted the food spilling into our little bowls, each child convinced he or she had received the smallest share. We were too busy squabbling to care about where the food came from, or to notice Ma's coarse, yellow hands, thickened by calluses.

Now I had no heart to accuse Ma of failing to think rationally. Watching her skinny children wolf down those soups and suck at the rib marrow for hours must have been enough for her to put up with the disgusting smells and deadly boredom of her job.

The stinging sensation spread to my nose, and tears welled up.

"Are you all right?" Uncle Gao looked at me kindly.

"I'm just not used to the chemical smell," I half-lied, wiping my eyes.

"No one likes it, even when they get used to it."

After dinner that night, I found a quiet moment. "Ma, I didn't know you were such a star at the factory dance parties." I was seeing her in a new light.

A smile blossomed across her tired face. "Oh yes, the dance parties were a big deal then. When the music started, my feet started to itch. The lads liked to dance with me because I was light as a swallow. Life was fun when I first joined the factory. We were young, patriotic, and high-spirited."

"I bet you had many admirers, didn't you, Ma? Was Uncle Gao one of them?"

"I was sought after by quite a few. Uncle Gao was always very kind to me."

My mother so rarely opened the door to her past, now I wanted to rush straight in.

"So why didn't you choose one of them?"

"I made a point of not marrying a man from the same factory. It would be too much."

It was my own voice, my own reasoning! "And your father seemed very knowledgeable and rather charming at first. How could I know he'd turn out to be an empty shell?"

"Didn't you have *any* ambition?" I fired another question, and hit a sore point. Her dreamy expression faded. She let loose a long sigh. "Everyone told me that 'my heart is higher than the sky but my fate is thinner than a piece of paper.' I have learned to concede to my fate. I know you are ambitious. Newborn calves are not afraid of tigers. But my child, don't aim too high. You'll just be disappointed."

She stroked my head with a gentleness I rarely knew. Some strands of my unruly hair tangled in her hand before falling free. She rose to walk toward the kitchen. For the first time, I noticed the fishtail wrinkles at the corner of her eyes. Her back was erect as usual, but she seemed to have aged three years in the months since her dancing shoes started to gather dust. Once again, she gave in to fate, grudgingly.

"Democracy isn't enough. Without a dictatorship to guard against saboteurs, we won't be able to maintain social stability." Inside the meeting hall, under the posters of Marx, Engels, Lenin, Stalin, and Chairman Mao, we had assembled again for Political Instructor Wang's sermon. He was reading out the latest directive from the central government about strengthening the socialist legal system in response to rising crime. From time to time, he would raise his gaze above his half-moon-shaped glasses, looking out toward the assembly like a hunting dog poised to attack.

There were still too many meetings of all sorts. No wonder the private companies, free of this political baggage, were doing much better than the state-owned sector.

I ached with impatience. I had so little time to waste, having signed up for three courses—Grammar, American and British History, and Intensive Reading—the maximum number allowed for one term at the Teach-Yourself University. Never had I imagined that the study of English would lend the frog a wider perspective. The walls of the well were shrinking down toward me; the light of other people's experience brightened my life.

Energized by my new goal, I tried to use every free moment to study. After supper at home, I would cycle back to the workshop through the darkness: there were no street lamps and no headlights on our bikes. I used to dread the middle section, along an unpaved road that ran beside the river, infamous for stories of rape, murder, accidents—even a ghost who would take off her head to comb her incredibly long hair. Several times, I fell off my bike when I bumped into a stone or rode into a ditch. At other times, I was spooked by young lovers suddenly emerging from the riverbank.

I drummed up courage with a Carpenters song. "Sing, sing a song, sing out loud, sing out strong, sing a good thing not bad, sing for you and me. La...la...la..."

I studied even under Wang's watchful eye. My tactic at meetings required a seat in a quiet corner toward the back, where I hid my book with *The People's Daily*.

While Wang went on about saboteurs, I was absorbed in a simplified English version of *Jane Eyre*, which I found packed with inspiration. I loved stories like *Jane Eyre* and *Great Expectations*, about little people from the bottom of the society fighting hard to improve their fate.

Reading novels in English satisfied both my need to study the language and my interest in literature, which was still growing. I had never heard anything back from the literary magazines. But I had no time to grieve: English was my priority now.

Red Rock had first whetted my appetite for learning English. After our encounter, I had bought simplified novels in English, but frustrated at my level, I had given up. Now I could devour these spiritual feasts—it was like relishing Nanjing salty duck at an authentic restaurant. A special kind of duck mind you, bred in the city, pickled for a certain time, and cooked in just the right way.

I bought these English novels at the foreign-language bookstore. Although Marxist poster boys still glowered from the walls, Richard Clayderman's easy-listening piano music had replaced the propaganda broadcasts. The Carpenters were among the first popular Western bands to go on sale. Classic novels were cheap since the concept of intellectual property was as distant as the dead foreign authors themselves. The footnotes in Chinese were generally useful, and often amusing. "Oliver had the bad habit of capitalist youth who like to judge or even rate the appearance of pretty girls," warned a footnote in *Love Story*, Erich Segal's best seller, on the page where Oliver gives his girlfriend's legs an "A."

I was extra keen on English novels, since the school's politically laced textbooks bored me numb. We learned how shocked Lenin was when he visited London and saw the huge difference between the West End and East End. "Two countries in one nation!" the future Soviet leader hissed angrily. "Capitalism came into the world, from head to toe, from every pore, with blood and dirt."

Our Intensive Reading curriculum predictably included Dickens's *Oliver Twist*, which I had read in Chinese at school. Even when most Western novels were forbidden, *An Orphan at the Foggy Capital*, the Chinese translation, was among the few permitted since it projected just the right image of capitalist London: cold, miserable, and unfair.

There were gems like *Jane Eyre*, luckily. Hidden in the back of the meeting room, I felt safe from Wang's flying spittle and swirling propaganda. I didn't understand every single word I was reading, but I got enough to appreciate Charlotte Brontë's masterpiece. When Jane thinks her beloved master Mr. Rochester is about to marry a rich society lady, she confesses her love in a moving speech. "Do you think, because I am poor, obscure, plain, and little, I am soulless and heartless?... If God had gifted me with some beauty, and much wealth, I should have made it as hard for you to leave me, as it is now for me to leave you...It is my spirit that addresses your spirit; just as if both had passed through the grave, and we stood at God's feet, equal—as we are!"

Tears came to my eyes: I felt for her; I saw myself in her; momentarily I felt I was the poor girl about to lose her love. With tear-blurred vision, I buried my head further into the book.

Suddenly, a colleague nudged me. For a moment, I didn't know where I was until I looked up to see Political Instructor Wang's sinister eyes glaring over me, his horse-like face pulled even longer.

"Stand up!" he yelled, snatching *Jane Eyre* from my grasp.

I stood up, red-faced, casually dashing off my tears with a fake yawn of boredom. But my fellow workers were far from bored. The eyes of several hundred people turned to enjoy the unexpected drama. Even the gossips stopped chatting and dozing workers shot awake.

"An English book!" he spat, shaking it violently, a disgusted look on his face. "Look at you, why do you dress up so fancifully for work? You like to worship foreign things, don't you? "

I was guilty of wearing a bright red woolen top and black skirt. To make matters worse, I had tied a silk scarf around my neck. Outside the well, women had just started to unbutton Mao's straitjacket and slip into more colorful and fashionable attire. But inside the factory fortress, a skirt was still too reyan an item. But I was determined not to be another faceless worker ant.

"I have the freedom to choose what I wear," I replied, despite my nerves. "I haven't broken any factory dress codes, have I?"

"Freedom? Some rotten ideas from the West have certainly gone to your head. This is a socialist factory. Reading a rotten foreign book during an important political meeting is a serious offense. You'll be punished. As for this book," he began ripping its pages to pieces like a possessed man. A deep conservative, Wang blamed capitalism for any negative fallout from the reforms, such as declining morals, growing money worship, and hedonistic youth. "If anyone dares to violate rules, that's the result!" He turned abruptly toward the rostrum. Behind his thin body, shreds of *Jane Eyre* glided to the ground, like white rose petals in a breeze.

A demerit was recorded in my personal file and my bonus was deducted. In defiance of Wang, I smuggled in a pocket-sized English–Chinese dictionary, a gift from Old Pan. When meetings dragged on, I would try to memorize new vocabulary from the "little yellow book," named after its cover. Pan had done just the same, noting every entry with a tick, and an approximate transliteration into Chinese, for he never had a chance to learn English at his village school. Next to England, he had penciled *ying ge lan*, which literally meant "hard burp rotten." At meetings, I had to stifle my laughter at his creative pronunciation. Lace became *la xi*, "diarrhea"; politics grew into *pao li ti ke si*, "run, power, kick, overcome, and die"—maybe not so wrong after all. Political Instructor Wang threw me sharp, disapproving glances. But I didn't care. I was losing my fear of the authorities. Paper tigers, I decided.

My public humiliation also served as a public announcement of my efforts to learn English. Amid the rumor and gossip that followed, the general consensus labeled me "a toad that dreams of swan meat." Once, after catching me speaking English to myself, a couple of workers hissed "Fake foreign devil!" an insulting term for any Chinese person trying to behave like a foreigner. People's admiration for the West was often tempered with fear, dislike, and jealousy. To comfort themselves, some brought up past glories and looked for signs of our superiority. One Chinese creation myth was popularly reworked as follows: Nuwa, a legendary superwoman, molded the first humans from balls of mud. But she burned the first batch, which became the African races; the second was underdone and resulted in the pasty-faced Europeans; the third was "just right," delivering today's Chinese.

Let people laugh. Frog or toad, I told myself that I had a vision, though not necessarily swan's meat, in mind.

All my life, I had been tinghua, listening to my parents, teachers, bosses, and the Party, following the prescribed path. Now, for the first time, I discovered that it was great fun to be a rebel. No wonder Chairman Mao famously said, "To rebel is justified!"

I wondered if there was an innate Chinese tendency toward conformity that made it easier for us to accept a dictatorial state—the People's Democratic Dictatorship, as our political system was formally called—or did dictatorship itself instill our complacency?

Conformity, often in the form of "collective spirit," was cultivated from birth. For a few months as a small child, I was dragged to the kindergarten in our village, which was run by the factory. "There will be toys to play with there," Ma wooed. There were a few, but our time for play was limited like everything else in the regimental establishment. Even the potties—cold metal spittoons—could only be used at an appointed hour each day, and we could not get off until instructed, sometimes fifteen minutes later, leaving sore, red rings on our naked behinds.

At school, we all sat with our hands behind our backs; when our teacher asked what we would do in the future, we would reply in unison: "We will strike hard for the course of Communism!"

Now, I came to see tinghua wasn't the greatest merit after all. If Jane Eyre had been so obedient to social convention, she would be forever confined to her role as a little governess. I couldn't say exactly when I had deserted my Soviet hero, the selfless Communist Pavel Korchaguin, for an "individualist" like Jane Eyre.

Maybe Wang was right: something from those "rotten Western books" had gotten into my head. Foreign language was probably more than just a tool.

FROM LEFT TO RIGHT: Lijia, her older sister Weija, her younger brother Xiaoshi, and her mother on the far right. Lijia and Weija are wearing skirts they borrowed from their neighbors.

A rare family picture.

Lijia, thirteen, with her siblings.

Lijia's mother in her youth.

Lijia's father in his youth.

Lijia with classmates from TV University. Prince Charming Ning, standing in the front row to the far right.

Lijia with Zhou Fang.

Lijia poses in front of the bronze Buddha her factory produced.

"I had changed my black heavy-framed glasses for the strangest pair I could find in town—large and irregularly shaped with sides that bent twice. Not particularly attractive, but certainly *reyan*."

Lijia, in a studio shot
at twenty-three

Lijia, front left, leading the demonstration
with workers from her factory in 1989.

Lijia with her parents and Nai, her grandmother, in the early 1990s.

Lijia at the launch of
China Remembers, which
she co-authored with
Calum MacLeod in 2000.

Chapter 20

The English Corner

"NO, you are WRONG!" Like many people who spoke English poorly, I tended to speak it loudly, as if sheer volume could compensate for lack of fluency. No wonder the English Corner always attracted crowds of onlookers—we sounded like we were quarreling! And quarreling in a strange foreign tongue. Presently, I was indeed arguing, over whether it was acceptable to criticize Lu Xun, the father of modern Chinese literature.

"I agree you on discipline, oh, sorry, on principle, it is okay to crit—sorry, I have trouble to say that word—cri-ti-cize him," he sounded out the syllables. "But not person attack."

In late summer of 1986, amid the arguments, broken grammar, and startling pronunciations at the English Corner, I met a producer, a Mr. Liu, from Jiangsu Provincial Television. English Corner, a free open-air gathering, lay a stone's throw from Liu's station in a small clearing beside Drum Tower Park, right in the heart of the city. There were such places now in most Chinese cities, places where people gathered to practice their English informally as the new trend to learn foreign languages swept the country. Ever since I signed up with the Teach-Yourself University, I had been coming here every Sunday after work. During the week, my kind boss would sometimes lend me the excuse of delivering a paycheck or some goodies to our sickly colleague Master Li, who lived north of Drum Tower. I loved slipping out from work to indulge myself in argument for the whole afternoon.

"Lu Xun had a famous of attacking others," I said, "though he was held"—I meant hailed—"as a hero by government, but he can't compose negative articles if he still living nowadays." Although freedom of speech remained an elusive dream, privately people had begun to express their views more freely, especially in unofficial venues like the English Corner.

"I see at your point," Liu said politely. "But it is good to have a few models, I mean heroes from China. Lu Xun is one of few. Already, many young people today think, well, how to say in English?" he paused for a moment, then continued in Chinese. "'The foreign moon is brighter than the Chinese moon' and too readily do they discard anything homemade." With a degree in Chinese literature, Liu was a self-appointed defender of Chinese culture and tradition.

"English, please." There was an unspoken rule that people who came to English Corner should try their best not to speak Chinese.

"All right, I'm not your match," he said in Chinese, frustrated that he couldn't express himself freely in English "I'll bring my colleague next time!"

Liu's English level was similar to mine, but he was perhaps less fluent orally. I was fired up and had been making steady progress. Unlike some, I wasn't shy about opening my mouth. With much more humiliating experiences under my belt, I didn't consider English errors at all embarrassing.

The opportunity to meet and argue with intelligent people drew me like a magnet to the English Corner. I watched, half amused and half surprised, as I became like a rooster, spoiling for a fight.

The following Sunday, Liu dragged along his colleague.

"Hi, I'm Charlie," Miao Qinglin said warmly, holding out his hand.

"Hi, I'm Lijia. Sorry, I haven't got an English name. I think my Chinese name is too pretty to give up. Li as in 'beautiful' and Jia as in 'fine.' Beautiful and fine lady, that's me!" Holding the front of my dress, I won a laugh with a theatrical curtsey.

Most Corner regulars had English names. Some christened themselves to sound like their Chinese names, such as "Charlie" for "Qinglin"; others preferred direct translation, like Stone or Flower, or inspirational role models like Margaret—Britain's "iron lady" was highly regarded in China. Fiction inspired others, like Scarlett, after *Gone With the Wind*, a hit in China as everywhere else, and Fanny from another classic. Some names made less sense, like the girl called Echo and the shy boy called Dick.

"Charlie after Charlie Chaplin?" I asked.

"Precise the case," he replied, twisting his long elegant hands in imitation of the comedian's famous screw-tightening scene.

Despite his average height, he had larger-than-life features. His big nose was slightly aggressive and his black spectacles seemed oversize, too. With his dark skin and lips, and a trendy striped shirt, Charlie could pass for a Southeast Asian.

"I like your long hair; you look like an artist," I told him, surprising myself: I couldn't imagine myself making such a remark to a young man in Chinese. It was just not something you did.

"Oh, I have no time to cut it." He brushed back his shining mane. His voice was deep and magnetic.

"Rubbish!" snapped Liu. "No time to cut hair? You keep long intention. Your attempting—is attempting the right word?—anyway, attempting pretty girls, perhaps?" He nudged at his colleague.

Miao turned to hit his mate. "Why attack me? We are supposed comrades-in-arms. I came to aid your help today."

Then, turning to me, he beamed. "I do like your glasses. They stand out."

"Oh, thank you." I self-consciously pushed them back up my nose. I had changed my black, heavy-framed glasses for the strangest pair I could find in town—large and irregularly shaped with sides that bent twice. Not particularly attractive, but certainly *reyan*. Since I was now regarded as weird at my factory, I might as well behave accordingly.

"Mr. Liu told me that you work at a factory. Do you really? I have never met a worker who is as colloquial as you are," Miao continued.

"He meant you are eloquent, not colloquial," Liu cut in.

"Yes, eloquent. You don't look like a worker," Miao fixed his gaze at me.

I felt under scrutiny. "Should I take that as a compliment?"

Here at the English Corner, I enjoyed telling people that I was a factory worker, which somehow sounded more impressive than, say, a middle school teacher. After all, you didn't meet many workers who could speak English, and not that badly by the Corner standard. "What do you think a worker should look like? An oil-stained uniform, and a peaked cap, holding an iron rod and singing 'we workers are powerful, hai, powerful!'" With an exaggerated deep voice, I started the famous "Song of the Workers." Liu and Miao soon joined in. "Every day, we are busy with work, hai, busy with work!" We laughed so much that we could hardly stand up.

"You are so funny today," noted Liu.

"I have met a few workers," said Miao. "We meet all kinds of people, don't we, Liu? Workers, number-one brother, I dreamed to becoming a worker when I was a peasant." Like most people his age, Miao was once a sent-down youth.

He returned to the city after gaining entry to Nanjing Normal College to study music; later he taught music at a school before joining the TV station when it recruited staff through open competition. Most of their colleagues had slipped in through the back door.

"You wouldn't dream becoming a worker now, I bet to say," I said enviously. "So cool to work of a TV station. You don't have strict rules, don't you? Do you know, hair like yours, a worker won't be able to enter our factory."

"That's just, uh," Miao switched to Chinese, "...super-ficial. We have other types of rules and control—the control of minds, which is far worse."

"Let's not talk about politics," Liu stepped in. "Anyway, Miss Zhang doesn't look like an obvious victim of repression. Look at your dress. What kind of dress code are we talking about?"

My dress was rather stylish one, a style I'd spotted in a fashion magazine and had copied, brilliantly, by our village dressmaker. I always dressed up when I attended Sunday's English Corner.

"'Wherever there is repression, there is rebellion,'" I cited a quotation by Chairman Mao while raising my skinny arm in the air. "Anyway, I'm not at my factory now."

Darkness had yet to fall when the two journalists left to shoot a performance by a visiting opera troupe. I felt sorry at parting after such a short meeting. Miao was interested in me, I could tell, and I found myself drawn to him, too.

On the following Sunday, I turned up early. But among the eager crowd I caught no sight of my journalist friends. I knew they were busy, often working weekends, when most cultural events took place. Then, it began to rain, and it rained for days, washing away my hopes of seeing Miao again.

"*Wei,* who are you looking for?" I heard Boss Lan shouting at the receiver. "*Ao,* it's for... Zhang Lijia." My colleagues fell about laughing as Lan tried to pronounce my name in standard Mandarin. A Mandarin speaker? Who could it be? Callers within the factory usually addressed me as Little Zhang. And judging from the intense interest of Boss Lan, it must be a man. My heart nearly leaped out of my throat.

"*Wei,* it's Zhang Lijia here." I picked up the phone and answered in standard Mandarin, too, like an educated person. My pronunciation was substandard, and was often mocked by my colleagues, but I was undaunted.

"Hi, there! It's Charlie here!" His voice, deep and beautiful, rang clearly through the line.

"Oh hi! How are you? What a surprise! Well, a pleasant surprise." I quickly switched to English.

He laughed at the other end of the line. "Are you free on Friday night? I'll be filming a show by Brigham Young University from America. I can get a couple of tickets if you're interested."

"A show from America? Oh, yes, please!"

Too excited to sit down, I walked over to the window. Outside, it was still raining. When raindrops hit the pond in the small garden, little ripples spread like dimples from a smile.

On Friday, I turned up in my best outfit—a red sleeveless dress made from fine silk. I had a black belt around my waist and a black silk ribbon, tied into a butterfly shape, decorating my neck. I liked striking colors, particularly red.

Miao was waiting in front of Nanjing's Great Hall of the People, the venue for the pantomime of our rubber-stamp legislature, along with all major cultural shows. "Where is your friend?" he asked, beaming at me.

"Uh, well, my friend couldn't make it," I told a white lie. I hadn't even invited anyone, just in case he'd ask me out for a drink after the show.

"He or she?" He queried in English, for in Chinese they sound identical—"*ta*."

"She," I replied.

"That's much better!" he beamed even more broadly. The color of my dress crept into my cheeks: we both understood the implication. And, from the sound of it, he didn't have a girlfriend either. How surprising, a man of his age and position?

The performance was lively and fun, especially the hula-dancing in straw skirts, but I paid more attention to Miao, who stood in the middle of the hall, operating a camera, though he was basically a producer. Liu wasn't there, but several of his colleagues were present, including a famous and attractive newsreader.

During intermission, when I went up to chat, Miao introduced me as "an expert in the English language." He said it in a flattering way, but I wondered if he would be embarrassed to introduce me as a factory worker.

No invitation to share a drink. After the show, he and his colleagues rushed into a van, its neon sign flashing "Jiangsu Provincial Television." But we made an appointment to meet up the following Tuesday, my day off. Before jumping into his van, he reminded me to watch the program the following night.

My eyes never strayed from the screen. *Strolling through the World of Art* was a prime-time program. What a star! Miao presented and narrated the program, which tonight was profiling the highly popular TV series *New Star*, based on a recent successful novel. In it, a Party secretary in a conservative county launches bold reforms as soon as he takes up the position, sacking incompetent officials and offering financial incentives.

While toeing the Party line, the drama gave a realistic picture of bureaucracy and corruption among government officials, and there was plenty of color, even love stories, to keep people watching. When Miao interviewed people in the street (I recognized the road outside his station), they suggested every official across China should watch and learn from the good communist.

I waited anxiously for our date. The day before, to my great disappointment, he called to say he that couldn't make it. But he promised to get in touch soon.

On Wednesday night, the harsh ringing jolted me out of my studies.

"*Wei*, hello?" I said nervously.

"Why did you say hello?" It was Miao! "Did you know it was me?"

"Yes, I did."

He laughed.

"I am finally a free man. Are you free now?"

"Sure!"

"Meet me at Zhonghua Citadel in fifteen minutes," he gave the quick order in Chinese.

The Citadel was only a few minutes' bike ride from my factory. Standing proudly in parts, and crumbling away in others, Nanjing's was the longest extant city wall in the world, thirty-three kilometers of stone that marked the old rural-urban divide. Zhonghua Citadel was its southern gate. As a little girl, I often climbed up there to fly kites with my cousin Weiping. The dragonfly kites he assembled with paper, bamboo, and sticky rice used to soar so high in the sky I feared they would never come home.

With my own spirits rising to similar heights, I turned

up at the citadel. In its shadow stood Miao, sweating and panting heavily.

"Where did you call from?"

"My office."

"My heaven! Did you fly?" That bike journey from north to south across the city could take me half an hour.

"I just couldn't wait to see you," he offered his explanation. As we shook hands, he held onto mine for a moment longer. "Are these typical workers' hands?"

"Yes. They smell of industrial oil if I don't wash them so carefully. And I have to keep my nails very short or they catch lots of grease. Where shall we go?"

"You're the local, you decide."

Here, on the edge of the city, there were no cafés, no teahouses where two people could sit for a chat. The only obvious place was Rain Flower Terrace, the same nearby hilly park that the lovebirds Wu and Xu had reportedly used. Unlike most parks in China, this one had no gates or closing time. We strolled along the main path after parking our bikes.

China's wealth of history and culture attaches a legend to almost every site. The story of Rain Flower Terrace went back to the Liang Dynasty. When Buddhist fever engulfed China, an enlightened monk came here to preach. His devotion converted so many people that heaven above was moved to rain flowers, which colored the pebbles where they fell.

We came to a site that marked butchery rather than beauty—a sculpture of revolutionary martyrs erected on a large raised platform. Like so many Chinese public works, this socialist realist art borrowed heavily from the Soviet Union. Carved from granite, and larger than life, these Communists, men and women, faced death without a flicker of fear: the Rain Flower Terrace was used as an execution ground by the Nationalists when Nanjing became their capital in 1927.

The winning Communists later turned the place into a "patriotic education base," constructing museums and other revolutionary monuments. In school, we came here every spring at Qingming Festival, a traditional time to remember the dead, sweep the tombs of martyrs, recall the Party's hard and glorious struggle to power, and give thanks for the peace and happiness the Party had bestowed.

"You know, I came here to film this statue early this year," said Miao. "I shot a little boy looking up at the sculpture. I like strong contrast, the little boy with the tall statue; something alive and something lifeless."

"What for?"

"Oh, some propaganda stuff." As he talked, he circled his elegant hands to create an imaginary lens. "Some of my colleagues are rather snobbish about cameramen, but I think a camera is the best toy a man can expect."

"Best toy for men, why not women?" I interrupted.

"Oh, you are sharp, hope you're not a feminist? A TV camera is simply too heavy for a woman. All the stations in China only hire men above five foot seven as cameramen." He resumed his theme enthusiastically. "There is something extremely satisfactory about telling your stories through the images you shoot."

"How fortunate when one loves one's job."

"Oh, yeah, I do love my job—very interesting and varied, and we get to meet all kinds of people."

"Such as beautiful actresses?" I suggested, "I saw you interview the stars of *New Star.*"

"Actresses," he shook his head, "you can't beat a fart out of them. Sometimes, we have to put words into their mouths."

"Do you really?"

"Otherwise, there's no story," he cackled. "So, what's it like to work for a rocket factory?"

"What? How do you know that?"

"I know lots of things," he said.

I threw a long look at him. In the semidarkness, I couldn't really see his expression. Had he always known the secret or did he dig it out because of his interest in me?

"You know what? I only saw a rocket once. And my job is boring beyond words."

We followed the paved path toward the top. At one point, we nearly bumped into each other. Just as quickly, we parted.

I explained my situation, and my frustration. "Sometimes I feel I'll go crazy if I stay there any longer."

"But you won't go crazy. When we were down in the village 'repairing the earth,' the situation was desperate. You can't imagine it. In the end, just about everyone survived." He talked about his rural exile and how he once nearly died, but for a barefoot doctor. Then, he turned to me, "I envy you for one thing, too—time. I want to study English, but work takes all my time."

"Why do you want to study English?" I asked.

"I want to go abroad to study, and then work in TV or film as a director. I like to boss people around. At times I also feel I'll go crazy if I stay at my TV station any longer. You can't imagine the restrictions, this not allowed, that not allowed; and there's plenty of rubbish to cover. I'll have to get out. Ideally, to America."

Chairman Mao once proudly declared, "The East wind prevails over the West wind." But the winds had reversed. Many educated people began to yearn for Western countries, in particular America, *Meiguo*, the beautiful country, in Chinese. After China opened its doors, we realized that, in this first-rank imperialist country we used to despise so much, people enjoyed a much higher standard of living than in China, far more advanced technology, as well as greater freedom, democracy, and civil rights. Overwhelmed, many began to admire America and the American way of life. The lucky ones with families or relatives abroad packed and left the country for a better life across the ocean. And many graduates tried to win scholarships to further their study in America.

"Why are you studying English? To go to America?" he asked.

"Me, going to America? Of course not. Impossible!" I confessed to him my "tool of struggle" plan: my hope to leave the factory by learning English and landing a job with a foreign-invested company.

"That sounds good."

It was one of those clear, warm nights in early autumn. An unseen cricket chorus washed over Rain Flower Terrace, somehow intensifying the silence. No human noise. We sat down on a bench near the peak, staring at the full golden moon hanging high in the sky.

"*Nijisui?*" He broke the silence, asking "how old are you?" but with a phrase used only for children.

"Three!" I giggled. "Actually, the ripe age of twenty-three." I was in fact only twenty-two, but the Chinese count a year inside one's mother.

"Little baby! I am thirty this year."

As he spoke, he carved the muddy ground with a stick. It took me a while to understand what he wrote: "Zhang Lijia, little friend." There is a prescribed order for the strokes that make up each Chinese character, from left to right, and top to bottom. But he wrote these characters in exactly the opposite order.

"Aiya, how did you do it?"

"Nothing, just a small trick," he demurred. "My parents made me do this to improve my memory. Later, while down in the countryside, I did lots of writing in the mud so that I wouldn't forget my characters. There were no pens or paper there."

It was getting late. We ought to have gone. But it was good to sit here in the quiet of the night and the music of his voice.

"Now tell me, what did you think of my program?" He changed the subject.

"Very impressive. My only suggestion is that your cameraman should not shoot from the side—it shows your 'general's belly,' you know."

"How dare you! My belly isn't that big yet!" he said with a grin and a pat of his belly. "Too many free banquets. My pot began to grow only after I joined the station."

"Also, there was that long shot of you walking up to vox-pop a couple. It stressed the funny way you waddle, like this," I got up to exaggerate his swaying amble. "No wonder you are named after Charlie Chaplin!" I burst out laughing.

He sprang up, too, making as if to hit me with his stick. I started to run away and he gave chase, laughing. When he caught me, he pulled me into his arms. He clumsily planted random kisses on my face. I kissed him back on the lips. It wasn't quite one of those masterful, heartthrobbing kisses one could watch in American films. Still, I felt so dizzy with happiness I had to rest my head on his shoulder.

When I lifted up my head, I said: "I don't understand why you haven't got a girlfriend, even with your potbelly." I could tell he was not an experienced kisser.

"I am simply too busy. Don't you know that falling in love is a game for those who have money and time?"

That was a famous line from *Fortress Besieged*.

"Were you also tricked by the moonlight tonight?" I questioned him nervously. The novel's hero, Fang Hongjiang, is fooled by the romance of the moon into kissing a girl he doesn't love.

"You silly melon, don't be too sensitive," he said gently. "I'm not a romantic like you. I just haven't met anyone who is as special as you."

His sweet talk hit the spot.

Chapter 21

Clouds and Rain

I stared at the telephone on Boss Lan's table, wondering if it would ever ring again. Miao had promised to call tonight, but it was eight already. Since I had fallen in love, the telephone had become my lifeline. I could call his office, but he was always out somewhere, interviewing or shooting on location. So I waited for his calls, infrequent at the best of times. During work hours, whenever my colleagues picked up the phone and called out "Zhang Lijia!" in badly mimicked standard Mandarin, my heart would leap up and then sink back down when I heard someone else's voice on the other end.

Then, unbelievably, the phone rang. "Meet me at the old place in fifteen minutes," came his deep voice.

Closing my books, I fled through the door like a gust of wind. Downstairs, under a ginkgo tree, I ran into Old Pan, on his way to my workshop with books under his arms. Months earlier, he had professed his love to me in a beautifully written poem. I had let him down as gently as I could. I held enormous affection and gratitude for him— he and his poems had saved me—but he never inspired sparks of love, even before Miao waddled into my life.

"Going out?" In the light from a downstairs workshop, the ginkgo cast faint, fan-shaped shadows on his face.

"Yes, I am meeting a friend, my boyfriend, actually." I was glowing with excitement.

He dropped his head, as if hit by some invisible force. "Sorry, I keep bothering you."

"No, no, I do want you to be my friend." I wished I could give him a friendly hug like friends did in foreign films. I still gladly read books he recommended, even though I focused my energy on studying English. Although our conversations were never personal, it was true that I might have given him some false hope. I had wanted to tell him about Miao, yet found it awkward to bring it up.

In Miao's arms, I soon forgot the heavy heart I had left under the gingko tree. Like other young lovers, we began to venture further into the dense woods of the Rain Flower Terrace.

One night, when Miao and I passed my factory on our way there, a daring idea made me screech to a halt. "Want to see my workshop?"

"Sure!" came his reply, "but how about the armed guards?"

"Just listen to me," I told him confidently, handing over my pass. "When you come to the gates, briefly dismount, like a dragonfly skimming the surface of the water, and flash the pass without showing the photo inside. Be calm and confident, and don't look at the guards. Got it?" I pulled up the corner of his coat to cover his long hair. The guards, unlike the secret police, had no right to interfere with an employee's hair. But it would certainly arouse suspicion.

Miao got in without any problem: confidence was never something he lacked.

"Sorry, I left my pass at home," I lied with my sweetest smile to the sentries. "I am from Work Unit Number Twenty-three." They were not nearly as frightening as they looked at first, particularly after I spotted a few of the young soldiers off-duty, strolling hand in hand: it was common for friends of the same sex to hold hands in public.

They had seen me before and waved me in. I rode in, wiping cold sweat on my forehead. If we were caught, the punishment would be severe.

Up in my workshop, I showed him how I checked the pressure gauges. Miao, listening, tried out one testing device. On top of my desk, he also spied my calligraphy set. Good handwriting was a reflection of one's education and sophistication. Conscious that mine was hardly an asset, I had recently started to practice calligraphy, encouraged by my friend Liu Weidong. Another of my efforts to cultivate myself and make good use of time: whenever my colleagues were too loud for me to study English, I would take up brush and ink.

"Calligraphy, just 'a plate of pickle,'" he boasted. "At fourteen, I won a big calligraphy competition. Shall I write a few characters for you to copy? Go on, make some ink for me."

I poured a little water onto an ink slab and began to grind it with an inkstone. For two thousand years, that had been the traditional way to prepare for the calligrapher's art, and it still provided better quality than ready-made ink.

While I softened the brush in a jar of water, he grinned at me. "Look, we are like a classic couple from the olden days! The ancient scholar always had a beauty to make the ink for him." Tracing each stroke with ease and grace, he began to write on the thin and absorbent calligraphy paper.

"Hai, fantastic!" My praise was wholehearted. "When did you begin to practice?"

"Since I was a child. My parents thought I was a genius so they made me learn all kinds of things. I began piano lessons when I was four. Didn't you ever learn a musical instrument?"

"Sadly no." At primary school, an enthusiastic music teacher once offered to teach me *pipa*, a plucked string instrument with a fretted fingerboard, for I had long, slim fingers. But Ma said we couldn't spare any money.

"Shame. A pipa costs nothing." It must be difficult for the son of a university professor to imagine life in a poor, working-class family.

"When you have your own child one day, send her to study music with me. All children should learn music, so that they'll appreciate the beauty of music when they grow up."

I let out a sour laugh. "She has nothing to do with you?"

"Oh, come on, you silly melon. Did I rule out the possibility I am the father?" He tickled me and I giggled. "Let's not talk about things too distant. Go on, it's your turn to write something."

Under his watchful eye, I gripped the brush and tried hard to trace out a few decent characters.

"Relax, you can't be so tense." He looked at my efforts and laughed. "Your handwriting is like a child's!"

I blushed. Next to his beautiful characters, my weak pictographs just magnified the gap between us—I was catching up with things he had already mastered in childhood.

"Let's pretend we are a classic couple," he sat me on his lap and held my hand. "Use the strength in your wrist. Before each stroke, try to work out the composition in your head. Steady."

I followed his instruction, relishing this unusual intimacy. Soon he began reaching inside my clothes. I tolerated his invading hands, even enjoying the sensation, until his grip grew tight. Breathing heavily, he tried to unzip my trousers. Startled by the violence of his actions, I stood to fight back: my arms had grown quite strong from wielding wrenches daily. I scratched his hands with my fingernails to free his grip. He refused, despite the dripping blood. Outraged, I turned to my last weapon— my teeth. He screamed and let go.

Sitting limply back in my chair, he looked like a defeated animal. "I, I'm so very sorry," he said after catching his breath. "I was overpowered by this urge I've never felt before. I am terribly ashamed of myself."

For a while I stood, stunned by what had happened. But looking at his bleeding hands and the bruise in his arm where I had sunk my teeth, I began to feel sorry for him. I went up to him to clean his wounds with my handkerchief. He embraced me and buried his head in my arms. "I love you!" He uttered the three words for the first time. Almost a whisper.

That whisper of love was enough for me to decide that Miao was going to be the first man in my life. When we had cuddled in the dense woods, and his breathing had become heavy, I knew what he was up to. But he had made no demands and his hands had never crept under my clothes. My own curious nature had often tempted me: I was restless from reading the love scenes in novels I had been devouring. I wanted to experience the rain and clouds with a man I loved. I had been waiting for too long.

I turned around to turn off the lamp on my desk. The comforting blanket of darkness enveloped us. I took Miao's bloodstained hand and guided it down.

"Why?" He asked.

"I love you." I replied, pulling off his jumper.

We lay down on an old wooden board, passed down to me by Ma, who used to sleep on it after lunch at the factory. It was the only useful part of her professional legacy—I had never made much use of her advice or the toolbox. But what would she think if she knew how I was using it? Oh, my poor mother, you have to forgive me. You were not allowed much fun in your life, but I would take matters into my own hands.

"Do you really love me?" I asked breathlessly.

"I love you, of course I do!" His voice quivered with emotion as he struggled to undo my bra.

Ever since I was a young girl, I had fantasized about my wedding night. In the glow of red candlelight, my bridegroom and I would sip wine from nuptial cups. (Even the discovery that I was allergic to alcohol had failed to dim this romantic illusion.) My marital bed would be silk-lined, shiny, and inviting. Roses in full blossom would radiate a sweet, heartfelt scent and the double happiness character would beam from a hundred paper cutouts.

But I became a "bride" on a hard wooden board, on the floor of my workshop, where the air was rank with industrial grease and the only wall decoration was a yellowing list of the rules I was breaking.

With his shaking hands, Miao removed my clothes one layer after another, like peeling petals from a flower. Naked now against the smooth, cold plank, I shivered, waiting for the long-anticipated ritual. Miao, once again, transformed into a charged animal, kissing and sniffing my body up and down, desperate to declare his physical love, searching for the right place—the "jade gate" as the Chinese poetically called it. When he finally did, I was struck by such a sharp pain that I screamed: nothing I had read prepared me for such agony. He stopped short and gagged me with his hand lest we disturb the watchman at the other end of the building.

"Sorry. I am so sorry," he murmured as he reluctantly withdrew. We held each other in darkness until his excitement subsided.

It was not my first night after all.

A few days later, we desperate lovers were back at my military sanctuary. We could have gone to Rain Flower Terrace, but it wasn't totally safe, since security patrols scoured the forest every night with powerful flashlights

to catch the "immoral" acts of unlucky lovers. A friend
from TV University was caught once in the small hours
of the night. She sat, fully dressed, on a stone bench with
a married engineer from her work unit on whom she had
a crush. But they were hauled to the local police station
and detained until their bosses were called. The incident
grew into a great sex scandal, although a doctor certified
that her hymen was intact. Also, it was getting too cold for
an outdoor tryst. We couldn't go to a hotel either, since
we would need a marriage certificate to get a room. Why
not risk my workshop again?

Better prepared this time, we eventually reunited on my
bridal board. The medical journals I had bought advised
first-timers to open the "jade gate" as wide as possible. My
muffled groans, of pain and growing pleasure, quickened
with the creaking complaints of the board as he penetrated
deep into my body. Both sounds were drowned out by the
spinning machines on the floor below. The shift workers
continued their nightly routine, while above their heads
I broke with mine, radically.

Miao offered to bike home with me for the first time, but
I declined because he had a long ride back to his parents'
flat at Nanjing University near Drum Tower Square. When
I rushed down the slope from the back gate, I felt I was
flying. Master Li, I'm a fox fairy now! I smiled to myself
in the darkness. How about Political Instructor Wang?
Nothing less than a "shameful and immoral act that can't
be tolerated by our country's law or the factory rules."
Screw the rules!

"I must have done something good!" I burst out singing
in my ecstasy, from the *Sound of Music*.

I wished I could sing aloud to the entire world: "I'm
a real woman now!"

Chapter 22

An Unsettling Time

"The students have taken to the streets!" Life lit up Big Zhang's sleepy eyes as he walked into our workshop one morning in mid-December. Blazing with excitement, Zhang described the demonstrations that had spread to our city from nearby Hefei in Anhui province.

Not that China's own media dared report. Only furtively, by shortwave radio—the BBC and the Voice of America—could Big Zhang pick up news of such disobedience. He paced up and down our workshop, bashing his enamel bowl with a metal spoon. "A movement!" he shouted. "It's time for a movement!"

He borrowed both the line and the action from an opportunist character in the hit film *Hibiscus Town*, who exploited the turmoil of the Cultural Revolution. In the final scene, however, the hooligan turns mad, calling for a "movement" up and down the town's narrow stone path. Mass movements in China have always left masses of victims behind.

"Aiya!" Boss Lan burst in breathlessly. "So many students at Drum Tower Square…"

"What are they doing? Are policemen trying to stop them?" I cut in.

"They are chanting slogans, wanting democracy! Democracy, can you believe it! Lots of policemen around, but not doing anything. The whole city center is snarled up, totally. So I got off my bus and walked all the way here." He filed his report, sitting on the wooden plank to change into slippers.

"Indeed, it's a movement!" Zhang shouted again excitedly.

"Have you taken the wrong medicine or what?" Lan snapped at Zhang.

"I'm not mad," Zhang roared. "You saw the students' movement with your own eyes. Don't you feel angry that we common people are made to suffer high inflation while corrupt officials and their families make huge, illegal profits?"

"Angry? What good is it to be angry?" said Boss Lan, putting on his white coat.

"Well, show your anger to the government, then. Don't be so indifferent." Zhang continued his speech, unheeding, as if delivering it to a large audience. "Our government hangs up a sheep's head but sells dog meat. Reform, improving people's living standards? How wonderful! Indeed, indeed! The simple fact is that we workers are working harder now, but our living standards are going down!"

"True," Master Lin added his gentle voice. "Before, I fed my whole family with my salary, no problem. But now, without any side income, they would eat chaff for half the year." His wife's family had rented a fishpond, which was bringing in some cash. While farmers had more or less benefited from Deng's reforms, many city workers did not share their joy. The recent talk of breaking the iron rice bowl only increased their anxiety.

"A movement is sweeping across China like a fire, in Hefei, Nanjing, Shanghai, and Beijing," Zhang declared solemnly. "We must support them!"

Among my colleagues, Zhang alone was interested in current affairs and politics. His excitement seemed exaggerated but real. In a strictly controlled society like ours, it was both shocking and fascinating to see anyone dare protest against the government.

My good friend Zhou Fang, also a shortwave-radio listener, kept me informed. The fire was sparked two weeks earlier by students from the prestigious Chinese University of Science and Technology in Hefei. They protested at their exclusion from the process of electing student union leaders and candidates for the provincial People's Congress, the puppet legislature that approved every Communist Party decision.

There had been growing signs of activism. Fang Lizhi, one of the university's vice presidents, was both a renowned astrophysicist and a passionate advocate of democracy. "Democracy is not granted from the top, but won by individuals," he famously urged. Professor Fang had been touring universities around the country, captivating audiences with shocking statements such as "The socialist movement, from Marx, to Lenin, to Stalin and Mao Zedong, failed." Free from the authorities' censorship, his daring lectures roused waves of excitement among students, who swarmed to him like moths drawn out of the darkness by a bright light.

In the wake of the Hefei protest, university students had responded in seventeen other cities across the country. How exciting! Too exciting to sit still. I asked leave from Boss Lan, using my flexitime.

"You're going to see the demonstration, right?" he guessed. "But just watch, don't get involved."

I called Fang at her workshop but she couldn't get away. Another friend, the tax officer Jiang He, agreed immediately, as I thought he would. We had often discussed the restless campus scene. "I was just thinking of calling you," he said.

Before leaving the workshop, I turned to Zhang. "Would you like to come along?"

He thought hard, but shook his head. "I'd better save my flexitime," he reasoned, resuming his usual lazy tone. "My wife is very pregnant. I'll need time off when the baby comes."

"Don't be so indifferent?" taunted Boss Lan, with a girlish giggle. "So typical of you! You can only make the noise of thunder, never the real rain."

The crowds grew thicker at New Street, right in the city center near Jiang He's tax bureau. I parked my bike and pressed on to Drum Tower Square, the heart of the action, with my old friend. "I have been watching all morning from my office window," he explained, his bright eyes glittering with excitement.

Jiang was a classmate from school and the first friend I ever made as an adult. Before, friendship meant sharing sunflower seeds and secrets that only mattered to little girls. Jiang was not only a playmate to enjoy outings with—we talked about everything and anything that interested or troubled us. I often popped over to his messy flat by Wuding Bridge, at the foot of the city wall, and roughly on my way home from the factory. There he would fire challenging questions and opinions at me. After China introduced a new enterprise tax to replace the fixed-profit remittance system, Jiang remembered that we used to equate tax with capitalism. No individual or enterprises paid any tax under Chinese communism. But changes were rolling in at a speed that dazzled people like Jiang who bothered to follow them all.

Jiang on his long legs, walked fast, urging me to hurry up. "Don't straggle along like a bound-foot granny!"

"But there's so much to see!"

Under the arch of parasol trees, thousands of students from Nanjing's major universities marched. They held flags and banners aloft, demanding: "We want real elections! We want democracy!"; "Get rid of corruption!"; "Control inflation!"; "Oppose nepotism!"

Like thousands of other onlookers, we followed and cheered the students from the sidewalk. Though most of the Old Hundred Names were less than interested in abstract concepts like democracy and human rights, they echoed the students' complaints. "It takes more than three days to freeze three inches of ice." Social discontent had been building for some time. Our society was battered by rampant graft, rising crime, and spiraling inflation, as well as ideological confusion. Many people were outraged that the fruits of reform were so unfairly distributed.

There was a sea of people at the Drum Tower Square. I elbowed my way through the thick crowds so that I could see the speakers while Jiang He stood tall at the back. Uncomfortable with his height, he often deliberately bent his legs in front of others. For once, he didn't have to.

"For thousands of years, we have accepted the system of dictatorship we inherited," a small student with a surprising sonorous voice was shouting excitedly to the microphone. "What have the reforms given us? What has Deng Xiaoping granted us? A little bit of freedom to make money. He does loosen our bonds now and then. But it's not enough. The whole system has not changed: it's the same old medicine with slight change of broth. We want true democracy—that's our basic human right. Only with democracy will China truly stand up and will Chinese become fully human!"

"Long live the democracy!" the crowds chanted.

By early afternoon, we were tired and hungry, our voices hoarse. But we simply couldn't desert this dramatic scene. We climbed a small hill inside Drum Tower Park to eat steamed buns stuffed with meat and vegetables.

The sky was high, the clouds pale. A thick layer of leaves covered the park, but no snow had yet fallen. A group of wild geese cried overhead, flying south before the real winter chill, expected any day. Their flying V formation resembled the Chinese character "*ren*"— people.

Looking at the formation, I said to Jiang He: "See, we are not fully human yet."

He laughed, spitting out the bun stuffing.

"Will democracy really work wonders, do you think?" I asked.

"I don't know. But I do think the lack of democracy has slowed down economic development."

I knew he was puzzled over Deng Xiaoping's creation of a "market economy with Chinese characteristics." "What does it mean?" he had once asked. "How can central planning and market regulation work together?"

Another loud cheer rose from the square. We looked down on the forest of student arms, rising and falling with each chant.

"I've never been to a protest before," I said.

"I have been to marches, but never protests," said Jiang.

The only marches we had attended were those organized by our schools or danwei, celebrating national anniversaries or Socialist achievements. How thrilling it must be to march in the street out of one's own will and shout something from one's heart.

We ate our stuffed buns, dreaming about an impossible world full of all kinds of freedoms and rights. From my colleague Big Zhang, I had heard that when Shanghai students demonstrated in the streets, they demanded that official newspapers report their protest truthfully.

"If we get freedom of the press, I'll certainly try to be a journalist," I declared with childish enthusiasm. "Can you imagine how exciting it would be to cover events like this?"

Among those hundred flowers recently blossomed in the literary garden was the country's first real investigative journalism, a movement led by Liu Binyan, a veteran journalist. Written in a literary style, his report "Between Man and Monsters" exposed a corrupt official who took bribes and embezzled several million yuan of public funds. It took the whole nation by storm and made Liu a household name. People loved such investigative stories even more than best-selling novels, for in a country where "mandarins can play with fire while commoners can't even light their oil lamps," as an old saying suggested, it was deeply satisfying to see officials and their corrupt ways exposed.

When I dreamed of becoming a journalist as a schoolgirl, it was because I thought I could write well and, perhaps naïvely, saw the glamorous side of being a "king without a crown," as journalists were sometimes called in Chinese. Those articles inspired me, and kept my childhood dream alive, although I knew my immediate goal was leaving the factory.

After that monumental night, I had expected a call, a note, or something like that from him. But nothing. A stone sinking into the ocean. I knew that Miao was working on location, filming the year's biggest TV show—the Spring Festival gala, which had become an integral part of China's Spring Festival celebration in recent years. Every local station copied the same format, competing to put on the best show with the biggest stars. But he was still in town. How could he ignore me after what had happened between us?

I became even more absentminded. Once, after finishing a gauge check, I forgot to loosen the valve. When I began unscrewing the gauge from the connector, oil shot out from the pipeline and splattered my white coat. Boss Lan hurried over to help mop up. "Be careful, Little Zhang. Are you daydreaming?"

I was, all the time. It was almost unbearable to stay alone at the workshop in the evening. The thought of him was a cricket hidden in the corner—I couldn't see it, but the noise was constant. I would stare at the floor, recalling every detail of our lovemaking.

After nearly three weeks, which registered as eternity, a call from Miao summoned me to a room in a smart hotel in the city center, where he was working on the gala.

"How are you doing, my silly melon?" When I turned up, he greeted me happily. Wasting no time, he pulled me straight toward his bed.

I pushed him away. "Why didn't you call me?"

"I've been too busy," he replied. "We've only had a few hours' sleep every night."

"Too busy to make a phone call?"

"I tried to call you many times, but your factory's line was always busy. Now I remember the number by heart." He repeated it. Correct. It was indeed hard to reach, though my extension was rarely busy.

"Come on, come to bed with me at once," he ordered.

When he held me in his arms, I began to cry. "I hate you for torturing me like this," I hit his chest. "You don't know how much I missed you."

Holding me tightly, he caressed me till I calmed down. Then, he took off his clothes and stood proudly in front of me, as if waiting for inspection. At my workshop, we had made love in the darkness. Now, in the gentle light filtering through the curtain, I saw a man's naked body for the first time. Like most Chinese men, he had little body hair apart from the private patch from which his manhood protruded unapologetically.

"You poor little girl. I'm sorry I can't play with you all the time." He embraced me. The warmth of his body softened me and the little kisses he planted on my neck released a tingle down my body.

"Did you miss me?" I asked as he hurriedly undressed me.

"Of course, I did, but you talk too much. I'm a man of action!"

The hotel taps defeated me. I came back for Miao's help, but found him blissfully asleep. He looked nicer in that state, his arrogance absent. I retreated to the bathroom and eventually succeeded in filling the tub for my first-ever bath. Soaking in the bubbles, I rubbed myself with creamy soap, feeling conscious of my body. I stayed there for what seemed like hours, enjoying a luxury I could never taste at home and reliving my newfound pleasures.

He was still asleep when I came out. I nudged him, tickled, and kissed him. "Hey, sleepyhead, wake up and talk to me."

Turning his body, he dragged me into the bed.

"Did you go see the demonstration yesterday?" I asked. "I heard there was a clash with the police. What happened, do you know?" Only a few days remained of 1986. Just the day before, another protest had erupted, drawing large crowds and police onto Nanjing's streets. The government seemed unsure about what to do, particularly since Hu Yaobang, the liberal-minded General Secretary of the Communist Party, appeared sympathetic toward the students.

"What? What demonstration?" He half-opened his eyes, squinting at me.

"What demonstration? The student demonstration, of course."

Suddenly fully awake, he brushed my arm off his chest. "How annoying! You woke me up just for the damned demonstration!"

My face turned from pink to red, irritated by the harsh tone. "I woke you up because I wanted to talk to you. I haven't seen you for weeks."

"Okay, talk about something sweet, not goddamned politics!"

"But aren't you amazed by the demonstration?"

"You silly melon! Why do you bother your little brain with such matters?" He turned his back to me and was about to fall asleep again. Was this the same man who recently had complained so bitterly about censorship?

Only after I threatened to leave and never return did he try to wake up and face me.

"I did hear the noises from the hotel. But I didn't have time to go out." He sat up in the bed without his glasses on, which made him look very different and somehow distant.

"You sound disinterested."

"This system does not allow me to be that interested. What can I do? Join in the demonstration, write a letter in support? I'd lose my job in no time."

I reminded him that, for centuries, China's intellectuals and scholars had been responsible for telling the ruler what his people needed, and advising him on the right course. I borrowed the sentence from an article by Fang Lizhi, the outspoken scientist, in which he criticized Chinese intellectuals for their weakness and lack of independence.

"Social responsibility? Sure," Miao agreed, "those who have a noble vision for making China better may be ready to make sacrifices, to try do something. But not me." He put on his glasses, as if they would help him think straight. "Once, when I was still down in the countryside, we were summoned to attend a meeting. It was all about learning from some hero—I can't remember his name now—anyway, some stupid egg who didn't deserve to be remembered. Supposedly, he was swept away by floods for trying to save a log. Yes, a log! A goddamn log. And I thought to myself, 'Why? Is my life worth less than a log?' This is a government that didn't and still doesn't know how to respect its people. You just wait and see, there will be a crackdown," he promised, chopping the air with his hand as he warmed to the theme. The student protest, he continued, was like "cracking a stone with an egg"—destined to fail, he predicted, because the Party would not tolerate anything that threatened their power. The student leaders would suffer. If they weren't locked up, they would at least be kicked out of their universities, with a permanent black mark on their files. And the worst thing was that nothing would change.

"I have wasted enough time 'repairing the earth.' If anything, I am now more determined to get out of this fucking country!" He slipped down in the bed. Soon his snoring grated on my ears.

I couldn't reach him.

I started to call him Chilly.

As the real winter chill set in, China's political atmosphere also turned cold. Party Secretary Hu Yaobang was ousted by hard-liners for condoning the student protests. The only result of the students' brave efforts was a harsh crackdown on bourgeois liberalism that punished intellectuals such as Fang Lizhi and my hero, journalist Liu Binyan, just as Miao had predicted.

Chapter 23

Party Passport

In a white chef's hat, Jiang He was grilling lamb kebabs over an iron trough of charcoal. The kebabs sizzled on bamboo sticks, sending columns of mouthwatering smoke into the air. He turned them swiftly to grill the other side, sprinkling on salt, chili powder, and cumin.

Without a license, or the slightest experience making kebabs, Jiang, the tax officer, had decided to open a kebab stall during the Spring Festival. He set up his stand in the square facing Confucius Temple and overlooking the Qinhuai River, which had been turned into an open-air food market. Steam escaped from circular bamboo steamers and half the sky flamed red with the flames from oil-drum stoves. Dozens of different stalls sold traditional Nanjing snacks: flavored sticky rice wrapped in lotus leaves, duck feet in five-spice sauce, and shredded bean curd with dried shrimp. Thanks to these famous snacks, Nanjing people had long earned the reputation of being *haochi*, loving good food, which came with a slightly negative connotation. In our defense, we would quote an ancestral saying: "The masses regard food as their heaven."

Jiang's only spot of trouble was lighting the charcoal on the first day, but a man selling dumplings at the next stall showed him how to light some newspaper first. After that, his venture had charged ahead with barely a hiccup—but plenty of satisfied burps.

Sun Ju, a classmate of ours, and I came to help as cashiers. It was no simple task. People stuffed money in our faces, as if fighting for the best bargain in the world. "Ten kebabs please, with chili." "Serve me first, I came earlier than he did!" Pushing away the intrusive arms, Ju was in her element, her cheeks crimson with excitement. "Stop it! Push, push, what for? Are you dying from hunger?" Even as her mouth spouted insults, her sparkling eyes smiled.

Ju and I used to share a desk. She happily gave up education after junior middle school to take over her mother's job as a clerk with the city's Sanitation and Management Bureau. As implied by her name, "chrysanthemum," Ju was a bubbly beauty, with a robust body and round breasts like the fragrant melons of South China. Yet night after night, she was content chatting with her mother and cracking melon seeds at home.

Two years ago a class reunion had brought us back together, and we now formed a gang of three. They went along with some of my crazier ideas, like swimming in the river as a storm raged overhead, or cycling for hours to visit ancient towns outside Nanjing.

As always, we were working well as a team, but I had joined the kebab venture simply to keep myself occupied. My romance was withering.

After the hotel-room episode, we settled into a routine: Miao would call and we would meet up, usually at the hotel. Instead of feeling grateful, like an emperor's chosen lady, I walked in complaining, seemingly the only thing in my power to do, since it was he who decided if, when, and where we would meet. My complaining, indeed, became our foreplay—there was no other ceremony before our clouds-and-rain session. In a matter of minutes, the clouds would disappear, the rain would pour, and he would fall into sound sleep, leaving me wondering why the occasional bits of racy literature I had read suggested something so exciting. He no longer bothered with any sweet talk.

The harder I tried to play a role in his life, the more we argued. I knew he wanted to go abroad and that I wasn't part of his plan. But my girlish vanity made me hesitate when I thought about leaving him: wasn't he a successful man, even a little famous?

If I'd idled at home, I'd have focused too much on troubling thoughts. There was little hope of seeing him over the festival—he was consumed by work.

Cheered by the bright red lanterns that decorated every shop front, I caught the festival spirit, which was prevailing, barely, over the gray sky and biting wind. Down the street, a blind masseur in a stained white coat was slapping a man's bald head; close by a dentist stood behind a table laden with tools, waiting for brave patients; a professional ear-picker coaxed wax from a client's ear, his head tilted before the metal probe, one eye tight shut till the painful tickle eased into deep satisfaction. Every kind of service meant money. Capitalism was singing triumphantly everywhere.

Money, money, money. People grew anxious and restless like ants on a hot pan. Even my literary friend Old Pan, who seemed to occupy a vague poetic world beyond earthy concerns, had tried—and failed—to run a fruit business. After being transferred from his cushy old post to a newly established bellows-expansion unit (he used to turn up only for class), Pan dreamed of making some quick money, then staying home to write. But he couldn't bring himself to cheat buyers as his partner, a former student, urged. Pan's misadventure closed after a single day.

Others showed more persistence in seizing new opportunities. Burning with acquisitiveness, Fitter Chen was the first among my friends to "jump into the sea," the popular term for anyone who gave up a steady state job for the risky business of private enterprise. He joined a so-called "suitcase company," buying and selling steel, fertilizer, and construction materials. Tens of thousands of such firms, each commanding little more than a suitcase, had surfaced across the country like a skin rash. Most disappeared just as quickly. Because of rapid industrial growth and an overheated economy, China was enduring an acute shortage of raw materials. Anyone who had access to materials in demand could make a fortune.

Even my friend Fang and I were swept along by the crazy wind. "Look, one of my father's colleagues heard someone needs polystyrene," she would call to say. "Could you ask around for a supplier?" I would then call Jiang He, Fitter Chen, my brother-in-law, his mates, my neighbors, basically everyone I knew. All such searches were wild goose chases, we eventually realized, and gave up.

But Jiang He was never really affected by the money craze. His kebab venture was more for a laugh than real profit. Every so often, he would urge Ju and me to take a break.

Arm in arm, we sampled our favorite snacks and wandered in the wake of the visitors who had descended from all over the city. The main streets, free from all vehicles, were packed with the bobbing black heads of merrymakers. Besieged by human energy and bustle, I found some comfort in the crowd.

The neighborhoods around Confucius Temple were becoming a hot spot for tourists. Framed by gray-tiled roofs and white walls with tops shaped vaguely like horse heads, the Ming- and Qing-era architecture had been restored along the main streets and riverbank. For the past thousand years, prostitutes had frequented this part of the river in fancy little dragon boats.

We visited the restored house of Fragrant Li, one of the eight most famous beauties of Qinhuai. Though it had been more than three hundred years since her death, her sweet scent did seem to linger between the pages of her books and on the instruments she once plucked so sensually. A traditional four-poster bed, carved in beautiful relief, offered a handy stage for people to imagine her epic tale of love with a talented young scholar. He betrayed her by surrendering to the Qing Dynasty, and in an angry rage, she destroyed her beautiful face, and therefore her livelihood, with a blade, but won herself eternal glory.

"Why do women always devote themselves to men who disappoint them?" I sighed to myself. From the window, I watched the modern dragon boats on the Qinhuai, hurrying tourist groups up and down the river, loudspeakers squawking out names and dates. Any trace of the river's romantic past was buried in the buzz of commerce. Even the river itself, once renowned for a shade of crystal green that inspired many poets, was now murky with industrial pollution.

An era without poetry.

At Beijing Mutton Restaurant, a row of glass jars caught my attention. In them, various intriguing objects soaked in yellowish alcohol: a coiled snake, a lizard, ginseng.

"Fancy any?" Jiang He asked.

"No, no, thank you very much," I said, waving my hands ferociously.

My friend was treating me to a big dinner, for my contribution to his kebab venture. And it was a real treat: like my fellow workers, I almost never ate out. The restaurant was a popular state-owned establishment, always crowded, although there were no reservations as such. If the tables were full, you would wait by the table with the least food left, begging the diners to leave with your hungry eyes. We were lucky. When the waitress spotted my friend's blue-gray tax officer's uniform, a table was set up for us in a corner.

Bright lights shone ruthlessly on the sweaty diners and illuminated the only decoration on the greasy wall—a scroll reading "Serve the people with your whole heart and whole mind." Yet the service was such that diners cleaned their own tables and fetched themselves bowls and chopsticks. Shouts rained down on every waitress who emerged from the blackened door leading to the kitchen. "Where is our food?" Without even looking up, she would shout back "Are you blind or what? Can't you see I am busy?"

Jiang He had been to this restaurant before. The more complicated China's tax system became, the more powerful the tax officers were, and thus the more frequently he dined out with various company bosses. He casually dipped a few thin slices of lamb into the copper hot pot, round and pregnant with burning charcoal, then stirred the meat in the soup boiling in the moat-like trough circling the pot. A final dip, in a saucer of sesame sauce, and into his mouth.

"Cheers!" My teacup and his beer glass clinked in the air.

After only one glass, his color started to rise. "I've just had the worst blow in my life, you know," he began slowly.

"What happened?" I had sensed that he wanted to discuss something serious when I found that Ju had not been invited.

"I've told you, haven't I? I wanted to get a master's degree in business at Nanjing University. But my danwei rejected my application."

Without a letter of introduction, he couldn't sit for the exam.

"Oh, no. Do you know why?"

"I think so." He lit a cigarette and frowned as the smoke climbed up his face. A heavy smoker, he stuck to Big Harvest, a cheap, strong Chinese brand—through his position, he could've secured desirable foreign cigarettes, but he dismissed them as not satisfying enough.

Last summer, Jiang He leapt into stardom at his tax bureau when he was awarded a degree in finance and economy from the Teach-Yourself University after just two years. His bosses needed someone like him to inspire others to devote themselves to the nation's modernization drive. Before long, the Communist Party secretary at the Bureau invited him to apply for Party membership. But Jiang refused. "What?" spluttered the experienced Party worker, rejecting the "great, glorious, and always correct" Chinese Communist Party? Why? Jiang had explained he was unsure whether joining the Party was what he wanted. He was sent home to reconsider. He returned with the same negative answer.

I remembered how that he had mentioned this, in a throwaway line last autumn. I had been immersed in my love affair, too distracted to respond properly. Still, I thought he was crazy. So did everyone else, save his father, a Party member himself.

"Didn't you understand the consequences?" I asked, raising my voice above the restaurant's bustle.

"I knew there would be some negative influence on my career, but not to what extent. I thought, naïvely, that it was a personal choice."

"Even I could tell you it's not personal. Why don't you come up with some excuse, say you aren't good enough for Party membership, pretend you're Christian, or something?"

Jiang assumed his characteristic expression, a childlike smile.

China's faith in communism had been crumbling like Nanjing's city wall. In a joke then circling via the small road, a son asked his father, "Dad, where is communism?" The father answered, "Can you see the edge of the sky, my son? That's communism. It does exist but you'll never reach it." Still, no one rejected the opportunity to join the Party. Membership meant, among other things, a fast-track career. That was why Party membership was often referred to as a Party passport.

"Do you know how my mother went mad?" he asked abruptly.

His mother looked rather mad, her short, wild hair sticking out like hedgehog prickles. Once I bumped into her at Jiang's flat, and she turned slowly, looked directly into my eyes, and squeezed my shoulders. He apologized afterward, explaining, "Her brain isn't normal." But I'd never known how, or why.

Taking his time, Jiang He told me the story. When he was a child, he accidentally broke a porcelain bust of Lin Biao, Chairman Mao's cheerleader-in-chief. A neighbor reported it, and though the authorities didn't punish him, his mother was tortured; perhaps worse still, his father, a navy officer, was forced to retire, ending a promising career. That was when the whole family returned to Nanjing, his father's hometown. Cooped up in the new, smaller apartment, Jiang's mother began to murmur to herself. "Whose fault is it? Not my son, not me, not my husband," she would go on, all day. "Who's at fault?"

"I began to think about this again recently," Jiang went on. "Chinese communists always boast about 'seeking truth and fact.' How could anyone who really sought the truth punish a woman for her young son's tiny error? At school we learned that communism was humanity's most noble and beautiful ideal. Now, I'm just not sure." He sucked deeply on his cigarette, then blew smoke rings. They floated, forming a chain that punctuated his question.

Similarly ruthless persecution, Jiang continued, had taken place in other socialist countries, which were also poor without exception, much poorer than the capitalist

West. And not just the West—our neighbors, the so-called Four Little Dragons of Asia—Hong Kong, Singapore, Taiwan, and South Korea all charged ahead, enjoying relative prosperity without the guidance of Marxism-Maoism. How could Marxist ideology lead China into modernization?

But as the restaurant grew noisier, Jiang's voice sounded smaller, and out of tune. "Four! Four! Five ... Six! Six! Six!" A group of men at a nearby table were playing a drinking game, guessing the total number of fingers thrust out each round. A young man with burning ears, obviously the loser, stood up in his chair and opened a bottle of beer with his teeth. Lifting the bottle skyward, he drank more than half in one gulp. The crowd cheered.

When the noise subsided, I offered my sympathy. I myself had gradually lost all interest in communism.

"I found study on my own too limiting," he confessed. "I need a tutor to give me advice and fellow students to discuss things with."

Jiang said he was puzzled about market mechanisms, multi-owner structures, capital, and social systems. He wanted to go to a proper university to find some answers.

"You should try. But how about the permission?" Only with Fang's forged letter of introduction had I been able to sign up with Teach-Yourself University. I guessed what he needed would be more difficult to fake.

He toyed with a slice of mutton bubbling in the hot-pot stew.

"If I quit my job, my neighborhood committee would surely provide me with permission." To support his argument, he quoted a story by Zhuang Zi, a philosopher: A wild pheasant in the marsh must go at least ten steps for one mouthful of food and another hundred steps for one mouthful of water. Nonetheless, it doesn't want to be trapped in a golden cage where there is abundant food.

What a bold plan. People usually gave up their jobs to pursue some enterprise that promised to make them money, not for the possibility of study.

"What did your father say?" I asked cautiously.

"Strongly opposed. How about you?"

"I am not sure, either. The competition will be very intense. And the students at the university definitely have an advantage over you; to start with, they know the professors already."

"You have no confidence in me?" His face turned as red as cooked mutton.

"No, no, no, I am just realistic. How about if you fail? You'll be jobless at home."

"I'll try again next year."

"How about money?"

"I made over two months' salary in just four days selling kebabs, you know that. And I wouldn't be ashamed to be a kebab seller."

I reminded him that there wouldn't be so many people without the festival. He hadn't felt embarrassed because he knew he would be a respected tax officer the next day. And he wouldn't feel fulfilled, working on the street permanently.

"Actually, I like being a tax officer," he resumed his slow talk. I often fought the urge to shake out the rest of his sentences. "The tax issue will become more important and there is a lot to learn. But I don't want to be stuck there forever. If I can study, I'll have other options, becoming an academic, running a factory, or whatever. If I don't study now, it'll be hard later, with a family and all that."

A family? We never talked about matters that personal, but I was certain that he didn't have a girlfriend, despite his popularity among his female colleagues. When there were dance parties at fancy dance halls organized by his tax bureau, he would often invite Ju and me to come along. The girls, drawn by his good looks and innocent charm, would fight to dance with him, or rather, to be dragged around by him, maintaining a respectable distance between them. "One, two, three, one, two, three," he stamped his feet, following the steps he was taught stiffly, as if pulling a rickshaw rather than a dance partner. I could feel the girls' barely controlled hostility toward us.

We biked home silently. Jiang He seemed a little down, probably because I hadn't endorsed his plan, however sympathetic I was. When we neared his flat, he asked if I'd stand on the bridge with him for a minute while he finished his last cigarette of the day.

"Sure."

He stood, as ever, with one leg slight bent. I felt a little uneasy about the intimate darkness imposed on us. It was a starry night. The river gushed beneath the bridge.

"You know I've admired you since the day I met you." His words came out in his usual slow way, but a little shaky. "I want you to be my girlfriend." He moved closer to me, holding my shoulder awkwardly with his right hand, then resting it there.

For a moment, I didn't know what to do. In the past two years, whenever I wondered if any love interest glued our gang of three together, the thought would quickly fade, like a trickle of water on hot sand. He went out of his way to pay equal attention to Ju and myself, though he was more ready to argue with me, more courteous to her. Living in the same neighborhood, they often visited each other. Ju was certainly far more attractive than me. We three had enjoyed such harmony and closeness. Now he was upsetting the balance.

I removed his hand from my shoulders.

"I am so, so sorry. We've been very close, almost like a brother and sister. And I hope we can remain like that. You are a very special friend to me, you know that."

Silence fell between us, heavier than the darkness.

After what felt like a long time, he said: "Is it because I'm not good enough for you?"

"Of course not! Please."

"I, I had wanted to tell you how much I love you. A hundred times, the words came to my mouth but I swallowed them. I worried I wasn't good enough for you. Now tonight I'm drunk, and I've opened my mouth. But please give me a chance, I'll try to be more worthy in the future." When I turned to look at him briefly, I could see something shining in his eyes.

"No, I do think of you very highly. It's just, you know, I fell in love with someone else. I slept with him. But we just split up—I'm still upset about it."

The final break had come when I felt that Chilly was patronizing me. He meant it when he called me a silly melon. One day, when I showed him a little poem I wrote about how I missed him, he glanced at it. "Such a little girl you are," came his dismissive comment. "You know some of my colleagues write beautifully." I had no doubt about it, as many of his colleagues had been hired for their writing skills. He had also laughed at my effort to learn how to read music, saying there was no need to pretend to be sophisticated. Chilly simply dismissed my ambitions. I had come to see, a little reluctantly, that he was dominating, self-centered, and cold. Yes, he was chilly.

My "Dear John" letter to him was more or less a copy of Jane's confession to Mr. Rochester. I wished I was more beautiful, I said, better educated, and of better social standing. But my spirit was equal to his, and I wanted to be treated as an equal. If I wasn't as important to him as he to me, I just had to give him up.

He replied by phoning me back one night—too busy to write—saying he was sorry, but it was probably best for both of us since he was not the romantic lover I was looking for.

It wasn't easy, but somehow it was more bearable than the first time around: at least I had been part of the decision-making process.

I finished my story and waited for Jiang to speak.

With a scratch a match flared to life. In a fleeting moment, I saw his frown as he dragged on yet another cigarette. "If you want me, I don't care whether you are a virgin or not."

I didn't know why I had revealed so much to him: maybe to show how serious I had been with the other man. It certainly wasn't a statement of self-censorship: sorry, you wouldn't want me now, I'm stained. The majority of Chinese men cared, as they'd been raised to, about their brides' virginity. In Chinese tradition, a bride was supposed to show a bloodstained white cloth to her mother-in-law on the morning after the wedding. The modern version was a strict medical examination. To get married, a couple not only needed permission from their danwei, but also a clean bill of health. Any disease listed on the form, hepatitis for instance, would prevent the union from taking place, and a split hymen could potentially spoil it, too.

I began crying silently, moved by his words, sorry for myself that Chilly didn't love me this way. Why did I always fall for guys hard as Red Rock or cold as Chilly?

Chapter 24

The Phoenix Feather

A series of hiccups attacked me—too much breakfast. Instead of my usual watery porridge, I'd enjoyed sesame bread and fried eggs, a treat normally reserved for crampy days during my period: my grandma believed that eggs, highly nutritious but too expensive to eat often, would compensate for the loss of blood, and thereby ease the pain.

This occasion, however, was far more serious—I was chasing a phoenix feather. There it was: an advertisement in *Jinling Evening News* for six English translators to work at the Jiangsu branch of China Import and Export Corporation, which had a monopoly on foreign trade. As in all good socialist states, the Chinese government generally doled out jobs. Open recruitments such as this, rare as phoenix feathers, usually came from firms with foreign investments. But few of them ventured to Nanjing, where the officials were infamously conservative.

Having passed the written exam, I had come today for the oral test. Standing outside assigned rooms among the daunting number of hopefuls, I tried hard to suppress my hiccups and my anxiety: we were waiting to be called for a one-on-one interview. Marx's quotation, "Foreign language is a tool of class struggle," came to my mind. Indeed, a struggle in the class, I smiled to myself. To house the thousand candidates, a school had been rented. Any jobs that were *wai*, foreign, always attracted hordes of people. A while back, when the Hilton Hotel in Shanghai advertised for a junior position, hundreds of overqualified university graduates applied.

My name was called. Under my bright red coat, my heart lurched.

"Good day!" a woman, well into her fifties, greeted me in the empty classroom. Another woman with permed hair sat next to her, writing notes.

"Er, good day," I replied after hesitation, pushing up my glasses. Were we supposed to say "How do you do" for the first meeting? So, I added "How do you do?"

"How do you do?" Her English was good, but with an accent I couldn't place. Wrinkles ran deep down her longish face. There was a rumpled elegance about her. She started simply, in the tone of a kind kindergarten teacher.

"I am twenty-three." My answers were short, precise. Like a proud toddler.

"I am a factory worker."

"Now, tell me briefly your story, please," she prompted.

I told her how I had become a worker, had been accepted to TV University, how I'd taken up English at Teach-Yourself University. My examiner listened carefully, almost encouragingly—or did I read too much into her occasional nods? As I spoke, I grew more confident.

Recently my oral English had enjoyed a small leap forward. Dr. Zhao, a woman doctor whom I'd met at English Corner, had introduced me to a casual English-speaking club attached to the Nanjing YMCA. Each Wednesday evening, a dozen of us gathered at the YMCA downtown to chat in English. Our teacher was a well-built, blond Canadian named James Graf, who smelled of clean laundry (few of his students had a washing machine, let alone fragrant imported detergent). An English teacher at River and Sea University, a school specializing in hydraulic engineering, he ran the club on a voluntary basis.

Teacher James, who insisted that we use his Christian name, didn't really teach, but organized and led discussions on a whole range of matters. One day, we discussed *Yellow Earth*, an internationally acclaimed film set on China's loess plateau, disliked by the authorities for "displaying a backward and ignorant aspect of the Chinese peasantry." Another day, we talked about books that had made an impact on our lives. We were always firing questions at him, from personal questions like why he let his daughters sleep alone in their rooms to questions about the Canadian voting system. Throughout our meetings, he would write up important or difficult words that came up on the blackboard. Whenever we used a difficult word or expressed an unusual view, he would reward us with a heartwarming "Well done!" None of us had ever encountered such an enthusiastic, encouraging, and amiable teacher. In front of him, we were freethinking, our tongues as glib as salesmen's.

When my elegant interviewer asked me what I hoped to gain from this job, I replied, "I hope it's a job that will allow me to realize my potential." "Realizing one's potential" was among the phrases James chalked up when we had talked about our future plans.

She looked impressed.

I walked out into the brisk spring air, feeling good about myself.

"Hush, quiet!" My family tried to silence me, but I couldn't stop showing off, beating the narrator to the lines I knew so well. Sitting too close to the TV, my whole family was watching a travel program about Peru.

No sooner had I lost the bid to become a professional translator than I secured my first translating job, for the international department of Jiangsu Provincial Television, helped by my guanxi there—Chilly. "Do you feel up to it?" Chilly had asked. "You can only listen to a cassette tape."

Eager, I had begged him: "Yes, please, let me try, let me!"

"Okay, then, no reward?"

I took the cassette from his hand and giggled a "no." Chilly always wanted to touch me, getting close whenever he had an opportunity: somehow, he thought that our sleeping together had granted him permanent access. We got along better these days, with nothing to demand from each other.

The job wasn't an easy bone to chew. Some parts of the program required countless replay before I caught the wording. Where I just couldn't get it, I had to turn to Teacher James, who was always more than willing to help. At the city library, I looked up more facts on Peru and checked the right translation of place names.

Translating is an excellent playground for people who enjoy toying with words and language, something I grew addicted to after Misty Poetry caught my imagination. I took my time picking words, a process described in Chinese as *tuiqiao*, "push, knock"—originating from a poet hesitating between pushing on a door or knocking, for the difference between these and many similar characters is subtle and intriguing.

Before handing in my work, I had known it by heart. Now, the temptation to spurt out these lines, my labor of love, was too strong to resist. Annoyed with my interruptions, my family was also deeply impressed and just as excited as me. At the end of the program, all eyes were fixed on the closing credits, until my name showed up: "Translator: Zhang Lijia."

"Look!" I shouted. "Did you see my name? I am a translator!" A translator! Having missed the boat to Foreign Language School, my journey to become a translator had been a difficult voyage. But here I was. Exhilarated, I began to dance wildly to the Latin rhythm of the closing theme music.

"Aiya, mother of mine! Our little Li will be famous!" lauded my mother.

"Amitufo…" Nai turned to her Buddhist mantra.

"Hao, hao," Father congratulated me, before returning to himself. "I could have told you one or two things about Peru…"

For the first time, my family saw something come of my endless, hitherto "pointless" study.

"Male, thirty-one years old, five-foot-eight-inches high, ca-cadre, features, features…What is this character?" Nai was slowly reading the lonely-heart ads on the central fold of *Jinling Evening News*, which she held at arm's length to accommodate her farsighted focus. Her round glasses, the same pair she used for embroidery, sat halfway down her nose. She turned to me, pointing at the character she didn't know.

"Regular features."

"Oh, yes, regular features, of course. With a proper university degree and a monthly income of nearly a thousand yuan. Oh, a thousand, not bad. Pity, he is an aged youth," Grandma summarized, as she did with each case. The "aged youth"—referring to those over thirty but unfortunately unmarried, many of them former sent-down youth—had become such an issue that work units began to organize parties to help them to find spouses.

Nai was getting better at reading the personal pages and their endless clichés. My lack of boyfriend troubled her deeply. Over and over again, Nai suffered attacks of jealousy when neighbors' daughters were married off amid the thunder of firecrackers. Even Little Flower, our old neighbor, had wed a butcher. Then Nai stumbled across the classifieds, or rather the "soliciting-marriage ads," as they were called, for every single advertiser had matrimony in mind. She recited them daily after supper, hoping that some man's fantastic descripiton would catch my fancy. "You aren't going to be an *laochunu*, are you?" she would ask me from time to time, a worried look on her oval-shaped face. A laochunu was an old maid—or literally, an old virgin.

"I am not, I swear," I would reply with a little smile.

I never mentioned my Chilly affair to my family. During a brief period when the romance was in full swing, I nearly blurted out his name. But I was glad now that I hadn't. For my family, introducing a boyfriend meant introducing the man I was to marry.

Put myself up for sale on the marriage pages? Never! I would rather die an old maid with a broken hymen. Look at those cold, calculating numbers and prizes: a household with ten thousand yuan in savings, Communist Party membership—the Party passport—a flat with a flush toilet, relatives abroad. They would demand a partner with matching bounty.

"Looking for, for, oh yes, I know," Nai went on, "a gentle lady, height between five-foot-three inches and five-foot-four-inches, pretty with double eyelids. Nanjing residence a must."

"Double eyelids? Well, Little Li hasn't got those," said my sister, joking at my expense. Weijia and Changyong were visiting for Nai's birthday meal, a steaming heap of noodles—a symbol of longevity.

"Little Li does, only not as obvious as yours!" Ma seemed more ready to jump to my defense since she'd seen my name flash on the TV screen.

The days of family warfare were more or less over. My brother Xiaoshi, the troublemaker in the family, had left home to join the army—he could no longer take life as a rootless ghost floating along the Yangtze. The People's

Liberation Army, gloriously called the "revolutionary furnace," sometimes did serve as a furnace to recast rotten eggs like him. If he could endure his three years' service in the antiriot section of the army, he would be assigned a decent job within the state-owned sector.

Even my parents had calmed down. Like two irregular gears, after a period of clashing, the sharp edges were worn off, and they were learning to coexist peacefully—for the most part.

What had most dramatically improved our quality of life was the new, long-overdue flat allocated to us that spring. On the ground floor of a newly constructed building, it had two bedrooms, but also a small sitting room, a toilet, and a kitchen to call our own. Nai quietly and contently put her bed in the common room to give me some privacy.

After the noodle bowls were cleared from the table, I presented Nai with a velvet box. "Happy birthday, Nai! I wish for your happiness to be as boundless as the Eastern Seas and your lifespan longer than that of the Southern Mountain!" I quoted the birthday-wish cliché.

"For me?" Nai opened the box and spotted a golden ring, glittering expensively. "Amituofo…"

With a struggle—the joint on her ring finger was unusually large—I slid it on. She admired it, dimples deep in her cheeks. "Half of my body is already buried in the yellow earth. What do I need such a fancy thing for?"

"To play mah-jongg with," I joked. Gold was a major status symbol, and one of Nai's mah-jongg friends showed off her gold ring continually.

"Is it twenty-four karat? Expensive?" Ma questioned.

"Not too bad."

"You should have told me, so we could buy the ring together for Nai," Weijia grunted later.

"Never mind, you can buy her a pair of golden earrings. I just made some extra money," I boasted.

I had taken on jobs through a translation company, translating cheaply made American cop or romance movies for shows at private video saloons. Heaven knows how these terrible films ended up in China. But it was fun to work on them—I made plenty of wild guesses whenever the fast-spoken slang grew impenetrable.

I discovered the pleasures of eating spicy noodles anytime I wanted, organizing outings with my expanding group of friends, and, above all, being generous with my family. Ever since the government had introduced state bonds, Ma and I had squabbled every year over fifty yuan worth. Supposedly a voluntary purchase, they were actually treated as a political task: the government badly needed to collect funds from the general public to feed the fast-growing economy. I tried to persuade Ma to keep it as an investment, a long-term, low-interest one. But she argued that it was just part of my job. Our tough negotiations usually saw her contribute thirty percent and me the rest. This year, however, I just paid the whole lot without even bringing it up.

Toying with her new ring, Nai returned to soliciting marriage. "Some man, thirty years old, five-foot-four-inches tall, with an uncle who is a cadre of minister level."

"Aha, a minister-level uncle. Little Li, he will have no problem in getting you a proper translator's job!" Weijia mocked me.

"No way—he's too short! I can't have a son-in-law who only comes up to my knees!" Father threw out a loud chuckle.

I read my newspaper, not responding.

"Honestly," sighed Ma, "I have no idea what kind of man will catch your fancy."

Chapter 25

A City on the Sea

Stylish and seductive, Shanghai was everything Nanjing was not. Some local youngsters learned to speak a few words of Shanghai dialect just to show how trendy they were.

The reason for my trip was far from fashionable: an irregular, large-faced pressure gauge, installed at an important position at the factory, had to be returned to the manufacturer for testing and repair.

I never refused any work trip. Even preparing for the logistics of travel filled me with excitement as it spelled a break from monotony. I had to visit the factory accountant to borrow money and exchange Jiangsu grain coupons for their nationwide equivalents. Rationing had been lifted on many items, but not grain, our main staple. Before any trip out of town, I also had to secure a letter of introduction from my danwei.

Only with this talisman could I secure a bed at the dismal hotel belonging to the Ministry of Aerospace, which accommodated employees at a subsidized price. Five stories of concrete, but not an inch of soul nor a breath of character. Buildings like this could be found anywhere in 1980s China. My four-bed dormitory on the top floor, the only floor for women, offered little beyond the beds themselves: a thermos, teacups, and an enamel washbasin under each bed. I used it to wash my face, with cold water from the tap and hot from the thermos, until one night I was woken by the drumming of liquid into the basin beside my roommate's bed—the toilet down the corridor was obviously too far for her.

I spent as little time there as possible. One evening, I set out in the last of the sunshine to explore the metropolis. When a "bendy" bus pulled up—two coaches joined by a concertina-like section—I joined the crowd pushing aboard, without knowing exactly where it was going. Buses were so infrequent you simply didn't want to miss one.

"Excuse me, does this bus go to Great World?" I tried to ask the woman conductor. The Great World was a large entertainment center housed in a colonial-style building. A must-see in Shanghai.

"Yes," she replied crossly as she collected fares.

"Could you let me know when we get there?"

Obviously not. The Shanghai dialect was famously soft, yet the conductor managed to spout it like gunfire. In her thirties, she was shaped like an umbrella, her thin, curve-less body sheltered by a shock of electrically curled hair, dry, fuzzy, and angry.

"I'll let you know," said a man in standard Mandarin. His voice was a little husky, but pleasant.

"That's kind of you." I turned to thank the man who stood, squashed, beside the steps by the door. I had noticed him at the bus stop, standing tall and straight among the crowds, like a crane among a batch of chickens.

"Did I detect a Nanjing accent?" he asked.

"Yes, I am from Nanjing!" I never managed to hide my local accent when speaking Mandarin. "And you?"

"Almost. I have been studying at Nanjing University for three years. Are you a student yourself?"

"No such luck. I work at a factory."

As the bus crawled along Shanghai's winding streets like an earth dragon, we swapped our reasons for being on it. He revealed that he'd come to Shanghai to look for a job after finishing his master's degree in chemical engineering.

"My best friend, Zhou Fang, also studied chemical engineering!" I said joyfully, as if this remote connection somehow made us less strangers. I was intrigued by the alien concept of looking for one's own job. At this, he winked and uttered the magic word guanxi. He was looking for a job in finance.

When the bus made a turn, he was suddenly illuminated by the setting sun. I could hardly help noticing how attractive he was. His big, spirited eyes radiated confidence, two bright windows in a square, lively face of pinkish skin. Even with crowds in the way, I could tell that he had an athletic build, tall and trim, with broad shoulders. A picture of masculine charm.

Golden sunlight poured on board. Passengers lucky enough to have a seat were mostly dozing, mouths agape, their heads jolting with every pothole. How could anyone sleep in such beautiful light?

My townsman made me laugh imitating the Nanjing dialect he had picked up. In what felt like a click of the fingers, I spotted the towering spire of Great World.

To my surprise, he jumped off the bus, too. "Guess what?" he explained cheerfully, "I have never gone inside to take a look. I will today."

The Great World Amusement Center was the epitome of Old Shanghai, once crowded with theaters, gambling dens, massage parlors, and dance halls. It was the heart of life in the "Whore of the Orient" until the Chinese Communist Party, itself secretly founded here in the French Concession, seized power. It kicked out the foreigners, reformed the prostitutes, and recast the Great World as a "Youth Palace" for "healthy" forms of entertainment like local opera, propaganda, and acrobatics.

But we were denied even this wholesome fare—a notice on the door said "closed for renovation."

"What a shame! I was so looking forward to the acrobats."

"Oh well. It must be destined that I'll never go inside," he said with exaggerated disappointment.

I decided to stroll down to the Bund, the embankment on the waterfront, the symbol of Shanghai and my favorite place in the city. "Surely you've been there?" I said, barely disguising the invitation.

"Yes, I have. But I'll walk down with you if you like. Such a beautiful day." He smiled, white teeth shining in the golden light.

"Excellent!"

"By the way, my name is Liang Jijin," he said, holding out his hand. We both laughed: we had chatted like old friends, without knowing each other's name.

"Zhang Lijia." I shook his strong and warm hand. I noticed his arms were rather hairy, but I chose to remark on his name instead. "Your name sounds like that director, Liang Yanjin."

"He's my elder brother!" Yanjin was a well-known "fourth-generation" filmmaker who had directed interesting titles like *Little Street*, and *Troubling Smiles*. The director was born in Yan'an, Liang revealed, the communist enclave and cradle of Mao's revolution, while he himself had been born in Ji'an, Jiangxi province. Jin, the second character of their forenames, was the old term for their father's home province of Shanxi.

"Maybe you should consider a new career as an actor," I joked. Since films were China's most popular form of entertainment, people adored film stars and directors.

"No such talent, unfortunately."

It was only the end of May, yet the summer, impatient and restless like Chinese themselves, was already in full swing. Girls' dresses billowed in the breeze like colorful flags. Shanghai women somehow looked more feminine than their sisters elsewhere in China. Perhaps they had lent the city its reputation as the "Paris of the East."

The promenade was filling with these bright women and their gallant admirers. Standing to face the river, the lovebirds held each other's waists, with arms crossed in an X. The men would whisper something to the girls, and the girls would cover their mouths, suppressing their giggles in a ladylike fashion. They never seemed bothered by other people's presence. You could often spy three couples sharing a single park bench but wrapped up in their own worlds, as if observing China's foreign policy—"peaceful coexistence and noninterference with each other."

Spotting a gap, Liang and I joined the line of lovers, but sat with a respectable distance between us. Monumental, European-style buildings loomed majestically from behind. Their owners were long dead, but these granite memories of capitalist empire still overshadowed a city that had not recovered its former vitality. Over the other side of the river, low-rise docks gave way to fields and mudflats stretching far beyond our view into the East China Sea.

Looking thoughtfully into the water, Liang began to talk about Shanghai's recent history, a subject that clearly fascinated him. For some nationalists, the city was a symbol of China's disgrace and humiliation. A fishing town turned treaty port, the gateway to the Yangtze River, only under the influence of invading cultures had Shanghai become a vibrant city. After the first Opium War, the British forced their first concession and an International Settlement followed. Trade in silk, tea, and opium boomed, and Shanghai sparked to life. It was here, under foreign rule, that the buds of modern industry and finance first sprouted. In order to modernize China, Liang said, we had to learn from the West. The question was how and to what extent.

"I feel we are standing at a crossroads, just like our forefathers back in the Self-Strengthening Movement in 1861."

I had been listening quietly until he mentioned Self-Strengthening. "Did you know that my factory was a product of the movement?" My patriotic education course had freshened up my history. After the Qing government dealt with the external threat by signing a peace settlement with the British and French, and with the internal threat by suppressing the Taiping Rebellion, the cruel truth had sunk in—China lagged far behind the West. True, the Chinese had invented gunpowder, but while we filled firecrackers to drive away evil spirits at Spring Festival, the West built artillery and gunboats to press us into those unfair treaties.

"How interesting, oh, yes of course, the defense industry was the emphasis of that movement." Liang complained that China's first modernization program, though it was daring, had been superficial: the ruling elite wanted the Western technology that could produce the magic ships and guns, but not the other aspects of the West that actually underpinned their success: their political institutions, the rule of law, and an open, questioning culture.

In his slightly husky voice, Liang spoke with ease and assurance. From time to time, I would turn to look at his handsome face, on which the golden light was fading. I was more impressed by the minute.

China's current government faced the same question—how far to go? In Liang's view, we needed to borrow both Western technology and other aspects of Western culture. In nineteenth century, as China gingerly launched its Self-Strengthening Movement, Japan was undergoing the Meiji Restoration, which turned out to be far more successful because Japan had bravely embraced industrial culture, too. In China, the principle "*zhongti xiyong*" holds sway—Western practice (*yong*) within the Chinese system (*ti*)—even today. But the problem was that Chinese ti didn't always accommodate the Western yong well.

"Economically, modernity means industrialization and free trade," Liang added, "yet Confucian doctrine teaches people to look down on business and competition, going for the middle way, the golden mean."

"Maybe we should work against feudalism rather than liberalism." Like a parrot, I repeated what Red Rock had told me years ago in Jinan. I still missed those arrogant lectures.

"You are absolutely right!" he agreed.

The sunset in the western sky flew to my cheeks. "Actually, a friend of mine, a boyfriend of mine, actually, a former boyfriend, thought so. He's liberal, even radical. For example, he thinks guanxi is a hangover from feudalism. He is a history student, you see. But why are you interested in history and economy? Your master's is in chemical engineering, isn't it?"

He sighed, saying that China's academic system was so inflexible that he'd had to carry on in the same subject as his bachelor's degree even though he had long lost interest in chemistry.

The mention of my former boyfriend turned our conversation personal. I started to tell him about my life unreservedly. My dear friend Zhou Fang had been serving me well as my counselor and priest, but I felt somehow I could be more honest and direct with this man I had just met. Liang listened attentively, making occasional remarks. Talking about my dingzhi drama, I said: "You see, my mother never understands the benefits of education."

"Do you still feel bitter about it?" He looked at me directly.

"Yes, a bit," I was a little afraid to meet his eyes: they could see through me, I was sure.

"I can understand you. But don't undervalue a mother's good intentions. Honestly, I think I became appreciative of my own parents more after I became a father myself. I have a two-year-old son."

He was married! He revealed the information in such a natural way, as if reporting what he had for supper. I was stung by disappointment. I began to scold myself. Don't be like your grandma, treating every man as a possible husband! Since I would never go to a proper university myself, I reasoned that reading good books and making clever friends was the next best thing. Why reject a worthwhile friend simply because of his wife?

Why give up this fascinating conversation to go back to my dismal hotel room to listen to women with thick accents chat about household chores?

Liang and I ended up spending the entire evening together. A pale moon rose as darkness fell, dusting the Huangpu River with glistening light. Faint whistles were blown from ships docking at piers upstream. In the gentleness of the night, he recounted his tough life.

Ten years my senior, Liang was the youngest of six children from an old cadre's family. After his father was attacked in the storm of the Cultural Revolution and his mother was detained, he mostly lived alone. He only escaped the muddy fields of the sent-down youth by joining the army after his father resumed his position. Once again, the revolutionary furnace served as a handy stepping-stone. From there, he was recommended to attend university under a program for students who were workers, peasants, and soldiers. He then worked as a technician at a Jiangxi factory before coming to Nanjing to study.

"So, you both benefited and suffered from your father's cadre background?"

"Oh, yes, honestly, I wouldn't have joined the army or gone to university so easily," Liang accepted. He said, in a way, he was also glad to have gone through hardship. When he was young, his family had a young houseboy at home, as well as a middle-aged servant whom they affectionately called *"Ayi,"* Auntie—a privilege enjoyed by every ranking cadre's family. Ayi shopped for them at special shops where no rationing limited their purchases. "I am ashamed to admit it, but I still need my family's guanxi to get a job I want. Your friend is right. Guanxi is a hangover of feudalism." He gently patted my bare shoulder. And I keenly felt the warmth there.

"Our society isn't normal. Sometimes, I tell myself if I can join the government, I'll try to help make it better. Am I a hypocrite or not?"

"I don't know you yet," I replied dumbly.

"I hope you will."

"You'd better find a good job in Nanjing, then. But if you are so interested in Shanghai, maybe you should get a job here?"

"We'll see."

Chapter 26

Jasmine

The faint fragrance of reed leaves floated in the air as Nai wrapped sticky rice into the pyramid-shaped dumplings eaten at the Dragon Boat Festival. The actual boat races, traditionally a central part of the celebration, had died out in our region, but every year Nai would still prepare the festival food, sticky rice with meat and soy sauce, or sweetened with dates, and we would peel off the long green leaves and relish them.

Tradition had it that Qu Yuan, a patriotic poet of distant times, drowned himself in a river after the fatuous emperor refused to listen to his warnings. Mourners cooked the dumplings and cast them into the river to distract hungry fish from Qu's corpse.

"Not having any?" Nai was surprised when I emerged in a daring strapless dress printed with pink flowers.

"No, I'm going out with some friends. Save some for me."

"Oh." She sighed and tied a string to another dumpling.

I attached a pair of cape jasmines to the first button of my white silk blouse. The sweet-scented flower with thin, long petals was always sold in pairs held together with a twist of wire. My affordable perfume. When I applied lipstick, I reminded myself that all this dressing up was for the venue, not the occasion. This wasn't a date. A week after I'd returned from Shanghai, Liang Jijin called to report that he'd secured a job with the Jiangsu

Economic Planning Commission. To celebrate, he invited me to dinner at the restaurant of my choice. I went for Victory, the best Western restaurant that accepted Chinese customers. A few blocks down the road, the Jinling Hotel served the best Western food—but only to its foreign guests, who were so far removed from ordinary Chinese they even used different banknotes, crisp FEC (foreign exchange certificates), worth far more than our grubby RMB (*renminbi*, or "people's money").

Outside the restaurant, on the second floor of the colonial Victory Hotel, Liang gave me a warm, comradely handshake. A young lady in a long black skirt and bow tie greeted us with a bow and lipsticked smile, before leading us into an air-conditioned dreamworld of chandeliers and flickering candles. On each snow-white tablecloth stood a single red rose in a bud vase. The soft sound of piano—even the pianist wore a suit—drifted into the dream.

"What do you want to eat?" Liang asked.

I was too busy looking around, feeling like a peasant overwhelmed by the splendor of an imperial palace.

I studied the menu, but the names of the dishes meant little to me. "You decide for me."

"How about the buffet? You can try a bit of everything that way."

On a long table covered with another brilliantly white cloth, the feast sat invitingly. I piled up my plate with roast beef, chicken legs, and prawns, ignoring salads and vegetables as I calculated they were cheap. On my way back to the seat, lured by the cakes, I also balanced an apple pie and a big spoonful of chocolate mousse on top of my overflowing plate. A Chinese palate can handle sweet and savory at the same time.

Sauce leaked onto the white tablecloth when I put down my plate. Liang, who had chosen a modest helping of starters, handed me a paper napkin. Leaning close, he advised in a low, playful tone: "You are allowed to have as many helpings as you like." And he winked at me before settling back into his chair. I felt the blush rise on my cheeks.

Gripping my knife and fork as tensely as a new recruit bearing his first rifle, I began stabbing the meat on my plate—these Western utensils were not as tinghua as chopsticks, were they?

Liang touched my hand lightly to attract my attention. "Look, start from the edge of the meat, cut a little bit at a time, like this."

I followed his example and it worked.

"Well, cheers! Congratulations on your new job," I toasted him. He touched his glass of wine to my water.

"Thank you. I am excited about the job. Delighted to stay. I've grown fond of your city, you know." The candlelight danced on his brilliant eyes.

"So, you've decided to go for the red hat route?" There were basically two choices for well-educated Chinese: the black hat route meant going abroad, to get the mortarboard used at graduation ceremonies in the West; the red hat meant working for the government to become a powerful official. "Oh, I almost forgot—you are a Party member." Liang joined the Party in the army, where it was much easier to obtain membership.

"To be honest with you, the job has little to do with my faith in communism." Liang sat back in his chair, folding his strong arms. Personal interest had dictated his taking the planning commission job. He reasoned that talents were needed in China's new economy. Emphasis was shifting from heavy industry to other sectors such as energy, infrastructure, and telecommunications, which had been ignored for far too long. Those who planned the economy should understand such trends and the workings of the market.

A smile cracked his handsome face. "I hope you won't think I'm Old Melon Wang who boasts how good his melons are."

"No, no, one conversation with you is better than ten years' reading." I flattered him with a cliché. Acutely aware of my own shallowness, I felt like a sponge soaking up water. "Do you think China will press ahead with the reforms?" In the wake of the anti-liberalism campaign, the political atmosphere had been tightened yet again.

Liang reasoned that Chinese politics often cycled between relaxation and tightening. He half-expected that the new Party chief Zhao Ziyang, liberal in his judgment, would soon come up with a blueprint for political reform. Moreover, Zhao was gathering around him the same kind of reform-minded advisers who had guided Deng Xiaoping's reform plans. "You'll be surprised how daring their ideas are—I think they're considering separating the Party and the administration. An orthodox Marxist like my dad would jump from his grave if he knew!" Liang flashed a bright smile. "In many ways, the advisers hold the steering wheel. I do admire them—they are the force that is changing China from within, probably more effectively than the dissidents."

Liang looked ahead to somewhere I couldn't see.

"So, you want to be part of the force?"

"Yes, if possible."

"Hope you won't end up like Qu Yuan." Throughout history, too many upright intellectuals like that patriotic poet had been punished by their rulers when they dared to offer honest opinions. I immediately regretted my blunt remarks.

His warm smile dazzled me. "Don't worry, I certainly won't jump from the Great Yangtze River Bridge!" The bridge was the most popular suicide spot in town.

I cast my eyes down on my plate and tucked into the food. "Delicious. Have you been to this restaurant before?"

"Yes, I've been here before."

Since he was so vague, I instantly thought he must've come with his wife.

As if reading my thoughts, he added. "A classmate from university took me here. He tried to persuade me to set up a company with him."

"Were you tempted?"

"Yes, of course, I was. But in the end, I feel that making money is just one way to show one's value, and a primitive way, to be blunt. I am still young, and I want to do things that really interest me."

What an oddity! He must be one of the few Chinese who were not moneygrubbing, *xiangqiankan*, literally, "looking at the money." The phrase had become the most popular wordplay in China: it sounded like "looking ahead," the favorite term of our communist leaders who wanted the anxious masses to look ahead to our bright future, and quietly put up with present-day difficulties.

A melodious piano solo rose again. The restaurant was half full, mostly with Western diners. A group of elderly travelers wearing the same ID badges suddenly burst out laughing, drowning the music.

"Look how colorfully dressed they are!" I remarked. One sizeable granny's dress was covered in neon flowers; another granny sported an eye-catching red scarf over her white T-shirt. In China, once they reached middle age, people never wore bright clothes, as if entering a permanent mourning period for the loss of their youth.

"I think the Americans are real individualists," Liang said. "For them, there isn't any certain color for any certain age." He took half a dozen books from his army canvas bag. "These are for your English study. I don't need them anymore."

Naturally I had told him about my plan to use English as my tool. He knew how hard it was trying to do anything different at a factory.

Flicking through the books, I found some English text-books, novels in English, and books for TOEFL, the Test of English as a Foreign Language, required by American universities. So, he had indeed tried the "black hat" route.

"Yes, I did ponder the idea. I took the test last year, but my score wasn't quite good enough, to be honest. I don't find it easy to learn English, at my age, you know. Or maybe my tongue is too stiff to pronounce any foreign sound. Anyhow, I've made up my mind that I'll be more useful staying here in China."

"Chairman Mao used the same argument when he decided to stay in China. Now some academics feel that China might be a different place, had he gone abroad for some Western education."

He smiled good-naturedly. "I don't think we can be compared under the same sun. Besides, it's complicated when the children of high-ranking leaders are sent abroad privately."

"Some workers at my factory already tease me for being 'a toad that wants to eat swan meat.' If they spot me studying a TOEFL book, they'll think I dream of going abroad, too. What would they say?" I chuckled myself. "'A toad that wants to jump to the moon?'"

"But do you really care what they say?"

"A bit, maybe. But I have so many fleas on me that I don't mind a new bite." I borrowed an idiom to show I was beyond caring.

"That's a good girl!" He enthused, eyes twinkling in the candlelight. It went down better than any of the desserts I had tried.

Liang insisted on paying for me, saying he had been earning money by teaching undergraduate classes at the university. "See, you owe me a dinner now. I am going home for a month. When I return, we'll have to meet up again."

"How can I thank you for the best dinner I ever had?"
"Sing a song, if you like."

Outside, the warm air felt very comforting. Standing under the whirling shadow of a parasol tree, I began to sing a famous folk song from the region.

Jasmine, oh, beautiful jasmine!
So many of them are blossoming on the branch,
white, fragrant and beautiful.
I am tempted to pick one blossom to wear in my hair,
but afraid the others may laugh at me.

In the scent of fresh jasmine rising from the flowers on my blouse, my singing sounded unusually sweet in the night air.

Chapter 27

Storm

Hidden in one corner of the factory yard, covered by a metal net, I glimpsed my future and it glittered in the sunlight. A stretch of flexible metal hose. Who would have imagined it would inspire such delight? Although I'd heard the term before, I'd never thought it to be an actual object, connecting two pipes at a right angle. Now I began to notice them across the factory as I skipped back to my workshop.

I could handle it every day, if I had to. I had just been called to the newly established flexible-metal-hose unit, where Director Du, a man with a shock of jet-black hair, received me warmly in his office. Eyeing me up and down, with a lengthy pause at my odd glasses, he concluded: "What a modern girl! We've heard a lot about you. Even foreigners are impressed by your good English. Is that right?"

I smiled. The story of foreigners singing my praise had swelled like puffed rice. A couple of months earlier, on a Liming-organized tour to an industrial exhibition, I met two Western backpackers who'd lost their way. After I pointed them in the right direction, they thanked me furiously, and then, to my colleagues, attempted to say "*tai bang le*," "great," holding up their thumbs. My colleagues had often heard me talking to myself in English, but to witness me in conversation with real, live foreign devils stunned them. For the rest of the day, Boss Lan frequently held up his thumb and imitated the foreigner's strange accent—"*Tai bang le*!"—to guaranteed laughter.

Was my luck finally turning?

"We have just imported some German-made machines," Director Du explained. "Can you help us translate the English brochure, for a fee, of course?"

"I would be honored."

Before letting me go, Du showed me his product and took care to explain how the hose was used in pipelines to compensate for displacement caused by temperature change, or whenever it proved awkward to install straight pipes.

Did Du intend to hire me for his work unit?

Before I knew it, I had earned myself a reputation. People sought me out to ask questions about studying English; mothers stopped me in the middle of the road so that their children could exchange a few pleasantries in English. Fewer and fewer people accused me of having a taste for swan meat. Some young girls even began to copy my self-styled fashion. My fame, however, had not translated into any job offers. When I failed in my first bid to become a professional translator, I hadn't been too upset. There would be more opportunities, I told myself.

Recently, Weijia had bumped into my elegant interviewer, a senior teacher at a nearby middle school, at a meeting for model teachers. Our names and physical likeness had soon led her to confess to Weijia that if only I'd been blessed with better guanxi, I would certainly have gotten the job. The news was cold comfort. Without connections or influential parents, I realized, I had little chance of securing a job through so-called "open competitions."

Du's in-house affair was my best bet. With a large dictionary in hand, I set down to tackle the technical translation before the deadline, just ten days away. Having worked on TV programs and films where I was free, even encouraged, to use flowery words and expressions, I felt reduced from cooking a feast to preparing a dose of Chinese herbal medicine—the only thing that mattered was dry precision. To handle the special terms I had to call a friend in the unit to ask how things worked. For the first time ever, my degree in mechanical engineering came in handy.

Soon after I handed over my neatly handwritten translation, Du summoned me again. He was direct. "Would you like to work for us as a translator?"

"Yes, I'd love to!" I shot back.

"We can't offer you a salary as high as in some foreign companies, but it's not bad, and you'll have opportunities to visit Germany." He pointed Germany on the world map that hung on his wall. "In the future, our products are going to be sold all over the world. If we combine advanced technology, with our advantage of cheap labor, we should be able to offer competitive prices. You'll see. We need talents like you." He patted my shoulder, with the air of a commander recruiting troops to conquer the world.

The flexible metal hose unit was the brainchild of our new factory director, Boss Cao, who, having decided that there was no future in relying on the state's limited allocation, was developing civilian products vigorously. As the tension of the Cold War eased, the demand for China's often outdated arms had diminished, and the military budget was cut. Nowadays even the army had started to march into business—you could have a raucous good time at a karaoke bar or disco run by one division or another.

Director Cao's strategy was to produce marketable civilian products that allowed the factory to utilize its existing expertise. The watering truck, one of the new products, was merely the truck used to transport liquid fuel for missiles with a few modifications. Flexible metal hose, in increasing demand, fit the same bill.

The unit that produced it, Ma wasted no time in discovering, was the most profitable in the factory, and its employees enjoyed the highest possible bonus.

She was delighted. I waited impatiently to be transferred.

The chanting barely stirred the quiet at Crowing Rooster Temple, on the eastern foot of Rooster Mountain. Beneath the temple's sloping roof, the nuns closed their eyes, bearing an expression above worldly concerns. With their shaved heads and dull gray robes, there was little to indicate they were women save their voices. An elderly nun, her face wrinkled like a walnut, beat out a rhythm on a hollow wooden fish. Most were old, except one pretty-faced girl. She must have been the latest convert, as the nunnery had only recently begun to accept nuns again. She would never worry about promotion and failure.

Liang and I were peeping into the chanting hall through intricate wooden carvings. Just as I had begun to wonder how a month could last so long, he had called, immediately upon his return to Nanjing. At my suggestion, we met up at the nunnery, ten minutes' ride from Drum Tower Square and set on a scenic hilltop. In a white T-shirt, he looked slightly tanned, handsome, and full of good spirits.

"How was your holiday?" I asked as we strolled around the temple compound.

"Not bad, but hardly a holiday. It was great to see my son. I can't believe how much he had grown! But I have to say I became bored after a while. I have more friends here now."

The Chinese scholar trees were blooming luxuriantly. When the wind blew, many of their tiny white petals drifted down like snowflakes.

"The flowers are edible, you know," I picked one up from a low branch and put it in my mouth. "My grandma used to make pancakes with these sweet flowers as the filling. Delicious!"

"Really!" he tried one himself. "Yes, not too bad," he said politely. "When you are poor, you just have to be resourceful. That's why we Chinese eat everything that moves. Our cuisine is very much a famine cuisine."

Liang had a good answer to every question. Somewhere up in the tree, a cicada was chirping away. Again, that aroma whirled out of my childhood. "We used to grill cicadas to eat. Really delicious."

"I'll skip that one," he laughed.

We sat down in the teahouse, originally a setting for Buddhist ceremonies. It was a traditional wooden structure with full-length carved doors and windows. Vermilion pillars, supporting the heavy beams, stood elegantly in a row, framing a solemn stage on which I could play out my recent misfortune.

The long silence from the flexible-metal-hose unit had worried me. When I gathered enough courage to telephone Director Du, he had said, "Aiya, Little Zhang, complicated, more complicated than I thought." He sounded hassled. "Is it true that your status is still worker?"

"Yes, it's true," I said sorrowfully, as if admitting to a future mother-in-law that I was barren. I was so carried away by hope that it hadn't occured to me that I wasn't actually qualified to perform the job of translator, classified as a cadre's position.

"Look, I haven't given up yet. I'll try to borrow you from your work unit."

A week later, a friend from the metal-hose unit told me that Du had been unexpectedly transferred to another factory. Rumor suggested that he had earned the nickname "Big Mouthed Du" for talking up too many unrealistic plans. Worse still, his ambition and ego displeased certain leaders.

Hoping against hope, I had contacted his deputy, who delivered the final disappointment. When Du tried to borrow me from my work unit, Political Instructor Wang had firmly refused to let me go on the grounds that I was needed. Needed? Anyone with half a child's brain could cope with my job.

"Oh, what a shame!" Liang said sympathetically. "I worked at a factory. I know how frustrating it can be."

He poured me a cup of hot jasmine tea. A swirl of tea leaves floated on the surface, then slowly sank down. In the summer, nothing beats tea for quenching thirst.

"Now, listen to me," he said. "If your ultimate goal is to find a translation job within the factory, then do whatever you can to improve your relationship with this Wang chap; but if your long-term goal is to jump out of the factory, then concentrate on that."

"I want to get out." The latest drama had made me more determined than ever.

"I'll keep my eyes open for you. What are the good parts of your current job?"

"I'm not too busy and I get along well with my direct boss, Lan." Since I'd earned the foreign devils' praise, Boss Lan had become even more accommodating, convinced that I was a gem wrongly stuck in the grease of his workshop.

"Excellent! Make the best use of that." Liang smiled at me, and the heavy fog that had been clouding my heart for days began to disperse.

With a dramatic thumping of drums, the chanting concluded. The crowds of pilgrims that circled the chanting hall flocked to the main yard. Some lit bamboo joss sticks from the golden flames of the carrot-shaped red candles. There were rows of them in large metal candleholders, standing tall like soldiers on stilts in battle formation. The worshippers, clasping their hands together in supplication, eyes closed, murmured mantras to themselves before throwing the joss sticks into a large copper incense burner, or adding burning candles to the formation. Fresh smoke would coil slowly up, obscuring their faces.

A soft breeze filled our nostrils with the scent of incense. From inside the teahouse, we watched the movement in the yard, sipping tea, wondering who these people were. Devoted believers, perhaps, on another pilgrimage, stocking up good karma for the lives ahead? Or more irregular worshippers, drawn to prayer by particular concerns, like promotion, marriage, a loved one's health?

Buddhism was enjoying a revival in China. In the street outside the temple, more shops opened up, selling candles, joss sticks, those fish-shaped wooden drums, and other ritual items. Once introduced to China from India in the second century, it had become domesticated. In time, it blended together with Taoism and Confucianism, and had dominated the spiritual lives of the Chinese ever since.

"Religion was probably never wiped from people's lives, even during the Cultural Revolution. Those people couldn't have turned into Buddhists overnight, don't you think?" Liang was always full of interesting questions.

"No, they couldn't." I told him about my grandma. Even if she didn't practice openly, she had always been a Buddhist in her bones. "She always believes that life is all about suffering, which is why she is so accepting of her fate. It must have helped her through the worst times."

"Throughout history, people have drawn strength from religion." After a pause, he asked: "Do you remember what Marx said about religion?"

"Religion is the opiate that poisons people." Of course I remembered the famous line with which he condemned millennia of human endeavor. We had all been taught the Marxist view that religion was the product of history and would die out, together with superstition, when society reached an advanced level.

Liang revealed that he'd once come across the famous phrase in an English book, but it read only "Religion is the opiate of the people." Maybe only the Chinese translation stressed the negative, he concluded. Anyway, Marx did believe that religion was an effect of economic pressures—it only served to comfort the poor, oppressed workers. "But look at America, highly developed economically, yet quite religious, too."

"Is it? What's your point?"

"Well, religion may not disappear even when the society reaches an advanced level." Ours was a confusing time, he said, since so much information had suddenly gushed in from outside, contradicting what we had learned.

I nodded, looking out of the window while digesting his words.

The teahouse overlooked Xuanwu Lake, the sparkling, jade-green surface of which stretched to Purple Mountain on the far side. It was so wide that one emperor marshaled a hundred thousand men there to conduct naval exercises on five hundred ships. Today there were only a few pleasure boats. In the late afternoon sun, ripples glistened like fish scales.

"What a perfect spot!" he enthused. "How did you find this place?"

I gave due credit to Pan Hai, my literary friend from the factory. Not a Nanjing native, Old Pan was keen to explore the city. On free days he came to Cock Crow Temple to read poetry, write his own, and ponder life-or-death matters. There was plenty of inspiration around. And, as famous as the temple itself, Rouge Well sat on the mountain's eastern slope. When a rival dynasty attacked at the end of the sixth century, the last Cheng emperor jumped into this well with his two favorite concubines to hide, but a trace of rouge on the well's lip betrayed them. Even today, the legend went, if you wiped the well with a white silk cloth, you would find a desperate, bloodred smear, the tear-splashed makeup of those doomed courtesans. Throughout Chinese history, civil strife has risen and fallen like a deadly tide, sweeping out corrupt and failed dictators. Without the romance of folk legend laced through it, the brutal reality of local history would have been much grimmer.

Despite its fancy name, the well was dry and insignificant these days, but I fell in love with the temple, amazed that a spiritual haven could survive amid the noise of a city center.

"I congratulate your friend," said Liang, "he sounds like an interesting character."

"He certainly is." I told Liang about Pan, his poems, and how I'd learned from him.

"Your mother should worry that your threshold will be flattened by boys," he joked.

"Hardly," I blushed, but pleased that he showed interest in my personal life. It lent me the excuse to pry into his personal life.

"What's your wife like?"

He thought for a while, resting his chin on his hand. I noticed again how hairy his arms were. Chilly, still my only real boyfriend, had very little body hair. It must feel different to touch hairy skin.

His verdict interrupted my unspeakable thoughts. "My wife is a teacher, a wonderful woman by anyone's standard, hardworking, educated, devoted to our family. She takes good care of my mother. And she never complains." He recited the long list of her virtues with little enthusiasm, like a teacher judging a hardworking but characterless student.

"So, you are a lucky man."

"To be honest with you…" he scratched his head, as if looking for the right words.

Our food came. "Look at that, almost too good to eat." Liang took a big spoonful.

We had vegetable noodles and two vegetarian dishes, all surprisingly delicious to carnivores like us. Buddha's teaching forbids taking any life, so no meat was served in the restaurant attached to the nunnery. Yet each dish bore a meaty name, and many were laid out in imitation of their meat-filled counterparts. Gongbao chicken, a classic Sichuan dish of diced chicken and peanuts in spicy chili sauce, became diced bean curd with peanuts in the same sauce. The red-cooked fish was mashed potato wrapped in bean curd skin with tomato sauce.

"I wonder if the meaty name of the dishes affects their taste." I felt stimulated when talking with Liang. There was little point in making any clever remarks to my colleagues. "Playing music to cows" was the apt Chinese phrase.

"Even I might consider becoming a Buddhist if I could eat food like this every day!"

Liang's cheerful boast reminded me of something. I fished a photograph from my bag. "Have you heard about the giant Buddha our factory is making?" I showed him proof, me smiling in front of a bronze head as big as a bus.

Our factory had taken part in a worldwide bid to cast a giant Buddha for the Precious Lotus Temple on Hong Kong's Lantau Island. Although he ran a military factory, how could our practical-minded leader sit and let this golden opportunity pass by? The Chinese always boasted of their three-thousand-year history of bronze making. The outstanding casting skills required in making the rockets had won us the bid. A year later, the largest outdoor bronze Buddha in the world, 112 feet high and 250 tons in weight, was born at the casting unit. Before its shipment to Hong Kong, our factory leaders had decided to treat all the employees to a photo with the massive icon. People had few pictures of themselves, let alone in front of such an extraordinary piece of art. To have a photo session for nearly ten thousand people was no small affair. Luckily mass organization was an art in communist China. Each work unit was assigned a day and a time, either before eight or after five-thirty. Once there, we stood in an orderly queue. When it was my turn, I had a few seconds to walk to a circle on the ground. I smiled at the camera; the photographer pressed the button; I moved away and the next smiler strode up. Another efficient assembly line.

"I have indeed heard about the Buddha. The papers were full of it. Hai, look, how impressive!" Liang said heartily while holding the photo. Even with the scaffolding, the Buddha looked splendid, with its all-seeing eyes half-closed and half a smile on its lips. But Liang's bright eyes focused on me instead of the Buddha. I wore a short denim skirt, my favorite garment—somehow, I identified with it as a fellow free spirit. My flesh-tinted stockings stopped shortly beneath it, leaving a gap of flesh in between. That was the fashion then.

Handing back the photo, he remarked, casually, "Isn't it a bit funny that your factory, a producer of missiles, got this big order to build a Buddha, the symbol of nonviolence?"

I had never thought about it.

The bright world darkened as powerful gusts rose from nowhere. Above us black clouds were rolling and billowing dramatically, dragons fighting across the sky's vast stage. Liang and I pedaled fast, hoping to beat the upcoming storm. He had insisted on taking me home, just like last time. The rain caught us on Eternal Happiness Road when we were more than halfway home. It came down so heavily the sky seemed to have sprung a leak. In a matter of seconds, people fled in all directions, leaving the streets deserted.

Dripping wet, we took refuge under the nearest building. Blown sideways by the wind, cold raindrops kept finding us beneath the thin strip of eave. Goose bumps crawled over my bare arms. Feeling as pathetic as a plucked chicken, I hugged myself, trying to keep warm, but also to cover my embarrassment—my thin dress had melted into a layer of transparent skin.

"Should I take off my T-shirt for you?"

"No, thank you." Turning to meet his eyes, I smiled bravely.

Swift as the wind, he turned to give me a back-cracking hug and kissed me full on the lips. Hit by this unexpected emotional storm, I felt caught in a trance. When my senses returned, I managed to say, between my chattering teeth, "But, but, you are married."

He stepped back, as if stunned by electricity. Outside the mercy of the eaves, he was soaked through almost immediately. But he stood still in the rain and didn't seem to care. Murmuring an apology, he added, in a voice more husky than usual: "I really didn't mean to offend you. I…"

I was startled when a flash of lightning showed he was crying.

Women's hearts are too soft to stand men's tears. I wanted to hold him and comfort him. But my sense of righteousness stood in the way. I might fantasize about how his hairy arms would feel to touch, but it was another matter to have those arms around me: he was married. I couldn't degrade myself by becoming a "third party," the disdainful new term for a woman having an affair with a married man. The general consensus was that marriage, the smallest cell of society, ought to be protected.

Did I love him? I wasn't sure. I had never dared approach that idea too closely. I did wonder briefly if Liang was interested in me, but just as quickly brushed aside the foolish notion, for fear of insulting him with the thought. He was always as sincere and comradely as his handshake. I kept telling myself it was a pure friendship, reminding myself of the benefits of having such an impressive friend. Still, I had to admit that I was deeply attracted to this handsome man. If he had fallen in love with me, I had done nothing to discourage him.

The rain continued to pour down, not in drops but lines, all tangled up like linen threads.

Chapter 28

The Third Party

The summer day lingered on and on. When the dark shadows of night finally emerged, I pedaled off again on my bike, in a cream-colored dress as thin as a cicada's wing.

Around the corner, in a small concrete square, I spotted my family. To escape the baking heat, they joined their neighbors outside on small bamboo chairs. The noisy gathering took place every night. Some even readied themselves to sleep the night outside on bamboo beds, despite the buzzing, biting mosquitoes.

Under the streetlights, Ma was "building the Great Wall"—stacking her mah-jongg tiles in a neat row. Unlike the other players, three crones hunched over their tiles, Ma sat with her back erect. Absorbed in the game, she ignored the beads of sweat gathering on her forehead. She wore a black-and-white dress, a gift from me. Inspired by the American grannies, I'd bought her a colorful dress, but she'd exchanged it for this more calmly patterned one: "Otherwise, people would think I was an old fox fairy."

Nai, in a sky-blue cotton top, stood watching over Ma's shoulder. She was never bothered by the heat: her calmness seemed to defeat it. She followed the game closely, but never commented or revealed information that might annoy the players. The key to a successful mah-jongg game was concealment. No wonder some people suggested that the game reflected China's inward-looking, inward-thinking Great Wall mentality.

The theory rang true in Ma's case. Since giving up ballroom dancing, she'd become ever more addicted to mah-jongg, a pastime I disliked for the way it attracted small-minded gossip. My smart mother ought to be after something bigger in life. So I tried to persuade her to take adult-education courses, to study calligraphy, or literature, but she claimed her eyesight was failing. "Besides, why should I learn new things?" she said. "Half of my body is already buried in the yellow earth." She had picked up Nai's favorite phrase. As her world was narrowing, so was her mind. She grew more and more like the illiterate grannies with whom she clattered mah-jongg tiles. She seemed to enjoy their company: they made her feel sophisticated by default.

Under the table, a coil was lit to drive mosquitoes away. The smoke circled around the players' bare legs like an invisible chain, binding them to the table as they built their Great Walls into the small hours.

In the crowded open space, other Wuding New Village residents were playing cards or Go. Kids sat on low stools, their heads crammed into school textbooks as they struggled to recognize characters in the dim light. Their parents sat or stood around, chatting, sipping tea, or fanning themselves ferociously.

In another corner, my father, clad only in a big pair of loose shorts that barely covered half his enormous potbelly, sang Beijing Opera with a group of old men. Some manipulated a pair of walnuts or metal balls in their hands, to maintain blood circulation and general good health. "Standing on top of the watchtower, I look down at the fine scenery, feather fan in my hand…" Holding a large palm fan as a prop, Father sang heartily, his lower jaw moving in that odd pattern. In summer, his fan stayed with him like a shadow. When his hands were busy, he shoved it down the back of his shorts.

I got off my bike to greet my family—I didn't want to appear too keen to get away. "I'm off now," I informed them.

"All right, don't ride too fast," Ma replied, her gaze never shifting from the line of her tiles. She was fondling a mah-jongg tile in her hand with a gentleness she never showed to her husband. "Mother of mine!" she suddenly spat, arching her two new moons. "My pieces are all over the place, like flowers scattered around by the Heavenly Maiden." Ma, too, enjoyed scattering a few fancy idioms, though her grannies rarely picked them up.

"Where's she going?" asked one player.

"She's off to her sister's place to study English. Didn't I tell you before, Little Li can translate foreign TV programs!" Ma boasted. "We are finished," she announced, referring to herself. "Only smart young people like her have got a future."

"Oh, not for a date, then," clucked Know-It-All Gao, a coarse and nosy granny who wore only a white singlet over her sagging breasts. A cigarette drooped between the thick, protruding lips that were responsible for most of the village gossip. As she talked, ash dusted down her front, while the smoke kept one eyelid clamped shut. Gao was a top agent in the bound-foot grannies detective team, the white-haired red armband brigade that patrolled the village for the neighborhood committee, spying for anything suspicious. Once Gao had caught a young man who hid in a tree to peep at women using a public toilet. She let no one forget that triumph.

I rode off before the women began their familiar exchange. Know-It-All Gao would surely ask if I had a boyfriend. Ma would say that I had lots of male friends and she couldn't keep up with me. In front of her friends, she liked to project the image of a modern parent. To her credit, my mother granted me more freedom than most parents, who tried to control their daughters' every move.

But had she known my plan that night...

At nine, Liang and I met up at Wuding Gate by the crumbling city wall. Without a word, he tailed behind me in the distance.

I was dripping with sweat, not only from the oppressive heat, but also from nervous anticipation. We were heading to my sister's empty flat, five minutes ride away from the old city gate. Weijia was on a trip to Lu Mountain for an official meeting: Chinese officials of all levels often found excuses to meet at the famous mountain retreat, further up the Yangtze River. Her devoted husband had insisted on accompanying his pregnant wife. As usual, whenever they were away, Weijia offered me the spare key, which opened the door both to material luxury, and the luxury of peace and privacy. At home we were battered by ear-splitting noise from nearby construction sites, which only reluctantly died down in the middle of the night.

Weijia had recently become an official. An eloquent speech at a model teacher's conference impressed a leader from the Qinhuai district government who transferred her to manage the Youth League work in his district, one of five in Nanjing. Smooth as polished jade, she fit into her new job immediately.

As soon as I held the string of silver keys in my hand, a daring idea flashed in my head: why not invite Liang to spend the night? I had long held the fantasy of sleeping in the arms of my lover, even for just one night, a dream Chilly had failed to fulfill.

"Lover" was a premature term for Liang, but we certainly had moved closer.

After the storm, I wasn't sure what to do. I had gone over to consult Chilly at his office, for he was the only person in the world that I could talk about matters of such indiscreet nature. "How stupid you are!" he jumped up from his desk. "What do you mean nice guy? Big gray wolf! Stay away from him, you silly melon!" he ordered with his usual authoritative air.

"Stop calling me 'silly melon.'"

"Anyway, if you miss that business," he winked at me, "you can always do it with me."

"You disgusting animal!" I told him off. I knew he was dating a music teacher, a university classmate of his.

"Disgusting animal? All men are disgusting animals, with only one thing on their mind, I tell you."

Whatever was in Liang's mind, I had decided to stay away from the emotional trauma of getting involved with a married man.

Then a letter from Liang tipped the balance.

I sincerely apologize if I have offended you, he wrote. *Let me tell you my story. My marriage to my wife seemed a very "natural" one. A good match by anyone's standard. She is the daughter of an old friend of my mother. We knew each other as kids. After my relationship with a girlfriend failed, I got together with her. Urged by my family, we got married before I came to Nanjing to study—my dying father very much hoped that his last child would solve "the marriage problem" before he passed away. She is a virtuous woman, a woman any man would feel lucky to have. We respect each other, though there is no passion. I am sure I'd have gotten along just fine in my lukewarm marriage, like millions of other couples. Then, I met you. You caught my eye the first time I saw you in Shanghai. You ran toward the bus. Your curly hair flew in the air and you looked like a free bird. I thought I could be a close friend of yours, an elder brother. But I fell in love with you. It was wrong of me. Being married, I have no right to love you. You are a wonderful girl who*

*deserves someone better. I don't think we can have a pure
friendship, as I once sincerely hoped. Therefore, I think we'd
better not see each other again. I'll cherish the happy memories
you brought me—they are very, very special to me.*

Panic!

Never see him again! I couldn't bear the idea. It suddenly
became clear that I had fallen in love with him in the golden
moment when he was lit by the setting sun on that crowded
Shanghai bus. I was in love with him before I knew it! For
me, love always struck fast. Recently, my friend Ju had
been introduced to a man who met her requirements as a
prospective husband: he had a university degree, income
over five hundred yuan per month, height above five foot
nine, and age under thirty. But inconceivably to me, they
met only so often, at parks and the like—a process termed
"cultivating feelings," as if love were a type of bacteria.

I had rushed to his dormitory at Nanjing University
that evening. He happened to be there, and alone. I threw
myself into his arms and we kissed. Somehow, without a
word of discussion, we had established that it was fine to
kiss as long as we didn't step over the final line—conducting
that rain-and-cloud business.

I had not expected such a battle to persuade him to go
along with my plan for us to spend the night together. It
wasn't appropriate, first of all, he said; secondly, people
might find out, thereby ruining my reputation. I argued
that it was no more inappropriate than anything we had
done to date, and that my reputation would survive if
we were careful. And finally, I needed his help with my
Teach-Yourself University exam, which was only a week
away. After I had showered him with kisses and tears, he
reluctantly gave in. One night only.

Weijia's building, assigned to them by her husband's
danwei, was small and quiet. In pitch darkness, I climbed to

the third-floor flat on my own, bumping into bikes and coal briquettes stacked in the landings, and then, having made sure the coast was clear, I crept downstairs to beckon Liang. Despite my promise, I knew I would be in deep trouble if any bound-foot detective or colleague of Changyong's caught sight of us. But danger also excited me—it had since my childhood. Though obedient at school, I grew bolder outside the gates. "Copying the leading sheep" was a game that dared you to follow someone's tricky or risky act. Whoever did the best became the leading sheep. I was often the only girl in the game. A long scar under my chin commemorated one heroic act—jumping down from a basketball backboard.

Once we made it to safety, we sighed with relief in a sweaty embrace. His kisses were salty, but I was hungry for them. We could've easily melted into the darkness, but he turned the bright light on. "I love you." He flashed a tender, almost apologetic smile. So, he wanted to play by the rules—nothing inappropriate.

While Liang had a shower—Weijia was one of the privileged few to enjoy a shower at home—I lay in bed, reveling in the sound of water splashing against the tiled floor.

The flat was a two-bedroom place. In sharp contrast to the dirty stairwell and drab exterior, it boasted chandeliers, leather sofas, and a massive sound system, which rarely made a sound—its presence as status symbol was enough. An electric fan swayed from one side to another, wafting a badly needed breeze.

We settled on the bed's bamboo matting, cooler to the skin than sheets. Hidden inside the white mosquito net, we were on a secluded island of our own. Nestling in his strong arms, I felt like a boat long at sea, finally anchored in a peaceful harbor. A dream fulfilled. I went to sleep blissfully.

I woke up in the morning to a still-surreal world. He pampered me, cooking a breakfast of fried eggs and savory pancake, carrying out chores in a brisk and natural style, as if they were his daily tasks.

Then, in the intimate, darkened room, we sat down to work: the bamboo curtains were drawn to keep out prying eyes. He was a demanding teacher, taking me through practice tests until I complained of a stiff neck.

He volunteered to give me a massage. When his thumbs pressed hard into my stiff shoulders, I gave a pained cry. Gradually, I relaxed as his fingers moved, pressing into my shoulders and neck. I didn't know when the kneading gave way to a gentle caress that generated an electric wave, scorching through my body. I closed my eyes to enjoy the sensation. My head was nearly touching his firm stomach. As more heat waves lapped my body, I could hear his heavy breathing. I stood up, seeking his lips. He kissed back with equal strength. I smelled his desire. My hand went down to feel it: a decent lady was not supposed to make such advance. But I didn't care. I just wanted him.

"Are you sure?" he asked.

"Yes, yes!"

Besieged, we crossed the forbidden final line with urgency. The stormy session was quick and explosive.

"Sorry, you got me excited for too many hours."

But I thanked him. We'd done it, we'd finally done it!

We lay still on the bamboo mat, half sleeping and half dreaming. Light penetrated through cracks in the bamboo curtain, together with the crackling noise of a welder in a nearby construction site. The defining noise of our time.

Weren't our bodies welded together just then?

I began to hum the folk song again. "Jasmine, oh, beautiful jasmine! I am tempted to pick one blossom to wear in my hair, but afraid the others may laugh at me."

Liang propped up with one arm to face me. "Of all

people, you are the one who would dare to pick up a jasmine to wear, without caring about other people's laughter."

I smiled in acknowledgement.

"I know you've wanted to make love. So have I. To be honest with you, if I had loved you any less than I do, I would have taken you a long time ago, believe me."

I rose to give him a tearful kiss.

"I've been thinking a great deal about our relationship. A funny one, isn't it?"

As he talked, he fanned me with a palm fan. I listened carefully while playing with the hair on his arms: we had never talked about our relationship properly. "If we'd stayed just friends, as we pretended, then we shouldn't kiss; if we admit that we are lovers, then what's the big difference between kissing and sex? But going that far, I just worried it wouldn't be fair to you."

"We love each other. That's the fairest deal in the world!" I said.

He confessed how often he'd had to battle his physical desires when we were together and how last night had tortured him. "You are such a fox fairy, irresistible! I nearly raped you last night."

"You should have," I grinned mischievously. "I would have enjoyed it." I touched the muscles on his arms, the result of years of bodybuilding, and asked: "I presume she enjoys that clouds-and-rain business with you, too, your wife, doesn't she?"

The smile disappeared from his handsome face. Liang revealed that in the beginning of their marriage, he thought his bride, a virgin until their wedding night, was just shy. He did his best to please her, but she remained uninterested, dutifully performing her conjugal obligations. "It has been a problem in our marriage, at least for me. But you can't divorce your wife on the grounds that she doesn't enjoy sex! A judge would laugh his teeth off." He let out a bitter laugh.

"Well, surely, sex is essential to the harmony in a relationship," I said.

"Yes, I presume so. I do wonder sometimes if our marriage would have survived till now if we had lived together all the time," he scratched his head. "She really is a good woman, probably just cold. I know women do enjoy clouds and rain, not just for the benefit of men."

"How do you know?" I poked him on the well-toned chest playfully, "From personal experience?"

He nodded. While down in the countryside, Liang was seduced by a much older woman, another sent-down youth in his commune. He wasn't sure if she liked him or only made use of him as a boy toy. Whatever the case was, she took care of him and made his life in that desolate village easier. "I was too young to know love anyway," he remarked on his distant youth, "but I enjoyed having sex with her, I am ashamed to say. Hai, do you want to hear a story?" He sat up.

"A story about sex?"

"Yes, sort of."

"A long time ago, there was a middle-aged monk who lived alone in a little temple hidden in a remote mountain. An enlightened monk and learned scholar, he refused all the temptations of the earthy world and totally devoted himself to Buddhism. His good reputation spread as far as the four seas. Then, one day, a young girl from a nearby village comes to worship. She's as pretty as peach blossom and fresh as morning dew. The monk is stunned by her innocent beauty. For some reason he can't explain, he invites her to the inner room where he advises her—then seduces her. 'What do you feel?' the monk asks the girl, who's lying dazzled underneath his body. At first she complains of a little pain. After a while, she cries: 'I feel pleasure, what is it then?' 'It's the devil,' the monk declares.

'Oh, master, please, I would love to have more devil!' the village girl pleads."

"More devil for me, too!" Straddling him, I also pled. We made love again. Like a great seducer, he teased me, aroused me, setting me on fire without letting me have him. "Women are *yin* who are slow to be aroused and slow to be satisfied," he quoted the Taoist theory of lovemaking. But words were no good for me. I groaned with pleasure and begged for his body. Finally, he slipped inside me as if it were the most natural thing in the world.

We were coated with a film of glistening sweat. Slippery as two eels, we once again welded together, perfectly. Thrusting, thrusting, we drove deeper into each other. As the flame turned white-hot, we exploded together. Beautiful sparks shot into the air.

Chapter 29

The Incident in the Park

The traffic problem was growing as fast as the economy itself. Wheezing buses and People's Liberation Army trucks now competed for space with motorized tricycles and Japanese-style pickup trucks. Open-engine tractors rumbled with noise and smoke, startling the ducks that were tied by their necks to the backs of motorbikes. Plodding along at a more traditional pace were horse or donkey carts full of watermelons; tricycles and streams of bicycles weaved in and out, barely avoiding each other and rarely bothering to notice red lights. Bells rang. Vehicles honked. Animals groaned and workers who had been sleeping soundly on top of trucks woke and joined the cursing: "Tamade!"

One evening, I ran into congestion at the end of Eternal Happiness Road. I had to carry my bike through narrow gaps in the jam to continue my journey north.

The street's name matched my mood. Intoxicated with love, I was feeling high up in the ninth heaven. The traffic jam, the baking heat, the boring routine, nothing could dampen my happiness.

I was so grateful for this love that I wanted to be a better person. At home, I did more chores than ever before; at work, my enthusiasm surprised and pleased Boss Lan. Twice a day, I cheerfully fetched sour plum juice from headquarters—the ice-cold drink was free to workers all throughout the summer.

Sometimes, I couldn't believe it was possible that such a handsome, gifted man had fallen in love with plain little me. Luckily there were reminders of him everywhere: books, little presents—pens, silk scarves—and phone calls at night if we didn't meet up.

Now firmly a "third party," I felt no shame. The absence of Liang's wife gave me plenty of space to pretend that she didn't even exist. I became more and more convinced that true love was justified, more so than a loveless marriage.

When Liang lent me an English edition of *Lady Chatterley's Lover* by D. H. Lawrence, I had taken it as an endorsement of our affair. Reveling in the passion between a sexually deprived upper-class lady and her husband's gamekeeper in nineteenth-century England, the book was passed like a baton between breathless literary lovers. Not exactly banned, it was nonetheless rarely on sale in bookshops. I had no idea how Liang obtained this battered copy. First, I wolfed down some juicy parts, then slowly read every line, every word, digesting all its richness. Whenever possible, Liang and I would read the book together, our senses aroused by the lyrical yet graphically described love scenes.

Logistics, not morality, became my major concern. We had few ways to secure badly needed privacy. We prayed for my sister's absence like drought-hit villagers praying for rain. Heavily pregnant, Weijia did go away for another weekend, to accompany her husband to a meeting in Shanghai. Cherishing the opportunity, we indulged ourselves in clouds and rain.

Liang had, fortunately, managed to keep his room in the dormitory, which he shared with a postgraduate student. It was a standard student room, a bunk bed, two desks, full of books all categorized on the shelves or piled up neatly on the desks. Clean and tidy.

Only when he knew for sure that his roommate would spend several hours at the laboratory were we able to make love there, hurriedly, nervously, and yet passionately, as if it were our last chance. He called me his "little fox fairy." In his husky voice, the negative term became tender and seductive. We tried our best to muffle the motions of love in his narrow, low bed. A world of other sounds floated in the open window: the basketball game in the court across the road; the tinkling of bicycle bells; the clank of metal spoons on enamel bowls in the washroom next door; and footsteps along the corridor, perhaps heading our way. A risky affair. Once someone knocked on the door—luckily, we were halfway decent. And when he answered, it was not the campus police, itching to record a sex crime, but a friend returning a book. Liang, without blinking an eye, introduced me as one of his many cousins.

Love made us more daring. "For the sake of sex, one's nerve could grow big enough to cover heaven," went the folk saying.

The charm of Xuanwu Lake belied its name—Dark Warrior, after the black dragon that had been spotted there, twice, in 449 CE. It was probably a lost Yangtze-River alligator, but in the Taoist views of the day, it was equated with the Dark Warrior, a turtle who ruled the northern constellation of the ancient world. The lake possesses a feminine beauty, its five islets linked by curving embankments and elegantly arched stone bridges. It stayed open till midnight as a favor to Nanjing's scorched citizens, suffering the "autumn tiger" heat of late August.

I was out of breath after the hour-long bike ride there. Punctual as ever, Liang already stood at the gate, absorbed in a book: whenever he found a free moment, he had a book on hand to fill it. He flashed a smile when he saw me. Hand in hand, we walked inside.

"How was your day?" he asked.

"I spent the whole day cleaning." The factory had recently become a candidate for provincial level "model" status, so the entire staff was mobilized to clean up before the inspection the next day. We mopped the floor; polished all the testing devices; climbed ladders to clean the windows till they shone like mirrors; and, worst of all, scrubbed off the yellow phlegm spat onto stairs and corridors by my colleague Little Ma.

Liang let out a hearty laugh. "I remember those pre-inspection cleanups. So Chinese, isn't it?"

"Never mind what I did. All I was thinking of was you!" We were just reaching a stone bridge. I leaped to the top, turned around, and kissed him.

He was quick to return my kiss. I knew he was uncomfortable with public affection, but he was always very tactful. "Thank you. Without the kiss, my day would be dull, too. Worse than dull, wasted. Yet another banquet," he continued as we walked along the lakeside toward somewhere more private. The key responsibility of his provincial planning commission was to approve projects, which gave it enormous power. To win approval, or simply to build useful relationships, people threw lavish banquets for Liang and his colleagues. "Revolution is not a dinner party," our great leader Chairman Mao once warned. But today's revolution seemed to be all about dinner parties—most business deals, official or private, were concluded at a banquet table crowed with expensive items—shark-fin or turtle soup, and drinks with medicinal benefits like bear-paw wine (considered generally good), snake-penis wine (a manhood enhancer) or snake-gallbladder wine (for improving eyesight).

"I couldn't wait to get out of it." Luckily, his banquets always started at five-thirty and never went more than two hours. That evening, some officials had gone on to a karaoke bar, but Liang had firmly declined the chance to sing and the singsong girls on offer—they were part of the appeal of karaoke bars that were springing up everywhere.

Liang had started his job several weeks earlier, and had already found it difficult adjusting from a relaxed academic regime to the nine-to-five official's life, in which, unlike at university, *not* speaking one's mind was the golden rule. Yet the most frustrating part was the bureaucracy and inefficiency, something he had underestimated before.

I sometimes worried that I might distract him from concentrating on his new job. But he claimed that he would suffocate without seeing me.

At the park, we found a perfect spot, an empty bench half hidden by a bushy Rose of Sharon, beside a pond where lily pads floated dreamily. The bright pink flowers had erupted into glorious full blossom.

Liang took a book from his canvas bag, a style favored by poor students and soldiers. Officials always carried black leather bags, a trademark of the elite. Yet out of this humble bag, he often plucked interesting articles or new books for me. Last time, he lent me the translated autobiography of American entrepreneur Lee Iacocca, bursting with individual initiative. Liang had become the connection between my small, stagnating well and a vibrant intellectual scene in the fast-changing world.

"For your friend Jiang He." Liang put the book into my hand.

"Nietzsche!" From the cover photo, I recognized the German philosopher's astonishing bushy moustache, shaped like the Chinese character for eight. *Death of God* was the startling title. I could hardly escape the philosopher's name, frequently cited in newspapers and journals. Like Teresa Deng to pop fans, Nietzsche and Freud were major stars to young intellectuals in China.

"I think he will find this interesting, or maybe you'd like to read it, too," Liang said.

My tax official friend had stayed, reluctantly, inside his golden cage and begun a correspondence course in accountancy to satisfy his thirst for knowledge. I had thought about introducing them, but decided against it: I would feel too embarrassed to admit to my friend that I was having an affair with a married man and I didn't want to lie either. I had to keep Liang secret, for the moment, at least.

Why recommend Jiang this particular book?

"Well, from what you've said, he's one of the many experiencing a 'faith crisis,'" Liang explained. All major religions were reviving, he said. Many people, like Jiang He, had become disillusioned with communism, which for many years was treated as a religion of sorts, Mao anointed as God. It was little wonder that dissatisfied intellectuals, having lived for so long under a single, ultimate authority, were now finding resonance in Nietzsche's call to reject traditions and reevaluate received values. "God is dead."

Liang talked excitedly, his brilliant eyes shining in the fading light.

I listened, enjoying the rhythms of the voice I loved without fully understanding.

"How clever you are!"

"No, no, I am not that clever," he smiled. "I just like to think."

Liang, unlike other men I'd known, had a way of showing me new things, and inspiring me to learn, without belittling me.

I circled my arm around him and he hugged back.

His mind, however, was still with Nietzsche. "You know, asceticism was one of the main reasons that he hated Christianity so much."

"And we are not ascetics, either." I sealed his lips with mine.

The curtain of the night fell, to the relief of countless young lovers fumbling in the undergrowth. Breeding as if by magic, the few first stars came to fill the sky, and fireflies darted about the low shrubs.

Xuanwu Lake was an enchanted place on such nights, its air sweetened by summer flowers.

In his strong arms, I felt so much like a woman, a loved, desired woman. I guided his hand down to my jade gate where a misty cloud had gathered. I panted as pleasure and need grew.

"Take me please. The devil is calling again," I whispered. His fingers were just "scratching an itchy leg through a boot"—not satisfying enough.

"No, not here," he pleaded.

"Please."

"NO!"

"But we've got nowhere to go. I cannot survive without you."

"I'll find a way, soon. But not now, please, my fox fairy."

But the little fox fairy had her way. While he talked about his responsibility to conduct our affair in a sensible fashion, I sneaked my hand into his trousers to grab what he called his little brother. This limp relative jumped to life in my hand. He groaned.

Standing face-to-face, we again welded together, perfectly. As the Rose of Sharon swayed with rhythm, our souls flew up to the heavens, where millions of stars' spying eyes glinted at the waves of heat shooting from our bodies.

But there were other spying eyes, too. And one glint became torchlight, piercing our privacy. "Shame, shame on you," shouted a burly man in a white singlet, appearing from nowhere and brutally dragging us back to reality, "what do you think this place is? If you are a legal couple, you can fuck at your home or hotel."

Quickly, I buttoned myself up. The man grabbed my arm with his fat hands, "You look like a decent girl, but are you?"

Shaken by this intrusion, I became angry by his insult. I would have pushed him if Liang didn't step in between, clutching his loose belt. "Big brother, let's have a man-to-man talk. Leave the lady alone. Can she go now?"

"Go?" he bellowed, "You're both coming with me to the police station. You've done the good deed. Now you have to face the consequences."

We exchanged concerned looks and slowly followed him along the main road. The man was pushing a bicycle, which only park workers could bring inside, but he lacked a security guard's uniform. We didn't dare challenge his identity as the last thing we wanted was to annoy him.

"What are you going to do with us, big brother?" Liang asked tentatively.

"The police will decide." The man let out a malicious smile, hoping for a scared reaction. I knew that in some cases people who'd been caught in public were sent to labor camp. I thought about my family, and big-mouthed Know-It-All Gao. Overnight, the whole village would know every detail. The shame would be too huge for my family to bear. How about Liang, his family's honor and his entire career?

"Come on, big brother, have a cigarette." Liang produced a pack of cigarettes, its fine packaging shining in the street lamp. The man hesitated for a moment, but took it with his short plump fingers when he noticed they were Chinas, the country's best brand. Liang bent down slightly to lit a cigarette for him. "You know, we actually got the marriage certificate ages ago. But we're still waiting for my danwei to assign a flat," Liang said calmly.

A convincing lie. Couples with marriage certificates at hand could wait for years for a home and one couldn't even get on the waiting list without a marriage certificate.

"So, you haven't had the wedding banquet yet?" the man asked.

"No, not yet." The ceremony to display the union to the public was an integral highlight of the wedding.

"So, you aren't really married, and so you can't do the business yet."

"Yes, I know," Liang said humbly, "but you know… Big brother, I know we're wrong and I promise that we'll never do it again. I swear by our beloved Chairman Mao!" For years, Mao was the closest thing to God in China, and his beliefs the only approved faith. Seeing the man's facial expression soften, Liang decided to try his luck. "It's getting late. Maybe we can pay a fine instead of going with you to the police station? I've got cash."

Sucking deeply on his cigarette, the man narrowed his eyes. "How much you got?"

Liang's eyes lit up. He took out his wallet and gave him everything he had, nearly four hundred yuan, possibly as much as the fat man made in a month.

The short plump hand snatched the money. I could almost detect a smile even as he tried to put on a straight face. "Need a receipt?"

"No, no need, big brother. Thank you very much."

In a second, he was back on his bike and pedaled away, leaving just a faint trail of smoke in the night air.

For a long while, we sat silently on the pavement beside our bikes. Smoke blurred Liang's handsome face. I had never seen him smoking before. Nestling against him, I contemplated our lucky escape.

Stubbing out his butt carefully on the pavement, he turned to me and held my hands. "Do you hope that we'll have a future together?"

"Of course, of course! But I don't dare bring it up with you." A lump moved in my throat. I took off my glasses and rested my forehead on his knees, wetting them with a stream of tears. I didn't know exactly why I was crying so uncontrollably—was I angry at him for underestimating my love; humiliated by my position as a third party; or just letting out the tension the evening's events had built up? All these feelings added drops to the stream.

We had never seriously discussed our future together. In a country with a divorce rate as low as one percent, getting one seemed as difficult as the Long March. In some ways, I felt it was enough that we loved each other. Deep in my heart, however, I would have loved to marry him and have a baby. I dreamed, every single day, about our son: somehow, I was convinced it was going to be a boy, and a modified version of his son—there was a photograph of him on Liang's desk, chasing a ball in his split pants. Our boy would have Liang's big bright eyes and thick dark eyebrows, and my little nose and curly hair: I never really liked my hair, but I thought the curls would look cute on a little boy.

There was little chance I'd get pregnant. When I was with Chilly, we risked conception every time—he'd just withdraw as climax shuddered near. But Liang was more careful. Apart from that first time at my sister's flat, he'd always used condoms. Contraceptives were not for sale, but distributed by family planning officials to married women in state-owned factories or government organizations. Unmarried people had no need of them, officials decreed, as they were not meant to have sex. But somehow, Liang managed to get these non-commodities. He always had his way.

"Sorry, my darling, I have not offered to marry you," he smoothed my back, but not my feelings. "You know, if I divorce my wife now, that would be the end of my career. I wouldn't be regarded as a moral person, and therefore not qualified for promotion. Also, she is looking after my old mother back at my hometown. Oh, please don't think I'm making excuses." He bent down to kiss my tearstained hands, murmuring how he loved me, how he had never experienced such unrestrained, passionate love in his whole life.

"Now, listen," he took both my hands, "I think the only way to have a future together is for both of us to go to America."

"America? How?" My eyes widened. Going to America— me, a little factory worker? I was twenty-three, with no special talents, no proper education, no achievements whatsoever. How could I get to America, the "beautiful country," where so very many Chinese dreamed of going?

"You are going to apply to study at an American university," Liang declared. All I needed to do was score well on the TOEFL test. As for him, if he behaved himself, he could likely be sent there as a government-sponsored visiting scholar. Once we were together in America, the land of freedom and opportunity, everything would be a lot easier.

"Do you really think so?"

"Yes, I do." He assured me assertively. "I personally much prefer Nietzsche to Schopenhauer because his attitude to life was so much more positive. If we are determined to do something, then we will!"

He squeezed my hand tightly as if hoping to pass his conviction on.

Chapter 30

Begging for Happiness

"Where? America! Mother of mine!" My mother's new moons shot up when I informed her of my grand new dream. She wouldn't have been more surprised if I had said I wanted to go to the moon.

"Why not?"

"Impossible, impossible!" Ma fanned herself ferociously with a palm fan. "You didn't even go to a proper university."

That was my own concern, too, but Liang assured me that TV University was as good as any so-called "proper university." In fact, in my application to an American university, he had suggested I stress how I'd taught myself. "Your experience has fully demonstrated your ability to learn, your initiative, and your intelligence, all of which mean more to Americans than anything else."

I repeated his words to Ma.

"But what about your worker status?"

"Doesn't matter. There is no such silly system in America. It's is a free country where everyone is equal."

She paused for a while, fanning herself and thinking hard. Going to America? There must be ten thousand problems to tackle, she hardly knew which to choose. "Surely, it will be harder than climbing to heaven. Do any of your classmates from TV University want to go there?"

"No one as far as I know, but I don't care. How can

a small sparrow know the ambition of a great roc?" I borrowed a Chinese idiom to encourage myself.

"America is very dangerous, isn't it? It's a place where dragons and fish are jumbled together. Robbery, murder, all those black people, how can a young girl like you fend for yourself there?"

"Don't believe the government propaganda! The crime rate may be higher, but it's not that bad." The government never forgot to criticize America when it had an opportunity to do so.

"Oh yes, and how much will university fees cost? Living costs, too? Terribly expensive country, isn't it? The total cost will be astronomical!" Ma waved her fan at the heavens. After overcoming the initial shock, her practical nature came into play.

"I don't know. Once I'm there, I can take on jobs in my spare time, working as a waitress or something. In America, wages are very high."

"Waitress, Little Li? Outrageous. You'll be the worst waitress in the world!" Father predicted, holding out his fan like a plate. "Here is your food, sir"—he said "sir" in English— "and crash!" He pressed his fan against my head.

"I am not 'sir,' but 'madam'!" I brushed off his fan, annoyed that he was trying again to show off his few English words. I was very clumsy and constantly spilled food on myself, yet waiting tables was the only job that I had heard Chinese students took up in America.

"Yes, madam, madam, I know that word, too!"

"Oh, just shut up!" Ma barked at her husband. "If you really were a learned man, we wouldn't worry about money so much, would we? You half-baked man, Kong Yiji!"

Tail between his legs, Father went outside.

Ma resumed her talk on money, something tangible, and vitally important in her book. "How much does the ticket to America cost?"

"Around five thousand yuan, or maybe less."

"Five thousand! Mother of mine! I won't save that much by the time I die. And you haven't got much yourself, I gather?"

Not much at all. "A beggar never spares food for the next meal," Ma used to warn, but it didn't stop me from spending every penny at my disposal.

But the financial difficulty was only a small bump compared to the mountain of challenges en route to America, or so Zhou Fang and I agreed. She was extremely supportive, for her fiancé, also a classmate of hers, shared the same dream and had been studying for the TOEFL. With a master's degree and a teaching position at a good university, he stood a much better chance than I did. Still, why not try?

"Maybe I can borrow some money from you, Weijia, and our relatives. It is effectively an investment. You know what? I am going to study business management! With that degree, I can make big money." I didn't know what business management meant. Liang chose the subject for me. He reasoned China urgently needed people with management skills, which would allow me to pick any high-paying job upon my return to the country. Studying journalism, on the other hand, would be unrealistic, because I stood little chance of competing with native speakers.

Nai had been scrubbing clothes on a washboard (we now owned a washing machine, but she insisted on washing her own clothes by hand). When our conversation made enough sense to her, she began to cry: "I just knew," she said, blowing her nose. "Look at the way you hold your chopsticks near the end." Since I was little, Nai had tried in vain to correct the way I held my chopsticks: according to superstitious belief, the way I did it instinctually foretold I would end up marrying far, far away from home. She also tried to correct my brother, who held his chopsticks too close to the tapered, eating end, which suggested that he would rely on his family too much. Not a good sign for a boy.

I went over, holding her coarse, soapy hands. "Nai, going to America is just an idea. It may never come true."

"It will, I know. Just like your Ma, once you set your mind on something a four-horse cart can't hold you back. Who's going to wash my hair then?" She wiped her tears. Since Nai didn't take proper showers regularly, every so often I would wash her hair at home in a basin, scratching and massaging her head. She would shut her eyes tight, moaning with pleasure, "Yes, harder, oh, so itchy!" It had long been a ritual that both of us enjoyed.

"So, come to America with me."

"I'm going nowhere. Don't understand the foreign farts. Half my body is already buried in the yellow earth."

She still didn't look her age, her hair black and her skin smooth. She was simply getting smaller. But her health was slowly declining. And her unselfish, unscientific approach didn't help. One night a few months earlier, she had suffered another minor heart attack. Unwilling to wake Ma up in the middle of the night, she just endured her discomfort quietly. The only precaution she took was to take off the ring I gave her. "It wouldn't come off if I died and my fingers went stiff!" she had explained, to our anger and laughter, the next day.

Now, looking at the dear face of my old grandma, I thought about how much I would miss her and the rest of my family, if I left. There were dishes that only Nai knew how to cook, like "lion's heads," and dumplings filled with shepherd's purse and minced pork. And I might never see her alive again.

But I had set my heart on America, where I would find freedom and love with Liang by my side.

The monster sat rigidly on a dirty wooden stool, a strange loop perched on her head. Hanging down from the loop were wires that linked to a device spouting alien noises. The rubbish woman stared at me as if I had three heads and six arms.

Dressed in a white skirt, I looked completely out of place in the rubbish dump. But it was the only place in the factory where I could listen to my English tapes without disturbance for a couple of hours.

I was studying for the TOEFL exam, or *Tuo fu*, "begging for happiness," as it was called in Chinese. Under Liang's guidance, I had signed up for a three-month intensive TOEFL course run by Nanjing University, one of many universities that had established test prep classes for the millions who shared my American dream.

My days now were filled with battles. The biggest one was to get my tired body out of bed in the morning. During the eight working hours, I functioned woodenly, but sprang to life the minute the off-work horn sounded. I would rush home, shoveling down my supper in five minutes, then jump back on my bike again, like a horse galloping without a stop. After a long ride, the sight of Nanjing University would invigorate me. The routine was repeated six times a week. An exhausting time indeed, but also a happy one. Hope had brightened my life.

When the class was over, Liang would often wait for me around a quiet corner, bringing me a roast sweet potato, golden persimmon, or bean curd mooncake: by then, my stomach would always be rumbling again. We would take a stroll in the campus's lovely garden or along a dark narrow street just outside the university, nicknamed Lovers' Lane. When his roommate was not around, only occasionally, we would spend some delirious time at his dormitory. No more open-air adventure ever since the park incident.

I had no idle time for parks anyway. I filled every moment pursuing my new goal.

To help with my listening comprehension, I borrowed my cousin Weiping's pillow-sized radio, a Japan-made Sony. When I turned to shortwave, the BBC news blasted out as if by magic. Imagine, the BBC, in London, the foggy capital of *Oliver Twist*! Reception was far from ideal. I had to fiddle constantly with tuning, changing the position of the radio or even shaking it to bring the sound back. Still, the magic box gave off such pleasure. Every morning began with "This is London" and a burst of cheerful music I soon grew fond of. Every night, I went to bed with clear BBC English in my head.

The news not only helped with my English but also provided me with good conversation material. In October 1987, when the Thirteenth Communist Party Congress took place, the BBC offered plenty of coverage about leadership changes and the long-awaited blueprint for political reform— just as Liang had hoped. He was pleased about Zhao's proposal to expand free-market mechanisms, abandoning the cautious "bigger birdcage" economic policy adopted earlier. "These ideas come straight from Zhao's think tank," Liang had informed me, "they would have been more daring if the conservatives haven't toned them down."

Unlike most of my fellow TOEFL students, who studied full-time, I had a job, and an increasingly busy one. A new policy had been introduced to encourage us to take on more work from outside the factory. Out of the extra profit we made, our factory received sixty percent, our work unit thirty, and the workshop ten. Yet even ten percent, insignificant though it may sound, could add up to a significant difference to our income. The market economy was reaching into every corner of society.

Now officially a model within the province, Liming was readying itself to bid for the greater glory of "national model factory." As part of a new campaign to tighten up discipline, plainclothes security personnel roamed workshop floors, alert for anyone sleeping, missing from their posts, or doing anything irrelevant to their jobs. They even hid inside the guardpost by the gates, in order to catch anyone who dared leave early. In the workshop, listening to my tapes with earphones on would be an open invitation for trouble. The only thing I could manage was to flip through Nietzsche's book. His emphasis on individualism and his belief in the power of will sent a timely and encouraging message to me.

My priority, however, was to keep up with my TOEFL course, which required at least a couple of hours' study during the day. How could I find time?

I had accidentally found a way to snatch some. One morning, a basket of rubbish in hand, I headed to the dump behind the back gate. A long trail of litter—food scraps, metal shavings, and a stream of black grease—extended from the dump like spilt intestines. Workers usually threw the waste from some distance to avoid getting their feet dirty and their senses disturbed. As I was about to shoot my rubbish into the air, a woman in a straw hat shouted at me from the entrance: "Tip off the rubbish here, woman!" She pointed at an open empty space behind her. Her job was to look after the rubbish dump.

I went over, rousing swarms of flies with each step. The actual rubbish dump, encircled by a parapet, was much less revolting. There were mostly scrap metal parts. Suddenly, the idea flashed in my mind—my hidden heaven! Who would come here?

The following day, I descended on the dumping ground again with a pack of cigarettes.

"For you."

"What for?" The rubbish woman took the bribe and asked in a strong rural accent.

"I want to borrow your place to study."

"Why? Even devils wouldn't come here to lay eggs! Well, please yourself." She had resumed her work. She had the unpleasant task of sorting out the rubbish so that scrap metal could be sold. The worst, dirtiest, and lowest jobs in the city were now taken by migrants like her.

After I sat on the stool, with my earphones on, the rubbish woman's red, infected eyes bugged. She stared at the loop and the wire. What was going on? The alien noise I made, following the tape, bewildered her further.

"Who are you?" She came up to me. "What are you doing here?"

I felt I owed her an explanation, so I put down my earphones.

"A worker from that building," I jabbed at the gray monster behind us. "I am studying."

"Studying foreign farts?" Standing there, her dry stick of a body hidden under her large straw hat, she looked like a scarecrow. Her haggard face was dotted with the light that seeped through the loose fabric of her hat. Despite her greasy canvas uniform, I could tell she was from a peasant family.

"Only English," I told her.

"Why?"

"I am trying to go to a foreign country called America."

"Why?"

"Why did you come to Nanjing?"

"Life is better here in a city."

"I heard life is even better over there."

"Is America far away?"

"Yes, far, far away, over the edge of the sky."

"Will you miss home?"

"I think I will. Do you miss home?"

"I do, particularly my little ones. I was still breastfeeding my little girl when I left home." Her eyes grew redder and her nose ran. Pressing her right index finger on her right nostril, she shot liquid out of her left nostril and repeated the process on the other side. She wiped her face with the back of her hands. "But two months' salary here is more than I could earn in a year at home."

I nodded.

"How many children have you got?"

"Me," I laughed, "none! I am not married yet. But I hope to go America with my boyfriend and we will get married there." I was dying to tell someone the secret that was bursting out of my chest.

I would sneak to the rubbish dump daily, with Boss Lan as my cover. It was only a hundred steps away, yet it felt like another world "where the sky is high and the emperor far away." I applied Tiger Balm to repel mosquitoes, and my earphones blocked the buzz of flies. Even the foul smell diminished as I concentrated my attention. Step by step, the TOEFL format became less strange.

For my break, I chatted with the rubbish woman. Despite her ancient looks, she was only thirty-six. A cousin had found her the job. In a village in central China, she left behind a husband, elderly parents, and four children aged from five to seventeen. She and her cousin lived in a rented makeshift shed by the river where there was no running water or electricity.

"Make sure your children finish their schooling," I advised.

"Don't know," she said, "But I know their bellies are full now."

Water runs from a high place to low-lying land, but people tend to move upward. How similar we were, I thought: she left her village for the city; I wanted to leave China for America. The only difference was that she migrated for her family, while I plotted for myself and for the sake of my love.

Chapter 31

Troubled Smile

One autumn afternoon, on another factory errand in Shanghai, I sat on a bus, replaying in my mind my incredible encounter with Liang in this city on the sea. The day had started just like any other day, with no sign or omen. Yet he had drifted into my life and changed it forever.

The sign for Shanghai Film Studio jerked me awake from my daydream. On an impulse, I leapt off the bus. The brother of my lover worked here as a director. Liang had promised to introduce him to me and said I would enjoy his company as he was "quite a character." Since I was here, having completed my gauge mission, why not just knock on his door?

The oldest and best film studio in China had an unglamorous lobby. An amiable man received me. He called up and, surprisingly, caught the busy director there. In minutes, the older Liang turned up. I had seen his photos in glossy film magazines. In real life, he was much shorter than his brother, but shared the same bright, sharp eyes. He was in his late forties. Wrinkles were creeping across his unshaven face, but he was nevertheless handsome, in a rough-edged way.

"Hi, my name is Zhang Lijia, a, a friend of Liang Jijin," I said a little uneasily.

He looked at me a little suspiciously, waiting for me to elaborate.

But I couldn't bring myself to say girlfriend. "Sorry, I thought he has mentioned me to you," my face turned red, "if you are busy, you don't have to…"

"He may have indeed mentioned you. But I'm rather forgetful at the best of times, let alone now. My life is in a complete mess. Come on, I love to meet my brother's friends. Usually interesting sorts." There was authority in his tone.

Estranged from his actress wife and teenage son, he lived alone in a flat inside the studio, as messy as he had hinted. Videotapes, pages from manuscripts, and books cluttered the room. Empty beer bottles and an ashtray hidden by cigarette butts crowded the glass coffee table: temporary, careless, unruly, the polar opposite of his brother's order-driven dormitory. There was none of the impressive art or decor I had anticipated either.

Liang cleared a corner on the sofa to let me sit down. "Sorry about the mess. I had a few guys over to talk about my next film."

"What's it about?" I asked.

"Some silly love story. Not quite sure about it." He began to move the bottles to the kitchen. When he re-emerged, I introduced myself once again awkwardly. But he paid no heed to my vague yet emphatic use of the word "friend."

"So, how is Number Six getting on with his flashy government job?" My Liang was the sixth born in their family.

"Oh, fine, but it's never easy to adapt a very different lifestyle."

"His conscious decision. He wants to become a big potato in the government, like our father." There was an apparent sense of satire in his tone.

"You don't approve?"

"Oh, no. It's just not my type of thing. I would go mad if I had to dress up, say things I don't mean, and try to please my bosses, ugh…" He creased up his face as if swallowing bitter Chinese medicine. "But he'll be fine," he continued, settling into an armchair opposite me. "He is the most adaptable one in our family."

I remembered a black comedy he directed a few years ago entitled *Troubled Smile* about how Chinese people, intellectuals in particular, had to pretend to be characters that were acceptable in society. Satirical and intelligent, it made people laugh—and then think. It did not make his name, but it was his best, in my view. I told him so, adding that I wasn't impressed by his latest film, *Singing in the Middle of the Night*, a love and horror story combined, set in 1930s Shanghai. "Hope you're not losing your sharpness?" I blurted out in my usual unsubtle way.

"Oh, dear, what an alarming remark!" he smiled, lighting a cigarette. He offered me one, but I turned it down. "Maybe you are right. My talent has depleted."

While he smoked, I sat there uneasily, not knowing where to put my two hands, or my two legs: should I go or gather my courage to reveal my third-party status? I looked around, as if searching for some clues. Everywhere my eyes landed on pictures of a ballerina, some stage photos in her tutu; others in casual clothes. In all of them, she looked stunning, a fact of which she was self-consciously aware.

"That's Tingting, the woman who is driving me crazy," the director picked up a framed photo of her, caressing it with his eyes. He began to tell me their story, fragments of which I had picked up from Liang. Their romance had started nearly two years ago at a friend's party where he spotted the young beauty, whose face was "prettier than cottonrose hibiscus," in his own flowery terms. Despite a twenty-year age gap, and opposition from all sides, the director filed for a divorce from his devoted wife. Only two months earlier, just as the divorce was going through, the ballerina had shifted her affections to a princeling of some sort, who showered her with expensive gifts and the promise of a helicopter.

"A helicopter, does it sound real?" he asked angrily. "You are a young lady, tell me what young ladies want?"

"Love, above everything else." I replied.

"She has all my love!"

"Well, maybe she feels insecure," I reasoned. A beautiful ballerina like Tingting, admired on and off stage, probably demanded plenty of attention. Maybe she felt she didn't get enough from him. I knew he could be a self-centered person. "Sorry for being direct, but you must be away often, and always surrounded by clouds of beauties. Or maybe she's simply attracted to money and power."

"Eh, interesting, I have never thought about these things before. Can I take you out for dinner?" He grabbed a checked scarf and hung it loosely around his neck, sealing his artistic image.

I gladly accepted, not only because I had nowhere else to go, but also because I had not completed my self-set mission—to learn more about my beloved man.

Around the corner from the studio, the restaurant was clearly a film crowd hangout. Faded posters of 1930s film stars filled the walls, with their permed hair, almost invisible smiles and fanciful *qipao*, the tight-fitting dress with high mandarin collar, split to the thigh. Their timeless, nostalgic beauty, a quality I also found in my grandma, made today's film stars look so plain. The music, grinding out of an old-fashioned gramophone, was all sentimental favorites from the pre-Communist era.

The head waitress, dressed in a lavish silk qipao, greeted us with a slight bow. Despite its conservative collar, the dress, highlighting the young woman's curves, was very seductive. The director's eyes fixed on her white legs, flashing between the daring split.

"Director Liang, what would you like to eat?" The waitress asked in sweet Shanghai dialect.

"My usual favorites," he replied, smiling at her without looking at the menu or consulting me. "Eh, the chicken feather must be fresh." The leafy vegetable, roughly shaped like a chicken feather, was very popular among Shanghaiese.

"How about you, miss?" she turned to me politely. No one knew at which point the stern term "comrade" was blown away by the strong winds of capitalism. Only officials continued to use it, on formal occasions.

"What Director Liang ordered is fine for me."

She bowed slightly, tripping away lightly like a butterfly.

After a few bites, I summoned all my courage. "Director Liang, er..." I blushed even before I began. "I mentioned I am a friend of Liang Jijin, I mean, I am his girlfriend."

The director halted chewing. After swallowing his mouthful of food, he raised a finger at me. "Seriously, you mean you've gone to bed?"

My face flamed with embarrassment and irritation at his blunt question. "Yes, we love each other. He must have mentioned his girlfriend to you."

He put down his chopsticks. "I am forgetful, but not of this kind of information. No, he didn't mention a word, I am afraid."

I was gripping a beautifully ironed napkin. As my heart sank, I let it loose on the table. It was all wrinkled, like a sad face about to cry. I tried in vain to straighten it. "I just don't understand. Really. He said that he had confessed our affair to you and you were very supportive..." I said, eyes still downcast at the napkin. I thought about the evening when Liang told me that he had revealed his secret to his director brother, the only family member who would understand him. "I can't wait to introduce you openly to all my family and friends," he had said with emotion. I'd been very moved. How come the director didn't know any of this?

"Supportive? Did you say supportive?" the director said loudly. "Support you to do what, get married?" he asked with a heavy dose of sarcasm.

"Yes, eventually." I told him about our plan of trying to go to America together.

"This is very interesting stuff," he said, eyes glowing with excitement. He lit a cigarette, in rich anticipation of a good drama. "I mean, it's totally out of character. Who would guess that Number Six would get involved in an affair?"

"What do you mean?"

"I mean he doesn't seem to be the emotional type who would go for an affair."

"You are married, you fell in love with your ballerina— why not your brother?" I told him how we met by chance, and how we were struck by love as if by lightning.

"Young lady," he patted my hand, "let me tell you the difference. I fell in love with my ballerina, so I decided to divorce my wife to marry her. Do you know what hell it is to get a divorce in China? Everyone I knew tried to stop me. My family threatened to cut ties with me. The only person who didn't beg me was my wife. She let me go graciously, even though she loved me. I am sorry that I broke her heart. But I wanted to pursue my love, my only chance for happiness. But somehow, I just don't think my brother would go through the same trouble or, worse, jeopardize his career." He sucked hard into his butt, stubbed it out, then rubbed his hands free of ash. Like his words, his movements were confident and assertive.

"Why?" I pleaded. "You don't know how much we love each other and how happy we are together." I told him, earnestly, stories of our time together. Liang was a perfect lover, caring, sensitive, funny, and a master at clouds and rain.

His brother listened patiently and then sighed. "Everyone thinks at some point that his or her love is the most beautiful and unique in the world, so special that even heaven should be moved. I did, and obviously you are right at that stage. True, I don't know your relationship, but I know my own brother," he looked me in the eye for the first time. "You are like a clear pool of water that one can see through, but not Number Six."

"I am totally lost. Tell me what kind of man he is."

"On the surface, he is a perfect gentleman, intelligent, friendly, and charming. He always knows the right thing to do and the right words to say. But..." he shifted in his chair and lit another cigarette. "But he can be calculating, and selfish. Bear in mind, he is extremely ambitious and driven. He will make sure he gets what he wants without sacrificing too much." To be fair, Number Six went through a lot as a young person, he added. In some ways, it was society that taught him to be cunning. The worst impact of the Cultural Revolution was that it destroyed Chinese people's integrity and honesty, the director concluded.

His words were threatening to destroy my dream, too. My defensive instincts flared. "How can I believe that your brother is as you describe?"

"You don't have to believe me. I am telling you this because I don't want you to get hurt. You are so young and naïve." He gently stroked my right hand, which was again gripping the napkin tightly, as if my life depended on it. I felt uneasy at his touch, but said nothing, waiting for him to spill more beans, however hurtful they might be.

"All right," Liang continued, "did he mention by any

chance that he had a beautiful girlfriend who was from a rather common background?"

"Yes, very briefly."

According to the director, Number Six dumped his girlfriend for his current wife, the daughter of a senior official, who more or less granted Liang a place at Nanjing University in a Master's program through the so-called "recommendation system," which ensured some "politically sound and academically outstanding" candidates, favored by the Party, entered university. In this way, he successfully jumped out of the factory he hated so much. "I could sympathize with him in some ways, but it was cruel to dump a girl who loved him wholeheartedly. She was totally devastated. I would forgive him if he loved his wife, but from the sound of it, he doesn't really."

Sitting there, I felt a sudden chill rise up my spine.

"Well, maybe your case is different and he truly loves you. When you both make your way to America, things may work out nicely for you. But," I was growing fearful of his "buts," "spending a few years abroad, gaining the 'gold plating,' is fine. But I would think he'd like to come back to pursue his ambition."

Since a degree from a Western university would surely attract multinational companies, going abroad to study was regarded as "gold plating," a way to boost one's commercial value. He didn't explain the implication of Liang's expected return to our relationship, but went on talking about himself.

"Look, I am a hundred times more famous than my brother in China. But in the eyes of my parents, I am no more than an opera actor making a lowly living in the Pear Garden. They are old-fashioned, antiques. For them, the only way to show a man's success is to work for the government as a high official. That's what they wanted Number Six to do."

"Are you jealous of your brother?" I was still trying to figure out why the director would splash dirty water at his own brother.

The director shook his head, explaining that he was nearly a grown-up man when Number Six was born. The youngest child did receive far more attention from the parents, who had earlier been too busy with their revolution. "But I am not as close to my family as he is. Number Six is a filial son, to give him credit."

I was half expecting him to say, "But it will make his divorce more difficult. The antique would hang herself rather than see her beloved son divorce the best wife in the world." But Liang just sat there, sipping beer, smoking his cigarette.

Through the haze of smoke, the faces of the old film stars on the wall became distorted and their smiles more obvious and knowing. Even the music grew irritating. I wanted to go.

Liang walked me to the nearest bus stop. I held my own arms against the night chill.

"Honestly, for your own sake, I advise you to think carefully about your relationship with my brother. He is too selfish to love anyone else." Walking closely by my side, he sounded like a doctor who was giving an injection to a sick child—it would hurt but was good for you. "You know, you very much remind me of Tingting. You both are naïve, stubborn, impulsive, and of course, lovely."

Before I knew it, he had already circled me with his right arm. I stopped to look at the hand on my shoulder and tried to remove it. In a second, he grabbed both of my arms and forced his intrusive tongue into my mouth. I flapped like a caught bird and kicked. Once free of his painful grip, I slapped him hard across his face. "You turtle egg, I am not a whore!"

I shot into the darkness like an arrow from the bow.

Chapter 32

Fish and Bear Paw

At the Black Forest Café, candles fluttered whenever the door moved. As I waited inside, my heart fluttered, too. Five to eight, five minutes until our appointment. I rehearsed in my head what I had to say.

Compared to most restaurants in China, where the lights were bright enough to play basketball, this place was cozy, the paintings on the walls barely visible in the dim light. The high-backed seats offered some privacy to the clientele, mostly young and trendy types who cared about atmosphere as much as the food. Several new establishments had opened to cater to their needs, adding more color to an increasingly lively urban landscape. Since it was conveniently located just south of the university, Liang and I had sometimes popped into the Black Forest for coffee when we tired of roaming the streets. The slightly bitter drink was new to both of us. We took a liking to it, with the help of milk and plenty of sugar.

Two minutes to eight, Liang turned up. Sitting down opposite me, he touched my hands, but I withdrew.

"What's wrong?" he pleaded, "I just knew something was up—you gave up your TOEFL class, right?"

As soon as I returned to Nanjing, I had arranged the meeting. I couldn't look him in the eye. If my glances lingered too long, I feared all my resolution would flee. He looked so handsome in a tight-fitting black jumper, so full of manly charm and energy. His eyes were burning brightly, but they were windows no more: I no longer felt I could see through to his soul.

"I met your brother in Shanghai." My voice was a little coarse from exhaustion.

"Oh, really, how come? Hope he didn't try to take advantage of you!" He made a nervous joke.

"Yes, he did. But that's not the reason I am so upset. What exactly did you tell him about me?"

I knew I had hit the nail on the head. He looked dumbfounded at first, then began to swear, something he had never done before. "Tamade! Damn him! I hope he's struck by thunder. He could have any woman he likes. Why lay his dirty claws on mine? What did he try to do? Did he ... ?"

"Nothing happened. I am not interested in discussing it. I want to know why you made up the whole story."

A brief but heavy silence. He scratched his head. After a long pause, he raised his head. "I am very sorry. To be honest with you, I did intend to tell him about us, the whole story. But this kind of matter is awkward to discuss over the phone. And I do believe that he would be very supportive of us."

"Well, you're wrong there. He doesn't believe for a moment you would do anything that might jeopardize your career."

"Do you believe him, then?"

"Yes, I do."

It seemed a head-on blow. "What else did my brother tell you?"

I mentioned his girlfriend and his marriage of convenience.

He nearly jumped. Then, he launched his defense: he had entered Nanjing University on his own merits. There was a recommendation system, but his score was high enough, he was sure of that. As for the former girlfriend, the whole story of their breaking up was far more complicated than the director knew. Indeed, he might have fancied her himself.

"Why, Lijia? I have known you and loved you for nearly half a year, and my brother is simply a stranger. What spell did he cast on you that you would choose to believe him instead of me?"

"He had no reason to lie to me."

"Yes, he did. He tried to paint a bad picture of me so that he could drag you to his bed."

I shook my head. Although the director did make a pass at me, it was an impulsive action, fuelled by drink. He simply wouldn't have bothered to knit a web of lies just to win me over.

"What do you want to do?" Liang asked, his voice husky.

"I am leaving you. Because you cheated me."

"I never cheated you. There is a distinction between white lies and cheating." Seeing my tired but firm face, he knew there wasn't much point in arguing. "It's unfair, Lijia. You've made up your mind even before the trial. Whatever I say makes no difference to you now."

I sighed. Back in my dismal hotel in Shanghai, I had suffered a sleepless night. I tossed about in the hard bed, tortured by anger, a sense of betrayal, and bewilderment. Why would Liang, my beloved, lie to me? Maybe he only pretended to be serious about me. I began to question his whole commitment.

I had learned other things from the director that contradicted his brother, such as the restriction on the children of high-ranking leaders going abroad. "No such thing!" the director had laughed. "America is full of the children of central government leaders!" Having no knowledge of such matters, I had accepted Liang's story. And their father's rank wasn't as high as I was led to believe.

He seemed very good at making up stories, like his tale of the monk seducing the mountain girl. Caught red-handed at Xuanwu Park, he calmly lied that we were actually married. I didn't mind these white lies so much, but why lie to me, the woman he loved, about important matters? Was he just a liar that couldn't be trusted?

Before the first birds sang in the morning, I had decided to end my love affair with Liang Jijin.

I always built up a perfect image of the man I fell for, papering over his imperfections. I'd done it even with Red Rock, my first love. Now, that image was falling away. I discovered the hidden and hideous side of Liang. I had been dazzled by his brilliance. When I was young, my family had a beautiful porcelain bowl, one of Nai's few antiques to survive that long, showing four boys in traditional clothing, each holding a character—fortune, power, longevity, and happiness—the top four desires in the traditional Chinese world. Because of the lovely bowl, the tasteless porridge we endured each morning seemed to taste better. Then, one day, Nai dropped it and a little piece was chipped off. In those days, there were still craftsmen who made a living by piecing broken porcelain together. But I had cried, not wanting it mended because no amount of mending would restore it to perfection. Now I would have to give him up like the cracked bowl.

"Why dump me like a meatless bone? I love you and I thought you loved me!" he persisted.

"I can't love a man whom I no longer trust." Before this meeting, I had indeed held some slim hope that Liang would somehow prove he wasn't what his brother said. Now, I knew he was, more or less.

"What can I do to make you to change your mind? Divorce my wife right now?"

Without really meaning to, I replied: "Yes, your marriage or me. You have to choose right now."

"You know it would be very difficult right now. She is looking after my ailing mother. Let's both try to go to America. Once I get there I can get you over, too. I promise I'll…"

But America failed to excite me, too. Without love, the halo of the beautiful country was fading.

A young couple walked into the café, the draft threatening our candle, casting a long, shaky shadow up the wall.

"You can't have a fish and bear paw at the same time." I rose to go, leaving him this morsel of conventional wisdom to bite. You can't have everything.

On the pavement outside, withered leaves from the parasol trees rattled in the wind. "The tree may crave calm, but the wind will not drop." Liang threw another Chinese idiom at me to summarize his helplessness. Things take their own course regardless of one's will.

"Can we at least stay friends?" He followed me.

"You know it's quite impossible."

"Then, let me take you home for the last time. I can't let a young lady go home alone at this late hour." He sounded gallant, yet pathetic.

"No, thank you. I can look after myself." I suddenly hated his good manners. If he believed I had wronged him, why would he bother to show kindness?

"You are well able to, that I know," he said, standing very close to me in the pavement, one hand caressing the handle of my bike. "I often marvel at your strong will. But sometimes I wish you wouldn't be so pigheaded."

My resolve was under direct threat, against the spell of his familiar smell. I had to fight so hard to suppress the urge to throw my tired body into his strong arms. Gathering my wits, I tried to push his hand away from my bike handle, but he held my hand. "Thank you, Lijia, the past few months have been the happiest time in my life."

I quickly got on my bike before my tears breached their gates. All the way home, a warm stream flowed down my face. Tailing behind me was Liang on his bike. I knew. I could feel the rays of his eyes.

"The lotus root snaps but its fibers stay joined," went an old saying. Liang sent me long, moving letters, trying to explain his position and begging me not to act on first impulse. The letters tortured me. I asked him to stop.

Without his smile, the sunshine in my life, I began to wither. I tried, mechanically, to carry on with my life as usual, going to work, checking the pressure gauges, riding to Nanjing University for TOEFL lessons. But I lost the enthusiasm. I had not visited the rubbish dump for a while. I was just a walking corpse.

One night, shortly before the end of my TOEFL class, it suddenly began to rain. The lucky ones who had taken the weather forecast seriously put on their raincoats and ducked into the curtain of rain. The majority stayed, trapped in the classroom. I walked to the door to join the others, watching the rain fall. All of a sudden, I saw Liang, standing tall and straight among the crowds, like a crane among a batch of chickens.

"I came to give you this," he said, offering a large umbrella with a wan smile. I hadn't seen him for nearly three weeks. To avoid the awkwardness of meeting in person, I had returned his books and some gifts he had given me by post. He seemed pallid, or so I imagined, and his manner slightly reserved. But his eyes were still brilliant and spirited as usual. "Sorry, I haven't got a raincoat for the bicycle. If you can manage to ride holding the umbrella, feel free to take it. Or better, wait until the rain stops. In this season, the heavy rain never lasts too long."

His husky voice wasn't over-friendly, just full of concern. Moved, I temporarily forgot this was the man I hated intensely. As I hesitated, he opened the umbrella and pulled me gently under its shelter. "Come on, please, wait for a bit in my room."

I walked beside him. Before we reached his dormitory, I was already in the warmth of his arms and the knowledge that his roommate was absent on a trip. How we used to will him away.

Everything in Liang's room was just the same. Once I was gone, his life could enjoy strict order again, I thought sourly. Looking around, my heart grew heavy with happy memories.

He sat me on his bunk bed, my usual seat, made me a cup of green tea, and sat down next to me. "Your hands are cold." He held both of my hands in his big warm hands, whispering. "So good to see you at such short range. In the past few weeks, I could only glimpse you in the TOEFL class. You were too far away, with too many heads in the way. Thank heaven and earth for the rain today! I was worried I'd never see you properly again. You know, I'll have to move to a flat assigned by my work unit next week."

My tears fell like the rain outside. "I am going to listen to my grandma's suggestion and get rid of my weeping mark. I have become so sentimental that every bit of emotion sets my tears off. Silly, really."

He pulled me into his arms, "Oh, darling, my little fox fairy, I am so sorry that I made you suffer. I never intended to."

In his comforting arms, I cried and cried until my bag of tears was empty. The next thing I knew we were impatiently tearing each other's clothes off. He touched me with an incredible tenderness and desperation. Three weeks' separation, three weeks of longing, love, and hatred all burst into passion. His bed groaned as we wrestled on it, groping toward the eruption of pleasure. "Please remember me, I love you," he whispered.

He marked my shoulder with his teeth once again. "Love got its teeth," he once had said to me, after sinking his into my shoulder at the peak of his excitement. "My mother used to bite my chubby legs when I was young. I am her last child. Only now, I know why."

This was his last mark. The threads, the fibers holding us together had to break.

Chapter 33

Unwanted Joy

"Congratulations! Really, you have *xi*!" The pretty nurse, who had left with my bottle of urine, returned to break the news. *Xi*, joy, is a subtle word for pregnancy. The confirmation would normally bring a bundle of joy, but not for an unmarried girl, who wasn't even in a stable relationship.

"Thank you." I twisted my grimace into something resembling a smile and took the test slip from her. There were only two lines on it, positive and negative, and filling the box beside positive was a single X—like those blood-red Xes splashed cross big character posters, detailing the crimes of prisoners doomed to capital punishment.

Outside the hospital, the brilliant sun made me dizzy. I opened my eyes to see my hometown in charming shape, with spring flowers blossoming everywhere.

Xi? I involuntarily rested a hand on my stomach, which remained as flat as a newly laid tarmac road. A baby was growing there? Hard to imagine. When my period was late, to my horror, I was forced to face the possibility. Each time I checked my unstained underwear, the horror would sink in deeper. Finally, I had braved a hospital trip, far away from home, only to confirm my worst fear.

To have a pregnancy test was as easy as spitting. But to abort that pregnancy wasn't. I had to produce an introduction letter from my danwei, to prove I was married and that my bosses consented to the abortion.

Xi, xi, xi? How to get rid of this unwanted joy? I asked myself again and again while I cycled home. China's strict controls on abortion had caused unspeakable suffering to women in my position. Some used a metal wire to fish out the fetus or squeezed it out with a large rolling pin to the stomach. Other women were obliged to turn to quack doctors with substandard practices. Driven by desperation, some even leapt to their death from the Great Yangtze River Bridge.

It was totally out of the question to keep an illegitimate child. He—or she—wouldn't be able to register his existence, get a residence permit, or go to school. A child born out of wedlock would bear a black mark, and be subject to humiliation from birth. But the humiliation would mostly likely fall on my family and me first: if my stomach swelled obviously, the factory's planning offiicals would drag me to the operation table.

To keep my life from ruin, I launched a self-rescue mission. Firstly I bought a fragment of deer horn musk at considerable expense—its strong aroma was supposed to trigger a miscarriage. I sniffed it greedily like a dog and kept it under my pillow at night. But nothing happened. The following night, I went to the dark riverside to jump down from the steep embankment, hoping to jerk the baby out of my body. Despite my military-style vigor, nothing happened. Later, I returned to dive into the river and soak myself in the smelly, cold water—icy water could induce an abortion, it was believed. I just caught a cold.

The baby clung persistently to its little life.

The next night, I turned up in front of my dear friend Zhou Fang's door. As always, I turned to her for help.

"Aiya, Lijia, *lai, lai*." Fang's mother opened the door and greeted me with a warm smile. Apart from the wrinkles in her kind face, she looked just like her daughter. "Little Fang, Lijia's here."

Fang appeared from her room, smiling broadly. No surprise. I often pedaled half an hour north and turned up at her doorstep without warning, to chat or seek advice on matters big and small. She was busier than usual, bustling about all day long with a demanding job, her fiancé's applications to American universities, and a bureaucratic war over her transfer to teach English at a technical school where her family had some guanxi. Yet she would never say no to me, or indeed anyone who was in need of help. Her resourcefulness and warmth had won her a large group of friends.

"Please put slippers on." To maintain the clean floor, Fang's family always took off their outdoor shoes. Their two-bedroom flat, allocated by the Polytech School where her father taught, had the same concrete floor and whitewashed walls as my home, but somehow felt cozy, thanks to the human warmth.

"Have you eaten?" Fang's mother brought me tea and sweets.

"I have, thank you, Auntie."

"Why are you so pale and thin?" she looked me up and down with concern. "Working too hard, eating too little? Should I heat up some food for you?"

With my face the color of pickled cucumber, I looked wan and sallow, I knew. The unbearable weight of xi was draining me like a bloodsucker. "Don't worry, Auntie. I'll soon join you for a proper meal." I had frequently enjoyed Fang's family's hospitality. The food was quite unremarkable, I had to say, for I had been spoiled by Nai's good cooking. But I relished the loving, calm atmosphere there, far removed from the often-tense conditions at my own home. Even their arguments were sugarcoated.

"Naughty old woman!" Fang's father would say to his wife when she tried to chop vegetables in the kitchen, "that's my job and I can do it better than you."

In Fang's own room, she seated me on the sole chair, and perched on the bed opposite herself.

"I have a lot to confess. How can I start, I..." I smiled one of my pathetic, fake smiles. So far, I had kept my secret love life from her, for fear of losing her friendship.

"Leniency to those who confess," she joked, like a policeman with a suspect.

With eyes cast down I began, briefly mentioning my two previous liaisons, but focusing on my affair with Liang, how we had met, fallen in love, and planned to go to America. "I thought your America plan was rather abrupt," Fang commented, "but then I also know how impatient you are."

I let out a rueful smile and continued the story that soon turned sour.

After breaking up with Liang, I had tumbled into an abyss of depression. In early December, my TOEFL class finished. While all my classmates were busily preparing for the exam in January, I didn't know what to do with myself. I got myself a part-time job in the evenings as a waitress at the Black Forest Café, just to keep myself occupied.

It was here that I had embarked on my first fling. A regular at the café, he was an artist in his late twenties, with a massive beard and bright tie-dyed T-shirt. One night, he chatted me up. A freelancer, he made a living by selling his art. "I have no danwei or anyone controlling me. I am a heavenly steed, roaring across the sky freely," he borrowed an idiom. When he invited me to see his art, I agreed.

At his flat, the foundation of his freewheeling lifestyle, he first showed me his unique works, which were like drawings, not by pencil lines, but different-sized copper wires. Surprisingly vivid. Then, he exhibited his naked body. "I am a hedonist, taking pleasure whenever I can." For the pleasure there was, I spent the night there. We both understood it was just for harmless fun.

I nervously observed my friend's face.

But she simply asked: "Did your mother ask why you didn't go home?"

"I said I was with you."

"Hai, I became your shield!"

Shield indeed. When I spent restless nights with Liang, taking advantage of his roommate's absence, I had sold Ma the same lie.

The fling flowered as briefly as the broad-leaved epiphyllum, famous for its fleeting blossom. The artist's laziness, lack of hygiene, and eccentric lifestyle proved a bit too much for me. But I enjoyed the sexual adventure, the first step out of my depression.

Since then, I had started to drift into a series of flings. I was surprised how easy it was to seduce or to be seduced. Boredom was to blame—if I had to find an excuse for my bad behavior. After Liang, I needed to create some ripple of excitement for myself. When I flirted with men, educated or artistic types preferably, I felt animated, almost happy. But if they foolishly grew serious, I ran away: I wasn't ready yet to fall in love again.

Almost to my horror, I found myself enjoying sex without any emotional attachment. Once upon a time, I wrote to Red Rock denouncing such behavior as "disgusting." I have become a real fox fairy, an animal, I thought to myself. Instinct howled inside my body.

Only then had I begun to understand the pearl of tears on Ma's face when she begged me to forget Red Rock because she didn't want her daughter to experience the misery of a living window like herself. Under that jack-o'-lantern, did she feel any sexual frustration? Did she slip her fingers down to her jade gate as I had done? Was her friendliness with men like Uncle Gao purely driven by the practical need to fix things at home? Did she have any affairs? I hoped she did. Being a woman just twelve days a year was not enough. But I would never know the answer—I could never bring myself to ask.

I knew for sure that she wouldn't approve of my flings. So, I had kept my dirty side from Ma and Fang.

"Now, you know what a rotten girl I really am," I said to Fang, at my tearful confession. I looked anxiously at my friend. She was pure, still a virgin, from what I could gather.

"Rotten, I haven't smelled anything rotten!" she threw a typical warm smile. "This guy Liang apparently left a big hole in your life. No, I don't think any less of you. I've always admired your courage."

"Thank you, my friend. You are too kind. I am in deep trouble," I continued uneasily. "I need your help. I have..." I couldn't bring myself to say xi. "I am pregnant! I am being punished."

"You are not!" she inhaled a gulp of cold air in terror and disbelief. When she gathered herself, she asked, "I don't mean to be nosy, but how about the baby's father?"

I shook my head. Since my split with Liang, I had grown careless. I almost forgot that I was a woman of childbearing age. Indeed, I sometimes doubted if I was able to bear a child since I was so thin. The baby was the result of an irresponsible one-night stand. When a work trip brought me to Hangzhou, a scenic city close to Shanghai, I had met a young academic from Shanghai who was staying at the same hotel. In the end, I had not even bothered to take his address.

"Don't worry, we'll work something out. How many weeks now?"

"Nearly seven, I guess."

"We'll have to be quick," she murmured to herself.

It only took one wail, echoing along the corridor, for the shivers down my spine to start shaking my body, like a grain on a sieve.

"Steady," came the scolding voice of a nurse, through the thin door. "No need to howl like that!"

Between her screams, the woman swore rudely. "Oh, you bastard, you animal. If you dare to fuck me again, I'll tear your balls off! Aiya, heavens, too painful…"

It sounded like she was a properly married woman, a victim of her husband's libido, I thought bitterly as I sat in the waiting room. There were several other women there, waiting to undergo the operation. Some were already crying in the arms of their men. I was the only one accompanied by another woman. "Don't worry, everything will be fine." Fang held my hand, hoping to calm me down. My friend thoughtfully brought a thermos of ginger soup cooked with brown sugar, believed to be good for women in my soon-to-be condition.

As instructed, I had arrived at seven-thirty in the evening, to see a certain Dr. Zhang at this small state-owned hospital, tucked away in the Western district. The wife of a friend of Fang's friend had made the arrangements, a favor that cost me two cartons of Marlboro cigarettes. There were many rules in China, but almost as many ways to get around them.

I was third in the queue. Number two started a nervous conversation. "Have you had an abortion before?"

"No."

"I have, once. As painful as death!" she assured me. "You know, we have actually got the proper papers. We're just waiting for my work unit to assign us a flat."

A familiar tale. Liang crept into my mind. What would he think of me if he found out that I got pregnant from a one-night stand? No, he should never find out. I would never see him again, anyway. Never again.

The door swung open with a bang and a rather large woman appeared in the doorway, looking pale as a ghost. Her husband, the cause of her suffering, rushed up, and she collapsed in his arms.

I began to shiver again. Soon, my name was called. I followed a young nurse into the small, low-ceilinged abortion room, pungent with disinfectant and blood. Instinctively, I shrank back from the operating table at its center, beside an ominous-looking machine. On the wall, under the red slogan "One couple, one child," there was a colorful poster of a mid-term baby inside a womb.

The nurse busied about the room, humming a popular song, "When I am missing you, my heart shivers..."

A thin-lipped, middle-aged woman, presumably Doctor Zhang, was inspecting a tray full of scalpels, their gleam cold and dazzling. A white cotton mask hung down from her left ear. After a minute she raised her head and asked, "Your medical record?"

I didn't have one. I got here through the back door, through guanxi. "I..." I opened my dry mouth, yet no legible words came out. A dying fish out of water.

"Oh, you are *that* woman," she said after a pause.

"Yes, I am. Thank you for taking the trouble, Doctor Zhang," I said humbly.

"That's quite all right," she replied with an air of great moral superiority. "Have you had any check-up or ultrasound?"

"No. But I knew for sure I am pregnant." I had already begun to experience severe morning sickness. In order not to arouse suspicion, I would sometimes swallow it back down, only to make myself more violently sick.

"Now, strip from the waist downward, then lie on the table. Be quick. We've got quite a few lined up today."

I stripped off my skirt, tights, and underwear, as fast as I could with shaking hands, my dignity peeling off with each layer. Lying on the operating bed, I placed my legs on the two stirrups. No holding back.

Doctor Zhang put her mask back on, ready to *datai*—"beat the fetus"—the painfully graphic Chinese term for abortion. "Da, da da, beat, beat, beat," my ears began to ring. I gripped the edge of the operation table, terrified I was to be butchered alive. No anesthesia. I heard the machine being switched on, then something cold and metal went deep inside me and stabbed my tender womb.

"Aah!" I yelped at the top of my lungs. My howl, piercing through the tired, thick air of the room, sounded just like the pigs in the slaughterhouse not far from our village. How I wished I could die like the pigs.

The next morning, I woke to the human noise of the neighborhood. It took some minutes before the montage of the abortion room returned before my eyes, then my other senses kicked in.

"It was growing very well." I kept hearing the cheerful remarks the nurse had made when she took the aborted fetus away. Chinese women attached little emotion to abortion, a common form of birth control. My sister had one and my mother three or four. I thought I would be overjoyed to be rid of it, like a tumor. But I was gripped by a hollow feeling.

The traditional wisdom demanded women in my position lie in bed in a darkened room, to avoid exposure to the sun or the slightest breath of wind. We were not supposed to touch cold water, read books, watch TV, or much else, because if a woman developed a problem at such a sensitive time, a backache or whatever, tradition held that the damage could be permanent. Weijia had followed such strict advice to the letter when she had her abortion, shortly after her wedding.

But I could afford none of these luxuries. I dragged my body out of bed and then onto my bike: I had to go to work as normal. I felt filled with lead. Without the baby, how could I weigh more?

"Aiya, Little Zhang, why are you looking so pale?" Boss Lan greeted me when I made my way to the workshop. "Study late last night?"

"No, woman's problem. I'll have to go to the hygiene room shortly," I replied with perfect assurance.

"We can't help with your woman's problem," he gave his girlish giggle. "Have fun at the hygiene room."

I slowly climbed upstairs to a modified toilet at the heart of the main compound. I was bleeding lightly, a consequence of the abortion.

"Zhang Lijia, from Work Unit Number Twenty-three," I showed my work pass to the woman behind the desk, cracking watermelon seeds. There was already a pile of husks on the concrete floor.

"*Haolai,*" The woman, short and round, her width almost equal to her height, took my pass and turned around to look for my file. Every month, when each woman in the factory had her period, she needed to report to family-planning staff, nicknamed the "period police," stationed at this hygiene room.

"Oh, you're rather late this month," she remarked, studying my card, dense with the dates of my monthly visits.

"Yes, I wonder why. Maybe I am just too tired," I replied.

"It happens," she said, popping another black seed into her mouth. I noticed there was a tiny bit missing from her upper front teeth, perhaps the result of years of cracking seeds. What else to engage her here?

She tailed me closely to the toilet, still chewing. Before squatting down to wash my private parts with hot water from pipes fitted with foot-controlled valves, I showed her my bloodstained sanitary towel. Most women might be embarrassed by the task, but she had been performing it for years and her face betrayed not the slightest trace of uneasiness. In fact, she often remarked on what she saw. "Oh, you've got a very heavy flow. Ask your mum to boil you some eggs." Or, "Aiya, what bushy hair you've got down there!" Privacy was a luxury no Chinese expected. Presently, she cranked her neck for a better look and said: "You've got some blood clots. No wonder you are late. Try black-boned chicken soup with ginseng." She fancied herself as an amateur gynecologist.

Any further delay, another couple weeks or so, she would've called the woman in charge of family planning at my work unit, reporting my case. Then, the family-planning officer would call me in to inquire about why I'd missed the monthly visit. Without a good reason, such as a work-related trip, I would have been taken to a gynecologist for a check-up. An old classmate of my sister's, unmarried at the time, was discovered to be pregnant in this way.

Satisfied, the period police issued me a bag of sanitary towels, free of charge. In the name of female workers' welfare, the system was our factory's interpretation of the strict family-planning policy introduced at the close of the 1970s, to tackle the overwhelming population problem. The methods chosen were urgent, often brutal, and ultimately very effective. Every danwei was responsible for any of its workers' violations, and they could bring serious consequences: had my pregnancy been discovered, our factory would have lost its model title, workers would've lost certain bonuses, and leaders their chance to climb higher on the ladder.

Holding the sanitary towels in my hand, I went downstairs. The lead that had been filling my legs suddenly went, leaving them weak.

With the accepted excuse of a "woman's problem," I used flexitime to take the afternoon off. I had a long sleep after lunch. But my dreams were troubled. Lying in bed the whole afternoon, I saw failure everywhere in the mirror of my life. My personal life was a mess and professionally, after fluttering about, chasing dreams, I remained trapped in the well of the gray Liming empire. Apart from the number of men I had slept with, what else could I boast of?

In the evening, Fang came to see me with royal jelly and dried longan pulp, an expensive delicacy.

"You shouldn't have bothered." Tears welled up. In my vulnerable state, I was deeply moved by her visit, as timely as "sending charcoal in snowy weather."

"Fed up with me already?" she joked.

"How do I deserve your friendship? I am so unworthy and have sunk so low!" Heavy feeling squeezed out my humor.

"Sunk low? What nonsense are you talking about?" she scolded me like a loving mother whose daughter had muddied her new dress. "When you are in a forest, you can't see it for the trees. Anyone would be impressed by what you've achieved." Fang started a list: how I had tried, unremittingly, all those years, to better myself; how I had obtained a good degree in mechanical engineering and another one in English from the Teach-Yourself University; how I had translated English TV programs and even gotten an article into print.

With the end of my love affair, my passion for English study dropped a thousand feet in one fall, but I filled the gap by taking up my writing again. Maybe suffering had lent it some substance, or maybe luck was with me—*Ningxia Youth* published my article about love and loss, "Thoughts on Qinghuai River." The monthly literary journal was based in Northwest China and ran interesting, even daring, articles.

"You often say you feel like a frog in a well," said Fang. "In my view, you are way beyond the well mentally, and physically, you can jump out any time you want."

I wasn't sure about "any time." I could have, last October. I was offered a job, right during the interview, by a Thai animal feed company that was running a big operation in China. But Liang had advised me to turn it down, arguing that the job, combining the role of interpreter, PR, and secretary, would be too demanding. "I could get you loads of jobs like that if you want," he boasted. I would be better off focusing on the TOEFL exam, pursuing a greater goal, and keeping my miserable job.

Would I ever get another opportunity like that?

"Of course, absolutely!" Fang said emphatically. "If you want it."

"I'll miss you like crazy when you leave the factory." Fang was soon to start her new life as a teacher at a technical school, but she was hardly enthusiastic. If she could study during work hours like me, she said, she wouldn't have bothered. "Lijia, you know your American dream is still feasible, even without this Liang guy, right? One can't give up eating for fear of choking."

America was beckoning Fang. Impressed by his outstanding score on the TOEFL, the University of Wisconsin had granted her fiancé a scholarship. Once he was there, Fang could follow him as a spouse; and once she was there, she would pull me over the Atlantic Ocean. "Let's go to America together!" my friend enthused.

I pondered Fang's invitation. When my love affair went dead, it seemed to have snuffed out all the aspiration in me. One can't give up eating for fear of choking, indeed.

"Yes, let's go!" I replied, gripping her hands tightly. They were small, almost fragile, like the rest of her, offering no clue to her life-affirming energy.

I actually did take the TOEFL exam in January 1988, because I'd paid for it months earlier. I scored better than I expected. And I was confident I could do even better the next time around.

Fang smiled, her eyes narrowing into lines behind her glasses. "You are far too energetic to sit still," she said.

"While waiting for my American dream, I'd like to translate a novel from English," I confessed, almost timidly. I was sure my friend could see the sparks in my eyes. There was a surging demand for newly-translated books, which were snatched up by keen readers as soon as they reached bookstores.

"That's a great idea!" Fang said.

My friend's kind words had lifted my spirit like wind filling a slack sail. "After surviving a major disaster, one is bound to have great fortune later in life," I reminded myself of the Chinese saying. I had survived this abortion; I could surely cope with whatever came my way.

I spent the next day in our tiny yard, resting and thinking about my future plan. Along the muddy border, nurtured by Nai's eggshells, red Chinese roses, white-edged morning glory, and bright-colored dahlia were all in full bloom, brilliant as silk brocade.

It was spring, after all.

Chapter 34

The Ocean Beckons

"River Elegy." On the YMCA blackboard, Teacher James chalked out the topic for the day's discussion, a hit TV documentary.

He then took his place in the circle—from the very beginning, he had refused to stand at the desk, facing us. The ceiling fan wafted around the scent of detergent, a smell I associate with him to this day. Teacher James's enthusiasm for his voluntary work was undiminished. It had taken a while for the alien concept of "volunteering" to sink in: why would he bother to take on extra work, away from his wife and two golden-haired daughters, without being paid a penny? But he claimed that our informal exchange, freer than the textbook regimen of his university class, was an excellent way to learn about China. His fascination with a country engulfed by change had brought him here in the first place.

"Everyone has watched the documentary, I presume?" James's flashing green eyes swept over a dozen of us.

"Yes, of course," we replied in one voice.

Ever since the six-part series, combining reportage, history, and sociology, had been aired earlier that summer, *River Elegy* had been a household name. Using the stagnant Yellow River as a metaphor, the documentary was highly critical of China's traditional culture, or "yellow civilization" as the makers of the documentary put it, which they represented as a landlocked mentality characterized by conservatism, isolationism, and despotism. They lavished praise on the "blue civilization," represented by industry, openness, transparency, individualism, and democracy.

"Now, tell me, why is it so popular? All my students are raving about it." He smiled. James's warm smile and athletic build reminded me strongly of Liang. Partly for his charm and partly for the stimulating debates he chaired, I had been turning up without fail to the Wednesday gatherings.

"It raises fundamental questions about our culture and values," a radio journalist fired the first shot. Unlike at school, we didn't have to raise our hands but simply spoke out when we had something to say.

"The documentary just hits the nail on the head. Why is China so poor and backward? It is all because of our mentality, our yellow civilization," remarked my quick-witted friend Doctor Zhao.

China's impotency had become an obsession of the intellectual class ever since it was exposed by British firepower during the Opium War, she said. Today, amid an economic downturn and rising social anxiety, *River Elegy* had stirred the big question again.

"Hmm...interesting" said James, "Are you saying that the program's popularity has a lot to do with the timing?"

Everyone agreed on that. The reforms were not going well. "Crossing the river by feeling the stones," was how Deng Xiaoping described his experimental socialist market economy. But at the moment, the stones seemed harder than ever to find.

As we chirped in enthusiastically, the temperature seemed to rise in the room.

James rose. "Do you mind if I open the big windows up there?"

"Yes," several people blurted out.

"Aha!" James smiled a mischievous smile while tapping his own forehead. "You mean, you don't want me to open the window?"

"No, not at all." We quickly corrected ourselves. Even though most members spoke pretty fluent English, we often fell into easy traps like this, particularly on occasions when we were focused on the content of the discussion rather than English grammar.

James wrote down the structure of the sentence and sat down again.

Following the thread, he said his students were more restless than ever. Recently, there had been a protest over rising costs. And there were more posters on campus, complaining about inflation and corruption, and demanding more human rights.

"Back to our topic," James turned to Doctor Zhao. "Okay, I understand that when things are not going well, people tend to find something to blame. But how can you blame a 'mentality' for a nation's poverty and backwardness?"

"I think the documentary does blame our system, too," said a university lecturer. "After all, our proletarian dictatorship system is still a dictatorship of some sort, not much better than an imperial one, don't you think? That's the hidden message."

"Wow!" exclaimed James, "I must say that China never fails to amaze me. If that's the case, I am surprised it's allowed to be broadcast at all."

Another member didn't see the hidden message, arguing that the documentary wasn't critical enough of the current system as it only lashed out at our ancestors and culture.

Small-road information suggested that there was indeed some heated debate among the top leaders about the program. In the end, reform-minded Zhao Ziyang gave the green light for public viewing.

The radio journalist remarked again: "It's time we gave

up the so-called 'Western application into the Chinese system.' Just as the Yellow River must flow into the sea, China must embrace Western civilization and march toward modernization." As he talked excitedly, more of his bushy hair flopped to his forehead.

While he was busy flinging his hair back, I seized the opportunity to step in. "Yes exactly. The Four Modernizations, we talk about it every day, but I doubt our leaders understand what modernization really means." I argued that modernity meant industrialization, free trade, and a whole system that supported them, such as rule of law and free media. The government had to address these issues sooner or later.

James nodded deeply, his green eyes flashing at me. He had been tremendously helpful in the translation project I had launched: translating an American novel about love entitled *No Love Lost,* a book I'd picked up, almost randomly, for its best-seller label. He patiently explained slang, difficult words, and cultural background. Showered by his encouragement, I grew more confident in expressing my views.

Both Red Rock and Liang had lectured me on the subject of modernization. Among the many commentaries that flooded the papers, one in particular amazed me. It pointed out that the paper's young writers borrowed theories from the West, among them, a theory of the origin of oriental despotism, which argued that the need to organize large numbers of people for water projects had provided the foundation for despotic states. So, that theory I had listened to in awe, on the bank of the Yellow River, wasn't really Red Rock's own. I was nevertheless more grateful than annoyed, as I was grateful to all three men I had fallen in love with, because they had each broadened my horizons.

Would *River Elegy,* too, open up Chinese people's minds?

Chapter 35

Leniency to Those Who Confess

The scratch of pen on paper was the only sound to fill the gaps between the policeman's questions and my halting answers. It was midmorning in mid-July, and the sun was already melting the streets outside. Here in Master Cheng's room, the grease-filled air was cool. An interrogation was underway. My crime? Organizing a demonstration by the workers from our factory to support the students in Tiananmen Square. A few days after our demonstration, on the dark night of June 4, 1989, the People's Liberation Army opened fire on the people, putting a bloody end to a democratic movement at the very heart of communist China.

The world was stunned, and China wept.

I had expected some kind of reprisal. Following the massacre, the government had launched a nationwide witchhunt against those who actively took part in the movement, which required everyone not only to confess his own actions but also to report what others did. Even the writers of *River Elegy* became wanted criminals and the documentary itself was banned for inciting anti-government sentiments. The bud of a "blue civilization" was brutally snapped.

I was still shocked, however, when the policeman had walked briskly into our workshop that morning. Asking for me, he impatiently gave only his surname, Zhou, and introduced his accomplice, Comrade Li, a female cadre from factory headquarters and a member of the special team investigating the "incident."

Demanding some privacy, this team of two established itself at Master Cheng's room, forcing him to abandon solitary confinement and join the rest of the group. Policeman Zhou seated himself behind Master Cheng's spotless desk, Comrade Li beside him, leaving me in a chair in the middle of the room, facing them alone. With nothing to lean on, I felt marooned on an isolated island.

"We have to ask you some questions. No need to worry," he said.

I could well imagine my panic-stricken face. Fear of the police was implanted into Chinese children by parents who threatened "the police will come to get you if you cry any more."

He started by establishing my identity, age, education, and status.

I watched them taking notes of my answers. My eyes anxiously swept the room, flitting from one large black iron window to another, and finally resting on the policeman. He looked young, but already possessed the arrogant air of someone who knew too well the power he held over the ordinary people.

The policeman looked up and asked in a more demanding voice. "So, why did you organize the demonstration?"

"I thought the student movement was patriotic and I wanted to show my support," I announced.

"But you not only took part, but also organized it. You, an ordinary worker? How come?"

"I am also a citizen."

"We heard that you are studying English. You must be aware that there's poison in the Western culture."

"Yes, I am aware."

"And you even translated a book. What is it about?"

In May, a letter from an editor from Ningxia People's

Publishing Company had greatly brightened my day. A friend from *Ningxia Youth* magazine made the introduction. The editor loved the novel *No Love Lost* and my translation, which was painstakingly polished by my literary friend Pan Hai. It would be published by the end of the year. With an air of a toad that was finally actually about to eat swan's meat, I spread the great news far and wide. "It's a love story set in America." I replied.

"A-mer-i-ca!" The policeman dragged out the word.

After a rattle of pages, he asked: "Are you a member of any foreign organization or group?"

"Of course not, why?" Given the government's paranoia about any uncensored organization, I knew it would invite trouble to mention the YMCA English-speaking Club. It wasn't an "organization" as such anyway.

"As you know, some foreign organizations would be only too happy if China changed its color. Did any foreign individual or organization encourage you in any way?"

"No, no one encouraged me," I continued to shake my head.

"So, it was all your idea?"

"Yes, my own idea."

The idea had only occurred to me after I went home for lunch that Sunday. It was May 28, 1989. Shoveling rice into my mouth, I watched the lunchtime news with my family. Everyone was addicted to news bulletins for the excitement of unfolding events captured live on television, something unprecedented in the People's Republic. One image stuck in my mind; arm in arm, sodden but elated, workers in the southern city of Guangzhou were protesting in the pouring rain, their mouths straining to shout support for the democracy movement.

The death of Hu Yaobang, the popular former secretary general who had been ousted in 1986 for his sympathetic view of the student protests, had triggered the drama. To mourn Hu's passing, students in Beijing marched to Tiananmen to lay wreaths, demanding his good reputation be restored. In the face of government silence, the demonstrations snowballed, and the protesters began to demand greater freedom and democracy. Like a match thrown onto kindling, the action by Beijing students sparked a chain reaction: students from all over the country took to the streets. They were soon joined by citizens from all walks of life. The Chinese people, who had never enjoyed any say in how they were governed, began to roar.

The movement intensified in mid-May after the students began a hunger strike. "Mother, we love food, but we love democracy even more," read one banner amid the sea of protestors in Tiananmen Square. The central government, restrained or paralyzed thus far, announced martial law on May 20. But it didn't work. The troops that entered the capital met such strong resistance from the citizens they were pushed back to the outskirts. In a stirring display of anger and defiance against the authorities, one million Beijing residents arose in protest. Most cities across the country followed suit.

It was an uncertain time, a critical time.

I was better informed that ever: a proud owner of a new shortwave radio, I listened to the BBC every day.

Even our own state media were being astonishingly frank. Taking advantage of the lack of unity among the top leaders, Chinese journalists removed the gag that had silenced them for decades. Otherwise, I wouldn't have seen the moving footage of protesters braving the pouring rain on that day.

"An impulsive action," I said to my interrogator, "I was very moved by what I saw on TV."

On that Sunday, upon returning to my workshop, I said to Big Zhang: "I wish I could go to the street to protest right now! I heard some factory workers have gone to the street in Nanjing."

"I heard, too." Big Zhang, as one would expect, had been chanting "Movement!" for days now, bashing his enamel bowl with a metal spoon. "Only in wind and thunder can the country show its vitality; alas, the ten thousand horses are all muted!" He quoted a Qing Dynasty poem. "Indeed, indeed, why don't you organize a demonstration for Liming workers? I'll join you with a few mates."

"Big Zhang, don't feed her rotten ideas!" Boss Lan barked. Our Mr. Goody-Goody rarely spoke in harsh tones. "Little Zhang," he turned to me, "you are not a student. It's too dangerous for you to go!"

During that time, my protective boss refused to let me out of his sight, lest I get into trouble. But every day after work, I would rush to the Drum Tower Square, Nanjing's Tiananmen, listening to the speeches and chanting slogans.

"Boss, you've watched *River Elegy*, haven't you?" I fired at him. "Doesn't it criticize us Chinese for our unwillingness to take part in political activities?"

"Taking part in political activities? That's inviting trouble!" Boss Lan replied in his high-pitched voice.

What was I waiting for? I had complained enough about the repressive regime; I had shared enough hot air with friends from the YMCA English-speaking Club, discussing how to be a modern citizen with a social conscience. It was high time for action!

I telephoned Fang, telling her that I wanted to organize a demonstration today after work. As foreign media were discussing rumors of imminent military crackdown, strong public support might just swing the tide.

In her usual calm voice, my friend admitted there was little point trying to dissuade me if I had made up my mind, but I should try to work together with the Youth League in the factory. In this way, a demonstration would be more effective and the risk shared.

The head of the Youth League in our work unit, a young graduate named Shi, responded enthusiastically to the idea, as if he had been craving the invitation. We contacted Luan, head of the factory branch. After some hesitation, Luan agreed, on the condition that the factory leaders consented, thus throwing the thorny question up to higher authorities: with the political winds so uncertain, no one at any level was sure whether to stop or support the protestors. The best survival tactic was to remain vague. But we took that luxury away from the factory leaders. After much discussion, they reached a decision: firstly, it would be best not to demonstrate; secondly if we insisted, then all demonstrators must only represent themselves, not the factory.

Only two hours remained before the off-work horn. My organizational skills, so far exercised for social outings with my friends, came in useful. I telephoned all the people I knew and asked them to tell their friends. Having tracked down cloth and bamboo poles for banners, I delegated the two Youth League cadres to obtain flags and make little strips of red cloth for armbands and headbands—a fashion necessity for the demonstrators.

I asked Liu Weidong, an excellent calligrapher, to help write the banners and slogans. "I'd love to help you," he said, "but it's too risky to get involved." There was unusual firmness in his soft voice. He was now rising steadily in the propaganda unit. "Don't go yourself, it's no good for you," he warned.

I thanked him and quickly hung up, before he had a chance to lecture me with the pearls of conventional wisdom: "the bird that flies first gets shot."

I took up my calligraphy set, resolved to complete the task. Thankfully, Big Zhang, who boasted decent calligraphy, stepped in and took on most of the brushwork.

Sitting on my isolated island, scenes from that extraordinary Sunday rose before my eyes. But I wasn't going to share them with Policeman Zhou and Comrade Li.

"How long did you have the idea before you carried it out?"

"I didn't plan it. I acted on impulse."

They both jotted down my words. In her late thirties, Li was dressed in a loose white shirt and black trousers. Her short hair was combed back, every strand in place, fixed by several hairpins. She didn't say very much, yet I could feel her hostility toward me.

"How many people joined the demonstration?" Zhou asked.

"I don't know. A few hundred, perhaps."

"Perhaps? Don't be vague," he snapped. "One hundred, two, three? Who are these people? Do you know them?"

"Probably between one hundred and two hundred. Sorry, I didn't count. Among the demonstrators, I knew Little Shi and Little Luan, the other two organizers, I trust you've heard." True, I didn't count. But I had been surprised and delighted to see well over two hundred people turn up at Gate One for the march. Among them were a big group came from my work unit, minus Big Zhang—his wife had called to forbid him from attending; several of my TV University classmates; Fang and friends from her work unit; and dozens of young men from the single people's dormitory, mostly university graduates mobilized by my literary friend Pan. But I dared not name a single one to my interrogators.

"Did the number of demonstrators stay the same?" The policeman narrowed his eyes.

"It did grow a bit."

Under the watchful eyes of many onlookers, including the anxious factory leaders, we, the marchers, set off as if for battle, defending a noble cause. This nationwide movement had drawn comparison with the May Fourth Movement of 1919, when thousands of students went to Tiananmen to protest against the Treaty of Versailles, which had transferred the authority over Germany's concessions in China to Japan. The students' outburst of anger soon ignited a mass movement that prevented the Chinese delegation from signing the treaty. It birthed a new, forceful nationalism.

Walking in the very front, I held a red flag, which fluttered in the wind like a roaring fire. I was exhilarated, feeling a sense of liberation that I had never experienced before. I couldn't help but hold my head high, my back straight and erect.

Behind me two workers carried a cloth banner strung high on bamboo sticks. Its brushwork read "Liming Youth Support Beijing." Others held placards, one announcing, "Here come the workers!" The little strips of bright red cloth tied to our arms and heads flamed in the wind.

Out on the main street, we melted into an endless flow of marchers. Before us walked students from a technical school; at our tail were several dozen workers from a glass-making factory. We waved flags at each other, delighted to find fellow workers supporting the cause.

Shortly after we turned a corner to march along China Road, a large group of workers from our factory caught up—they simply didn't want their leaders to see them. "Welcome, warmest welcome!" shouted Little Shi through a loudspeaker. Marchers greeted the newcomers with cheers and applause.

Throughout the one-hour march, the Liming contingent swelled. We later learned that ours was the largest demonstration by workers in Nanjing during the whole democracy movement.

Another rattle of pages. The policeman asked slowly: "The number grew only a bit, did you say?" He looked rather pleased with himself, like an animal toying with its prey. He was taking his time, waiting for the right moment to attack.

"More than a bit." I tried to play down the number, as if the seriousness of my crime would shrink with the size.

"There is no point in lying, let me warn you. How many exactly?" he asked in a harsher tone.

"A couple hundred more joined in later. But I really don't know for sure."

"What kind of slogans did you shout?"

"The usual ones."

"Like what?"

"'Support students, oppose martial law,' 'Down with corruption,' 'Long live democracy.'" I listed the safe slogans.

Little Shi, who led the slogan chanting, did start with them. Later, however, as more people joined in and the atmosphere grew more excitable, some Liming workers began to complain that our slogans were "as weak as horse piss." On impulse, Little Shi let rip: "Down with the repressive government!" "Anyone who dares to crack down on the democracy movement will be condemned for ten thousand years!" Fully aware that these slogans jumped the safe boundary, we all repeated them loudly, like naughty boys enjoying the thrill of forbidden action. A few workers even named names, like "Premier Li Peng will die of ten thousand slow cuts!" Each daring slogan provoked loud cheers and gales of laughter among the onlookers lining the pavements, some showing V signs in the air. Why not? Why couldn't we Chinese say something close to our hearts, just for once?

"ZHANG LIJIA!" The policeman struck the table so hard the porcelain teacups jumped. "I advise you not to play any tricks with us. To tell you the truth, we know everything already. I trust you know our policy: leniency to those who confess their crimes and severity to those who refuse." A cliché for sure, but no less threatening for that.

I could feel the flame of anger leaping from inside me. "Am I a criminal, then? What are the charges?" I pushed my glasses back up my nose.

"Criminal? Did I say that?" he replied less harshly. "In China, one needs permission to protest in the street. Did you have permission?"

"No."

"So, you did violate the law." He took off his hat, to twirl in his hand. The metal badge glistened with a cold flash of authority. "We are just trying to establish the nature of this incident. You'd better cooperate. I don't like this toothpaste-squeezing style. Why don't you tell us all about the demonstration, from the beginning right to the end, without any reservation."

I started to recount that day, focusing on the obvious and harmless parts. I remembered what my former lover Liang once told me, in the wake of the park incident: never volunteer any information when facing a policeman. "The more you confess, the more trouble you'll have."

After a lunch break, the interrogation resumed.

"We understand that you gave a speech at Drum Tower Square."

My surprised look seemed to please him.

"What exactly did you say that won you such applause?"

"I, ah, I can't remember exactly."

I remembered every impassioned word. It was the first time I'd given a speech since my school days. There, I used to parrot the promises of the young pioneers, how faithfully we would carry on the revolutionary cause. But this speech, I didn't prepare at all. It sprang straight from the heart.

When we reached Drum Tower Square, the central stage in town, some organizers from the Autonomous Union of Nanjing Students received us. Their organizational work was sorely needed, as marching contingents poured into the square from all quarters, like hundreds of rivers emptying into the sea. Each newly arrived group had to address the gathering crowds. I was given the honor of representing our factory.

Standing at a raised platform in the middle of the square, I looked around. The whole place was so thick with people that barely a drop of water could've trickled through. The students sat neatly on the ground under their university flags. Onlookers occupied every inch of space surrounding the square, including the nearby open space where my English Corner lay. Some had even climbed high up in the trees where they perched, watching. Every face was glowing with excitement; every pair of eyes sparkled with hope.

Could the patriotism and the will of people once again form a force powerful enough to change history?

My eyes brimmed with tears. Holding the microphone tightly, I forced myself to calm down. "I am an ordinary worker from Nanjing's Liming Machinery Manufacture," I introduced myself. My voice was shaking with excitement and nerves.

"Our ancestors told us that 'every man has a share in the responsibility for the fate of his country.' Now, our country is at a critical point and we felt we just had to do something. We workers are supposedly the masters of the nation. But do we have a say in our government? Can we express our views freely? Can we vote for our leaders? The answer is no, no, and NO! Even the length of our hair and the width of our trouser legs are subject to control. We have been locked in the shackles of dictatorship for too long. The students bravely went to the street, demanding democracy so that they could smash the shackles and let us live as free and true human beings. Their action is not *dongluan*, turmoil, but patriotic behavior. Today, we came here to show our wholehearted support for the students in Tiananmen and to salute them and you, all of you here today for participating in this noblest cause! The Chinese people have finally stood up! Victory will be with us! Long live democracy!"

"Long live democracy!" Every single voice in the square joined in the roar. It reverberated across the nine heavens, shaking the whole world.

"Well, I am afraid you will have to try very hard to recall what you said."

The forest of arms disappeared. The bobbing heads shrank into one rigid face.

In what he described as a "squeezing-toothpaste" fashion, I described my speech a little more.

"Was there a poem or something?" the policeman demanded.

"Answer" was the title of the poem. Ever since my literary friend Old Pan introduced Bei Dao's poem to me, I had loved it, and remembered every line by heart. Its solemn mood, and spirit of defiance and dignity, had struck a chord with the students on Tiananmen Square. Here in Nanjing, there was no better way to close my speech. "Let me tell you, world, / I—do—not—believe! / If a thousand challenges lie at your feet, / Count me as number one thousand and one!"

"I read a famous Misty poem after the speech," I confessed.

"Misty poem?" he repeated, twirling the hat in his hand,

his face lacking the certainty of a few minutes earlier. "What is it? An underground poem? Any reactionary tendencies?"

"It's an officially published poem and it suited our mood."

Policeman Zhou threw his hat on the desk. "I would advise you to be honest. I get information not only from you, but also from many others. Leniency only to those who confess, remember!"

"I remember," I replied. I really didn't want to offend the police. He had power over me and I was afraid of him. I pushed back my glasses only to find they still were sitting on the bridge of my nose.

The remaining questions went more smoothly. At last, he pushed his notebook with the official heading Nanjing Public Security Bureau toward me: "Have a look if my record is correct."

I scanned through his handwritten notes, hasty and arrogant with strokes all over the place like brandished claws.

"Fine," I said, relieved that the end was close.

"Now, make your fingerprint here." He produced a box of bloodred ink.

I stood stupefied for a moment. I'd seen many films in which the criminals had to leave their fingerprints in ink. The imprint of humiliation. I dipped my index finger in the ink and pressed it onto his notebook. It looked so conclusive. I knew that the fingerprint, together with this interrogation, would lurk forever in my personal file, a persistent threat for years to come. What about my American dream?

Slowly I saw the red ink turned into a red flag, fluttering in the wind. I was proud of what I'd done.

I handed Policeman Zhou his notebook back, held my head up, and my back straight and erect. Just like my mother.

Acknowledgments

I'd like to thank Anthony Sheil for seeing the potential in this book. You always managed to come up with sound editorial advice after each of my drafts. I have benefited from your expertise, nurturing, and encouragement. My mentor Ian Johnson, as always, offered excellent suggestions. I feel fortunate to have had Blake Morrison as a teacher at Goldsmiths' MA in Creative and Life Writing Program. Your critique and tips were very useful and inspiring.

I am grateful to Chris Wood for sending me to interview James Atlas for the *South China Morning Post*. Indeed, I am deeply grateful to James himself for taking me on board. I'd like to thank Jessica Fjeld for doing a grand editing job. And I want to thank many family and friends for their support as I crawled out of the darkest passage in my life, in particular, Lucy Kynge and Mure Dickie.

Biggest hug to my girls May and Kirsty. Thank you for being the most entertaining of angels. The biggest thanks, however, is reserved for my ex-husband Calum MacLeod. Thank you for changing my life; thank you for your love and support over the years while I struggled to complete this book; and thank you for the first-class polishing job you did on it. Without you, there wouldn't have been this book.